THE
TAKING
OF
HILL 159 . . .

Masses of tanks were visibly forming for attack on all sides of the hill. The artillery barrage was intense, and constant dive-bombing by British Typhoons had been under way since sunup.

〉 〉 〉

As the Canadians began to challenge the handful of Panzers still able to put up a fight, the German commander, Gen. Kurt Meyer, felt a sudden sensation of pain. His head had been wounded by a shell fragment and blood was pouring down over his face. His aides managed to get him back to an aid station. As soon as the wound was bandaged, Meyer headed back toward defensive positions. But it was already too late. The positions were being overrun as General Simonds of the Canadian First Army poured more and more of his tanks and troops over the hill and down the road leading from Hill 159 into Falaise. For Meyer and the remnants of his once-proud 12th SS Panzer Division, the only choice was retreat ...

AUGUST 1944

AUGUST 1944
THE CAMPAIGN FOR FRANCE

ROBERT A. MILLER

WARNER BOOKS

A Warner Communications Company

To Mary Lu,
who introduced me to history

 A Warner Communications Company

Printed in the United States of America

First Warner Books Printing: November, 1989

10 9 8 7 6 5 4 3 2 1

CONTENTS

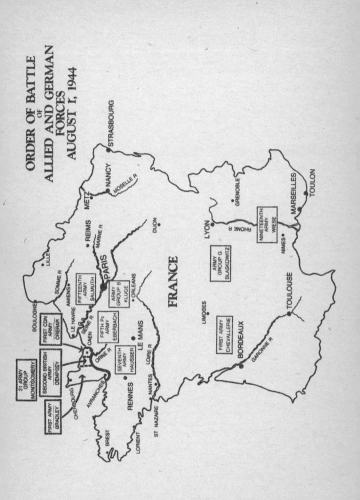

ORDER OF BATTLE
OF
ALLIED AND GERMAN
FORCES
AUGUST 1, 1944

FRANCE

STRASBOURG

NANCY
MOSELLE R

METZ

REIMS

MARNE R

DIJON

LYON

RHONE R

GRENOBLE

MARSEILLES

TOULON

NINETEENTH
ARMY
WIESE

NIMES

ARMY
GROUP G
BLASKOWITZ

TOULOUSE

LIMOGES

GARONNE R

BORDEAUX

FIRST ARMY
CHEVALLERIE

LILLE

SOMME R

BOULOGNE

AMIENS

PARIS

FIFTEENTH
ARMY
SALMUTH

SEINE R

LE HAVRE

ARMY
GROUP B
KLUGE

ORLEANS

FIRST CDN
ARMY
CRERAR

CAEN

ORNE R

FIFTH Pz
ARMY
EBERBACH

LE MANS

LOIRE R

SECOND BRITISH
ARMY
DEMPSEY

21 ARMY
GROUP
MONTGOMERY

CHERBOURG

AVRANCHES

FIRST ARMY
BRADLEY

SEVENTH
ARMY
HAUSSER

RENNES

NANTES

ST NAZAIRE

LORIENT

BREST

PROLOGUE

In the six years' duration of the Second World War, numerous time periods or particular dates have been described by historians as critical to the outcome of the war. The spring of 1940, which saw the fall of France and the beginning of Nazi domination of the European continent, was one such period. The German invasion of Russia in June 1941 was another. The attack on Pearl Harbor and the Japanese sweep throughout the Pacific in late 1941 and early 1942 must certainly be considered a major influence on the progress of the war. Some historians have claimed that the Battle of Midway in June 1942 was a pivotal event, at least in the war between the United States and Japan. The period most frequently mentioned as the turning point in the fortunes of the various contestants has been the fall of 1942. The Russians' successful defense of Stalingrad, the British victory at El Alamein, the American invasion of North Africa, and the Guadalcanal campaign in the South Pacific all occurred within a month or two of each other, and their combined influence on the course of the war was significant.

Another period deserves to take its place alongside these well-known moments in history. It is the month of August 1944. The Allied campaign in northern Europe, which began with the invasion of Normandy, sealed the fate of the Axis powers. More than any other campaign of the war, it was decisive—it tipped the scales between victory and defeat. Furthermore, it was through the hedgerows and across the plains of France during the month of August that the ultimate outcome of this crucial campaign was decided. The events of these thirty-one days had a major impact on the outcome of World War II.

As background to more fully appreciate the significance of these crucial days of August, it would be worthwhile to review briefly the story of the planning and development of the European campaign. It had a rather long and tortuous history, leading up to the climatic day when American, British, and Canadian troops stormed ashore on the beaches of Normandy. The story began just a few months after the Japanese attack on Pearl Harbor.

It is to be considered that the principal target for our first major offensive should be Germany, to be attacked through western Europe. This answer is based on the following reasons:

(1) It involves the shortest possible sea routes, thus placing a minimum strain upon shipping. . . .

(2) No matter where our forces are employed, the lines of communication to England must be kept reasonably safe. Therefore, a theater in western Europe does not require a dispersion of escorting and other protective equipment, air and naval.

(3) An early beginning toward building up, in Great Britain, air and ground forces, and a forward base, will from the very beginning, carry a certain threat against Germany which should prevent complete concentration against Russia. . . .

(4) Land communications for the invading force are superior to those to be found in any other area from which either enemy can be attacked. . . .

(5) The forward base in England is already supplied with air fields from which a large air force can operate in order to gain, along the coast, the air superiority that is absolutely vital to a successful landing. . . .

(6) The plan offers the only feasible method for employing offensively a major portion of the British combat power. . . .

(7) It attempts to attack our principal enemy while he is engaged on several fronts; hence, speed in preparation is important.

The great objection to the plan is the difficulty of organizing, on the shores of western Europe, a force of sufficient strength to meet the hostile opposition that could be brought against it.

The success of the plan depends on the following:

a. Complete agreement among the Combined Chiefs of Staff that this constitutes our eventual task; and a determination to accomplish all the preparatory work demanded. Proper adjustment of training and production schedules.

b. Overwhelming air support.

c. Ample landing craft.

d. Ample shipping to support the operations from the beginning and to bring U.S. reinforcements rapidly into the theater.

e. Husbanding of combat power—to acquire the necessary strength, and avoid the evils of unjustified dispersion. . . .[1]

The above memorandum, dated March 25, 1942, was to Army Chief of Staff Gen. George C. Marshall from the Operations Division of the War Department. Formerly known as the War Plans Division, the Operations Division (OPD) was entrusted with broad powers to formulate worldwide strategy and direct military operations. This memorandum represented one of the earliest concrete proposals with respect to long-range military strategy since the attack on Pearl Harbor had brought the United States into active participation in the war. It highlighted two important concepts that were to serve as the basic foundation of American military policy throughout the war: the defeat of Germany was to receive priority over the war against Japan in the Pacific, and this defeat could be accomplished most effectively by a major invasion of the continent of western Europe. The author of the memorandum was the new commander of OPD, Brig. Gen. Dwight D. Eisenhower.

Marshall had lunch at the White House the day he received the memorandum. Along with the president, Secretary of the

Army Henry Stimson, Secretary of the Navy Frank Knox, Adm. Ernest King, Gen. Hap Arnold, and Harry Hopkins were also present. Marshall presented the arguments in favor of an attack across the English Channel as outlined in Eisenhower's memo and received Roosevelt's approval to proceed with the planning. Within a week, Marshall and Stimson were back at the White House with a final draft of the proposals, which received Roosevelt's enthusiastic endorsement. Code name BOLERO, the plan called for the invasion of Europe in the summer of 1943 and included a subsidiary plan for a smaller landing in 1942, should events on the continent make such an operation appear feasible.

Marshall and Hopkins went to London in the middle of April in order to secure British support for the plan. At a late-night meeting at Chequers, Prime Minister Winston Churchill was the essence of cordiality and told his American guests that he "had no hesitation in accepting the plan."[2] Encouraged by this apparent support of the British allies, Marshall returned with orders for Eisenhower and OPD to put maximum effort into converting the plans into action. Then, at the end of May, he ordered Eisenhower to London to review the problems involved in building up sufficient forces for BOLERO. After a ten-day trip, Eisenhower returned with a recommendation that a position of commander of the European Theater of Operations (ETO) be established to organize, train, and command the American forces to be assigned to the theater. Marshall agreed and, after several days of consideration, appointed Eisenhower to the command.

While Eisenhower was crossing the Atlantic to London in the latter part of June to assume his new command, another very distinguished person was traveling in the opposite direction. Winston Churchill was on his way to Washington. British-American concurrence about European military strategy was about to come to an end. The British acceptance of BOLERO in April was based more on their desire to see American troops moving to British soil and delight over the American adoption of the "European first" strategy than on any agreement with the idea of a cross-channel attack. In fact, they were strongly opposed. Memories of heavy British casualties in France during World War I weighed heavily on

Churchill and the senior British military commanders. They believed that a strategy of smaller attacks on the periphery of the continent (i.e., Scandinavia and the Mediterranean) would be just as effective in ultimately forcing the collapse of the German enemy, without the heavy casualties they foresaw resulting from the cross-channel attack.

It was a bleak summer for British military fortunes, and Churchill recognized in this adversity a way to bend Allied European strategy in a direction more compatible with British interest. The British Eighth Army had its back to the wall in northern Africa, and Field Marshal Erwin Rommel was threatening to overrun Egypt and the Nile Valley. Such a loss would be a severe disaster to the entire Allied cause. Meanwhile, nothing had happened in Europe to make any kind of invasion of the continent even remotely possible during 1942. Churchill pointed out that it was unreasonable to permit the growing American forces to remain idle during 1942, particularly while the Russian army was fighting for its life in front of Stalingrad. Therefore, did it not make sense to stage an American landing in North Africa to take the pressure off the British Eighth Army and to begin to build a formidable Allied presence in the Mediterranean area? After several days of discussions with the persuasive Churchill at both the White House and Roosevelt's family home in Hyde Park, New York, the president agreed, and the American forces that Marshall had planned on using to invade the continent began to be siphoned off to the Mediterranean theater.

With this decision, there began an eighteen-month period of contention and disagreement between the British and American high commands over European military strategy and launching an invasion of the European continent. As the commitment to the Mediterranean theater grew, the possibilities of a cross-channel attack became more remote. Throughout this period, Marshall was the adamant, unremitting advocate of invasion, but he was constantly frustrated by his British counterparts. At one point, he even threatened to withdraw American support from the European theater and concentrate on the war in the Pacific. Roosevelt refused to support such a move, however, and Marshall was forced to relent.

At the Allied conference in Casablanca in January 1943,

the British did agree to the establishment of a combined Allied planning staff to develop plans for a cross-channel attack. Called COSSAC (Chief of Staff to the Supreme Allied Commander), it was headed by British Lt. Gen. Frederick Morgan, who was to include both British and Americans on his staff. COSSAC started serious work in April and by August had developed an invasion plan named OVERLORD, which was quite similar to the plan eventually adopted. D day was to be in May 1944.

It was not, however, until November 1943 at the three-power conference in Teheran that OVERLORD became cast in stone. In the face of heavy pressure from Stalin, who would not believe that the plan was firm until a commander had been named, British resistance faded. Roosevelt surprised everyone by appointing Eisenhower instead of Marshall to the post of supreme commander. (Faced with failing health and a growing dependence on Marshall's management of the global war, he was unwilling to allow Marshall to leave Washington and therefore was unable to offer the general the prize that he most earnestly desired.) The plan to invade the European continent had finally become a reality.

After a brief trip to the States, Eisenhower arrived in London on January 15, 1944, to assume his duties as supreme commander, Allied Expeditionary Force. There was much to be done. Fortunately, most of his subordinates were already on the job and many of the problems were being dealt with when he arrived. One problem in particular had received concentrated attention from General Montgomery, designated commander of the land forces for the invasion. The invasion plan developed by General Morgan's COSSAC staff called for a three-division attack along a twenty-five-mile stretch of the Normandy coast in front of the French cities of Caen and Bayeux. Both Eisenhower and Montgomery were concerned that such an attack would lack strength and cover too narrow a front. They preferred a five-division attack and extension of the front to include the eastern coast of the Cotentin Peninsula.

For such an increase in the size of the landing force, there was a price to be paid. The limitation imposed on Morgan's planners had been the availability of landing craft, at that time the scarcest item in the inventory of invasion necessities.

An increase from three to five divisions would obviously require a substantial increase in the availability of such craft. Intensive efforts were put forth to speed new construction and to beg, borrow, or steal from other theaters of war. While these efforts met with some success, there was only one real solution to the problem—to delay the invasion date to allow time for additional craft to be delivered. By the end of January, the decision had been made to delay D day from May to June.

Another problem for the supreme commander had to do with the invasion of southern France, which had been added to the invasion plan largely at the insistence of the American High Command in order to further broaden the attack and provide additional port facilities. Eisenhower had to deal with two basic problems. First of all, the British were strongly opposed to the whole idea. They saw the plan as withdrawing resources from the Italian campaign, which was important to their concept of attacking the "soft underbelly" of Europe. The British, and most particularly Winston Churchill, favored a campaign from Italy north to Central Europe in an effort to maintain Allied political control of that important region in postwar Europe. Eisenhower spent countless hours with the prime minister on the subject and, in the end, only the fact that it was an "American and French show" enabled the operation to proceed over British objections.

The second problem was that ANVIL, as the operation was named, suffered from the same landing craft shortage that plagued OVERLORD. The two attacks were originally planned to take place at the same time, but it quickly became clear that there were insufficient landing craft to support both attacks simultaneously. Again, there was only one way out of the dilemma—to delay the landing in southern France so that many of the same landing craft could be used in both assaults. A delay of at least a month was agreed upon, but ANVIL remained a source of contention between the Allies right up until the day the landing took place.

The title Supreme Commander was intended to denote that Eisenhower had control of all forces in the European theater—not only the forces of the different Allies but of the different services (army, navy, air force) as well. One troubling exception arose. The Strategic Air Forces (both British and American) maintained that they should be excluded from Eisenhower's control, and they received considerable backing in this position from the British. The argument centered around the concept, deeply felt by the airmen, that the war would ultimately be won by the heavy bombing of German strategic and industrial resources. While Eisenhower did not disagree with the importance of strategic bombing, he felt he should have control of *all* Allied resources, particularly during the period immediately prior to D day. He planned a heavy attack on the French rail and other transportation facilities in an effort to isolate the invasion area from enemy reinforcement. After much discussion over several weeks, Eisenhower did win his point, and it was agreed that, for the critical period before and after the invasion, the Strategic Air Force commanders would be under his control.

Countless other problems faced Eisenhower as the clock wound down to the month of June: problems of security, disagreements over the use of airborne troops in the invasion, development of plans to deceive the enemy about Allied intentions, political difficulties with the various French factions, and, of course, the all-important task of training the troops for an operation for which there was no precedent in all the annals of military warfare. Amphibious warfare, in itself, was not new. By the summer of 1944, the Allies had made numerous landings in the Pacific and Mediterranean theaters and learned much about the problems of assaulting enemy-held beaches. However, nothing even approaching the scale of the proposed Normandy assault had ever been attempted. Furthermore, the assault was to be made against a German army that had had plenty of time to prepare and that after five years of war remained the most formidable military organization of all time.

When viewed in retrospect, the success of the Normandy landings on June 6, 1944, tends to mask the tremendous risk the undertaking represented and how close to disastrous failure it came on that summer morning, particularly at Omaha Beach. More than 5,000 ships and 200,000 men were committed directly to the operation. Millions more had been involved in the years of planning and buildup preceding D day. If the Allies had been unsuccessful in establishing a viable beachhead on the Normandy coast, the cost to the continued prosecution of the total war would have been incalculable. The British opposition to the cross-channel attack would have been vindicated, and another attempt at invasion would certainly have been unlikely for at least a year, if not longer. This would have given Hitler the opportunity to throw the vast majority of his forces against the advancing Russian army. Dissension among the Allies would certainly have increased to levels of bitter recrimination. Confronted by the bulk of the German army, Stalin would have been sorely tempted to negotiate a separate peace with Hitler, and the Americans would undoubtedly have turned to the Pacific as their major theater of operations. War weariness and disillusion would have grown rapidly among the Allies as they foresaw little likelihood of an early end of the war. These and other possible consequences would have materially changed the future course of the war and the makeup of the postwar world.

A tremendous gamble was being played out on the Normandy beaches as the Allies sought to gain a foothold on the coast of France. However, the risks to the success of the Normandy invasion did not end on D day. Progress off the beaches was slower than expected across the entire front, with the possible exception of the Cotentin Peninsula. The German defense was fierce and effective, and they had uncommitted reserves available that could be thrown against the Allies. With the help of tactical air superiority, naval gunfire support, and the success of the Allied programs for deceiving the enemy, the Allies were barely able to maintain their beachhead and begin the buildup of their forces. Hitler was uncertain about committing his reserves because of the fear of additional landings, and those that he did commit had a difficult time reaching the front in the face of heavy air attacks.

For the first forty-five days of the invasion, the issue remained in doubt. The city of Caen, scheduled to be taken on D day, was not secured until late July. The Germans had concentrated their strength, particularly their Panzer divisions, against the British forces trying to take the city. Meanwhile, the Americans were finding the going extremely difficult through the hilly, wooded "bocage" country of Normandy, and only the capture of Cherbourg was accomplished on schedule. As July was drawing to a close, Eisenhower and his forces had little to cheer about. Progress had been slow, fighting difficult, and casualties heavy. They were well behind the schedule of advance called for by the invasion plans. There was no assurance that the Allied position on the continent could be maintained and every indication that the cost of doing so was going to be very high. The situation was cause for serious concern among the Allied High Command.

And yet, if one were to turn the clock forward just slightly over thirty days, the contrast would be overwhelming. By the end of August, there was no longer any question whatsoever that the invasion was a success—beyond even the most optimistic hopes of the invasion planners. The German invaders had been driven entirely out of France with the exception of a small area near the German border. The Allied armies were advancing at a pace unequaled in previous military experience. Several German armies had been practically destroyed. The most important strategic problem now facing the Allied High Command was that of crossing the Rhine River into Germany itself. Hopes were even being expressed that the war with Germany could be over by Christmas.

One is hard-pressed to find in military history such a dramatic change in circumstances in so short a period of time in a battle of such size and scope. August 1944 was truly a remarkable month. While the war in western Europe was to continue for nine more months, final victory was assured by the series of events that occurred during August. It was a month of bewildering activity—rapid buildup of Allied forces, the coming of age of the American army as an outstanding military organization, dramatic alterations and basic changes in Allied military strategy, unparalleled movement of forces, the flowering of the concept of unified Allied command in spite of frequent clashes of personality among its leaders. It also witnessed the utter defeat of the German army in France, the disastrous consequences of the assumption by Hitler of direct control over his armies, and the frequently outstanding fighting quality of many German individual fighting units.

The purpose of this book is to chronicle the history of the month of August in some detail. It is hoped that a fuller appreciation of the significance of the month's events can be provided by examining the day-by-day activities from several different points of view and through the eyes of a number of the participants. While the American point of view has been predominant, British, French, Canadian, and German viewpoints have also been included.

The narrative is chronological in nature. This approach does have its disadvantages in terms of providing a coherent analysis of particular campaigns. The campaign in Brittany, for example, could be better understood were it to be followed in one narrative from beginning to end. However, the war was fought day by day. The military personnel from general to private had to react to events as they occurred and had not the luxury of subsequent analysis or time to consider. The timing and interdependence of events are important in order to truly appreciate the impact on the participants and to understand more fully their decisions and actions in the light of these events.

It is also hoped that the chronological approach will somehow or other lead to a better appreciation of the enormity of the sweep of events that occurred during the month. Certainly, some of the campaigns in Russia were larger in scale if considered only in the light of the number of troops engaged. However, when you add the variety and complexity represented in the campaign in western Europe, it must be considered as one of the most monumental undertakings in the history of mankind. No period in the 336 days from the landing in Normandy until the German surrender better illustrates this fact than the 31 days of August 1944.

Tuesday, AUGUST 1

August 1, 1944, was an important day in the life of Lt. Gen. Omar N. Bradley. On this day (noon was the precise time) he was to relinquish command of the United States First Army in order to take charge of the Twelfth Army Group, which was to have responsibility for all United States Army forces in Normandy. It represented a command of twenty-one infantry and armored divisions plus numerous command, staff, and supporting units (a force of more than 900,000 men), which would more than double by the time the army reached the Elbe River in Germany nine months later.

Almost a year before, Gen. George C. Marshall had picked Bradley as the man to command the American troops in the assault on the European continent. At the time, Bradley had been a corps commander in Sicily and was genuinely surprised to have been chosen for such an important command. "It was astonishing the way he [Marshall] remembered me from [Fort] Benning,"[1] he had said at the time. It was at Fort Benning in the early 1930s that Marshall had begun keeping his "little black book,"[2] which contained a list of his selections of the most promising young officers in the army. Bradley's name had occupied a leading position on that list since its inception—a surprising choice, perhaps, but the product of years of careful judgment and selection.

Months of training, planning, and organizing in England

prior to the invasion and almost two months leading the First Army through the difficult early stages of the campaign—these were the experiences that Bradley brought to the important task he was about to undertake. He brought other things as well. In the words of General Eisenhower, he "displayed qualities of steadfastness, drive, professional skill, and a capacity for human understanding which became so obvious to his subordinates and his superiors alike that the American teamwork forged on the many battlefields of the Normandy beachhead was never thereafter seriously shaken."[3] The "Soldiers' General" was ready for the job.

As Bradley climbed into his jeep to take the fifteen-mile ride from the First Army headquarters a few miles north of Saint-Lô to his new headquarters at Twelfth Army Group, he had a mind full of plans for the future. But as his driver carefully picked his way through the ruins of Saint-Lô and past the villages of Saint-Gilles, La Chappelle, Marigny, and other scenes of recent fighting, Bradley could not help thinking back to recent events. This was D day + 56. The invasion—not yet two months old—had not gone quite the way the planners at Supreme Headquarters, Allied Expeditionary Forces (SHAEF) had projected.

As the jeep wound down the narrow roads of the Normandy countryside, Bradley was visibly reminded of one of the major obstacles that no one at SHAEF, or anywhere else, had prepared him for—the Normandy hedgerows. He described them this way:

> Across the neck of the Normandy peninsula, the hedgerows formed a natural line of defense more formidable than even Rommel could have contrived. For centuries the broad, rich flatlands had been divided and subdivided into tiny pastures whose earthen walls had grown into ramparts. Often the height and thickness of a tank, these hedgerows were crowned with a thorny growth of trees and brambles. Their roots had bound the packed earth as steel mesh reinforces concrete.
>
> Many were backed by deep drainage ditches and these the enemy utilized as a built-in system of communication trenches. To advance from pasture to pasture it became necessary for us to break a path through

those ramparts in the face of savage and well concealed enemy fire. Not even in Tunisia had we found more exasperating defensive terrain. Collins called it no less formidable than the jungles of Guadalcanal.[4]

For an army that was highly mechanized, whose strategy was based on speed and rapid deployment, these hedgerows were both maddening and deadly. Tanks were not only useless but on many occasions were sitting ducks. It was a type of terrain ideally suited for defense, and the Germans used it well.

As so often happened during the war, it was American ingenuity that found the closest thing to a solution. A twenty-nine-year-old sergeant from New York City named Curtis Culin, Jr., developed a series of tusklike prongs that fit onto the front of a tank. These prongs bit into the hedgerow, enabling the tank to plow through the dirt rather than climb up the bank and expose its underside to enemy fire. It was a very simple solution—but one that came too late to have a major impact on the "Battle of the Hedgerows."

As Bradley's jeep drove down the road crowded with American GIs, other thoughts came to mind. In contrast to their British allies, as well as to their German opponents, these American troops were green. Most of them had had no combat experience before setting foot on Normandy soil. Omar Bradley knew this and felt deeply the burden it placed on him. One of his most difficult decisions had been to assign the "Big Red One"—the 1st Infantry Division—to the Omaha Beach landing. They had landed in North Africa in 1942 and Sicily in 1943 and looked on another landing on the European mainland in 1944 as stretching their odds of survival beyond reasonable limits. The men found it difficult to understand why they should be picked again when so many other divisions were now available. But they were the only division with battle experience, and Bradley felt that he could not risk a landing without at least part of the force having been through it before. While he won no laurels from the troops of the Big Red One, the difficulties at the Omaha Beach landing gave him the grim satisfaction that his decision had been right.

The combination of green troops and an officer corps (from

general to lieutenant) that was also short on practical experience was bound to be doubly troublesome. True—it was possible to move officers around in an effort to broaden their experience, and some of the general officers in the Twelfth Army Group had seen duty in North Africa, Sicily, and even the Pacific theater. However, in this rapidly growing army there was a serious shortage of battle-experienced officers at all levels.

An example of this problem was the 90th Infantry Division. It had landed across Utah Beach on D + 2. Its mission: to cut across the Cherbourg peninsula. Its performance was poor; its attacks halfhearted and disorganized. From the moment the division landed, it had failed to meet its objectives. The commander, Brig. Gen. Jay MacKelvie, in the job only two months, as his predecessor had gone on to corps command, was relieved on the fourth day after the landing. His corps commander, Maj. Gen. J. Lawton "Lightning Joe" Collins, not known for his patience with subordinates, replaced MacKelvie with his own deputy at the VII Corps, Maj. Gen. Eugene Landrum, in the hopes that he could "clean house" and get the division in fighting shape. After little more than a month, however, it was clear that the job was not being done, and morale was sinking fast. There was serious consideration given to taking the unprecedented step of breaking up the division and assigning the troops elsewhere. Then Bradley located a man whose career he had followed since the Sicily campaign—Brig. Gen. Raymond S. McLain—a National Guard officer who had shown real promise as a division artillery commander in Sicily. He had been given the 90th Division job just two days before, and Bradley was cautiously confident he could get the job done where others had failed.

Still another picture flashed across Bradley's mind—the trip he had made on June 22 back to Omaha Beach, where he was "appalled by the desolation for it vastly exceeded that of D day."[5] A great storm had racked the English Channel for two days, destroying one of the two large artificial harbors designed and built by the British and causing serious damage to the other. Unfortunately for Bradley, the harbor at Omaha Beach was the one destroyed. Since delivery across the beaches was still the only significant source of supply, everything from troop landings to food supplies was affected. But the biggest problem was ammunition. The general would not soon forget the frustration he felt when he had to call off an attack down the Cotentin Peninsula by Major General Middleton's VIII Corps because of lack of ammunition, knowing full well that during this delay the Germans were steadily adding troops and ammunition to their side of the line. Inadequate supplies to the fighting front were a problem that would plague Bradley for months to come, but Mother Nature had made it particularly difficult during the past six weeks.

In spite of all the gloomy thoughts, the general did have many reasons to smile as he approached his new command post a few miles north of the cathedral city of Coutances. First, there was the capture of Saint-Lô. It had been a costly campaign—the city was in absolute ruins, and there were more than 5,000 American casualties. But because of the city's strategic location, its capture was a necessary forerunner to the task of breaking out of the Normandy grip that had held the armies since D day.

Key to accomplishing the breakout was a plan called COBRA. It envisaged a massive attack on a very narrow front, preceded by a saturation bombing attack made possible by the Allies' almost absolute control of the air over Normandy. With the capture of Saint-Lô, a jumping-off place for the attack was established on a road running northwest from that city to the town of Periers. The saturation and breakthrough area was to be 7,000 yards wide and 2,500 yards deep. The attack was to be launched by four battle-tested infantry divisions plus elements of two armored divisions—all under the control of the VII Corps and Joe Collins. A powerful force, indeed, for such a small front.

Bradley, Collins, and their staffs had formulated this novel plan with the help of an air force major general named Pete Quesada—a name that always brought a smile to Bradley's lips. Pete was one air force general who believed wholeheartedly in air-to-ground support, while most of his compatriots looked upon it as an evil to be avoided at all costs —an inefficient use of plane and pilot. He kept his command post close to the ground troops that his planes were to support, and as a result he and Bradley saw quite a bit of each other. In brainstorming about the COBRA operation, the two of them had come up with an idea that was to have an important influence on COBRA, and subsequent operations as well. The problem was to provide effective air cover for tank operations when rapid movement through changing terrain was involved. Quesada remembered the conversation this way:

> Quesada: "Look, Brad, if you will concentrate your armor, I'll tell you what I'll do. I will keep over every column that you establish a flight of bombers from daylight until dark."
> Bradley: "You will?"
> Q: "Yes, I will."
> B: "For every column that I establish?"
> Q: "Yes, and further than that, Brad, we'll do something else that I think will be of tremendous help. We will put in the lead tank of every column an aircraft radio and fix it so they can talk to the flight that is above them which will be there from dawn to dusk."
> B: "Terrific. You'll do that? Can you do it?"
> Q: "Yes. Furthermore, in order for that talk to be meaningful to the pilot, I'll put an aviator in the tank."[6]

When Bradley ordered a couple of tanks sent to the IX Tactical Air Force headquarters so that the radio installation could be worked out, the officer on the receiving end thought the general must have made a mistake, and he sent the tanks to the 9th Infantry Division instead. What would the air force want with tanks? When the 9th Infantry said the tanks were not for them, the officer called the General back. When the orders were repeated—IX Tactical Air Force—he could only comment, "Well, I'll be damned."[7]

The idea worked, and as tank operations became more rapid, daring, and innovative during the coming months, the marriage between Bradley's tanks and Quesada's friendly "eyes in the sky" became complete.

With all its hope and promise, the COBRA operation had begun on a note of disappointment. Poor flying weather caused several postponements, and when on July 24 the postponement came a little late, word failed to reach some of the planes. The result was the loss of some element of surprise to the enemy, and because many bombs were dropped short, there were 25 men killed and 131 wounded in the 30th Division, one of the units that was to lead the attack.

Bradley had a vehement argument with the air force over the direction of the bombing attack. He wanted the bombing run to be parallel to the line separating the armies in order to protect his men from short bomb drops. The air force preferred to fly perpendicular to the line so that their planes would be over the target area for a shorter period and therefore be less exposed to antiaircraft fire. Perpendicular was the direction that was used. Bradley, who felt he had been promised a parallel drop, was to say as much as thirty-five years later, "I have seldom been so angry. It was duplicity—a shocking breach of good faith."[8]

Duplicity or not, the attack was launched the next day with another perpendicular drop during which an even larger number of American troops were killed and injured. But the preponderant bulk of the air attack fell on the German army, and the effect was earth-shattering, to say the least. It still took two days of very heavy fighting in this bombed-out area before cracks in the German line began to develop. Joe Collins's VII Corps, both armored and infantry, moved southwest towards Coutances and the west coast of the Normandy peninsula. This threatened to cut off elements of the German Seventh Army that were defending this part of the line. When Major General Middleton's VIII Corps then attacked from the north along the western coast, the German retreat became a rout. The VIII Corps, struggling to move fast along crowded roads, managed to capture intact two key bridges over the Sée and the Sélune rivers. This enabled the American forces to turn into the Brittany peninsula at Avranches and past the monastery of Mont-Saint-Michel. The left hinge of the German defense in Normandy had been shattered.

The jeep came to a stop in front of a wheeled caravan type of office that was to serve as Bradley's command post through much of the European campaign. He was greeted by the members of the Twelfth Army Group Staff, most of whom he had known and worked with as far back as the days in North Africa: Lev Allen, chief of staff; Red O'Hare, G-1

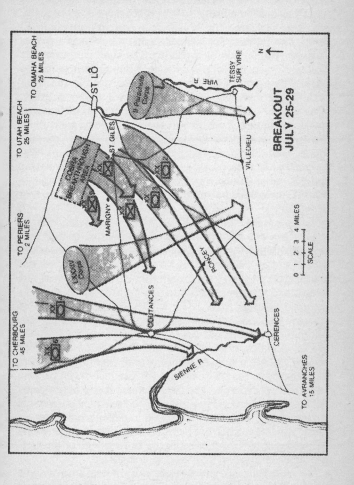

**BREAKOUT
JULY 25-29**

(Administration and Personnel); Ed Sibert, G-2 (Intelligence); Frank Kibler, G-3 (Operations). They had been working together as a unit organizing the Twelfth Army Group for some time. This made the activation of the group easy and efficient, and they were ready for business when the general arrived.

Certainly there was plenty to do. The word on everyone's mind was ''exploit''—how to exploit this great opportunity that had developed over the past few days. From the point of view of army organization, Bradley was in good shape. As he moved into Twelfth Army Group Command, the rapidly growing United States forces in Normandy were to be split into two armies—the First, under Lt. Gen. Courtney Hodges, and the Third, under the best known and most controversial of American field generals, George Patton. Patton's army was to be on the right (west) of the line and consist of the VIII Corps already committed, the XV Corps just coming on the scene, and two other corps (XII and XX) to be in action in a matter of days. The First Army under Hodges with the V, VII, and XIX Corps represented the bulk of the troops involved in the recent fighting. Both army commanders (Patton and Hodges) had been working for several weeks under Bradley with the troops now under their command and were able to ''hit the ground running'' when their commands became official.

As the general and his staff reviewed the situation, one opportunity and one potential problem clearly emerged in the light of recent events. The opportunity was to break out into Brittany, with the primary goal being to capture the several important ports on the peninsula—Brest, Saint-Malo, Lorient, and Saint-Nazaire. This achievement was a major component of the SHAEF invasion plan because of the logistical problems represented by maintaining such a large army on the Continent. Supply over the beaches was deemed to be inadequate at best, and certainly the July storm had made it an even riskier bet.

The potential problem was more tactical than strategic. As the American troops turned the corner into Brittany, they were in effect turning their backs on the enemy. The narrow corridor down which the VIII Corps had raced to turn the corner at Avranches needed to be expanded and the corner itself protected from possible enemy attack. These were the matters that the Twelfth Army Group Staff addressed on this, the first morning of their active existence.

From his headquarters at Chateau La Roche Guyon, Field Marshal Guenther von Kluge had a lovely view overlooking the northward bend of the Seine River as it wound its way from Paris to the sea. The chateau—seat of the Dukes of Rochefoucauld—was built into the chalk cliffs that rose steeply from the river. The ruins of the original Norman castle of the eleventh century dominated the cliff above the castle's more recent successor.

On this day, however, the beauty and tranquility of the scene were lost on von Kluge. He had problems everywhere he turned. He had little reason for optimism or hope, and mixed feelings about the chain of events that had brought him here.

An army commander on the Russian front, he had been seriously wounded in an automobile accident near Minsk in the fall of 1943. Laid up for months, he was finally ready to return to duty when Hitler lost patience with Field Marshal Gerd von Runstedt, his overall commander of the western front. A hero of the 1940 blitzkrieg of western Europe, von Runstedt was both disdainful of Hitler and at odds with his grand strategy for conducting the war.[9]

Von Kluge was sent to the headquarters of *Oberbefehlshaber West (OB West)* on the outskirts of Paris to assume command. As commander of *OB West*, von Kluge had operational control of all German ground forces in western Europe and reported directly to Oberkommando der Wehrmacht (OKW), Hitler's military high command. Reporting to von Kluge were two army groups. *Army Group G* was responsible for the defense of southern France. *Army Group B*'s area of responsibility covered northern France, Belgium, and the Netherlands, including the defense of the Atlantic Wall, of which Normandy was a part. The commander of *Army Group B* was Field Marshal Erwin Rommel.

Another automobile accident was to play an important part in von Kluge's career. This time it was Rommel who on July 17 was seriously injured when his car crashed while attempting to evade a low-level bombing attack on a road in the Normandy countryside.

In view of the critical importance of the Normandy front, von Kluge decided, with Hitler's concurrence, to take over command of *Army Group B* as well as *OB West*. In order to be in closer touch with the battle, he moved his personal headquarters to Chateau La Roche Guyon, which had served as headquarters for *Army Group B* under Rommel. He left his chief of staff, Lieutenant General Blumentritt, in charge of the Paris headquarters of *OB West*.

Back at the chateau after two days at the front, von Kluge knew full well how serious a dilemma he faced. The American breakthrough down the west coast of the Normandy peninsula had exposed the left flank of his defense, and all his efforts to plug the gap seemed fruitless.

He was particularly displeased with Colonel General Hausser, the *Seventh Army* commander whose troops represented the bulk of the forces in Normandy. Von Kluge had warned Hausser several days before against using his Panzer divisions as front-line defensive units. "If there is a breakthrough anywhere along the line, you will have no way to react," von Kluge had told Hausser. "Your Panzer divisions should be used as a mobile reserve against any penetration." Hausser, on the other hand, felt that "tanks formed the backbone of the position: built into the ground, they served as anti-tank guns." The two divisions stayed in line.[10]

Von Kluge would like to have replaced Hausser, but because Hausser was one of Himmler's SS commanders, von Kluge either was unable or felt it politically unwise to do so. However, he had made some command changes several days before. He replaced the *LXXXIV Corps* commander (Lt. Gen. Dietrich von Choltitz) as well as Hausser's chief of staff (Maj. Gen. Max Pemsel). Pemsel's replacement (Maj. Gen. Rudolph von Gersdorff) had left La Roche Guyon just three days before with some specific orders for Hausser concerning his defensive movements, which were the subject of von Kluge's most serious displeasure with his subordinate.

Von Kluge had emphasized the importance of the *LXXXIV Corps* (the left wing of the *Seventh Army*) withdrawing south in order to protect the key cities of Avranches and Pontaubault—the gateway for the Allies' turning movement into Brittany. Von Gersdorff, with these orders in his pocket, had arrived too late to deliver them, and all other forms of communication had been totally disrupted. As a result, von Kluge's orders were in vain.

Analyzing the situation on his own, Hausser was concerned that if he withdrew straight south, the Americans would drive a wedge between the *LXXXIV Corps* on the left and the rest of his *Seventh Army*. With this potential danger in mind, he ordered a withdrawal to the southeast, hoping thereby to keep his army intact.

The results were as von Kluge had feared. Not only was the way into Brittany left unguarded; there were other disastrous consequences. While the U.S. Third Army was heading south for Avranches and Pontaubault, the First Army on its left had been active as well. Spearheaded by two armored divisions, the troops were driving south against savage resistance from the bulk of the German *Seventh Army*. The 2nd Armored Division had made rapid progress and on July 29 and 30 found themselves directly across the route of the retreating left flank of Hausser's army in the vicinity of the small village of Roncey. In two days and nights of bitter fighting, the Germans lost more than 1,500 dead and 4,000 captured plus a large number of their vehicles, including tanks.[11]

Frustrated by lack of information and breakdowns in all communications, and scrambling to somehow find troops to plug the growing breach in his defensive position, von Kluge indeed had his hands full. "It's a madhouse here." "You can't imagine what it's like." "It's a crazy situation."[12] These were the words he had used in describing the situation to General Blumentritt back in Paris. Trying to create some order out of all the chaos would have consumed all the general's time and energy this first day of August except that pressures were arising from other sources as well.

On the previous day, Col. Gen. Alfred Jodl, chief of staff of the German army, had journeyed to Rastenburg in East Prussia—site of Adolph Hitler's Wolfschanze ("Wolf's Lair") secret headquarters. It was here just eleven days earlier that the unsuccessful attempt on Hitler's life had taken place. As a result of the bombing, the Führer was still suffering physical problems that were to plague him for the rest of his life. But the major effect of this misadventure was to add emphasis to his growing distrust of his generals, many of whom had been involved in the plot. More and more, Hitler was assuming for himself complete control of the prosecution of the war.

Jodl's visit was to discuss overall military strategy, but the Normandy problem was at the top of the agenda. Hitler's solution to the problems in Normandy was to hold the line everywhere at all costs. He ordered all the Brittany ports to be defended "to the last man." He refused to even consider a strategy favored by a number of his top military advisors —withdrawal to a defensive line north of the Seine River. However, he had agreed after a month or more of urging by von Runstedt, Rommel, and von Kluge to move a number of divisions to Normandy from the *Fifteenth Army* in the Calais-Boulogne area. These divisions had been held there to defend against an anticipated second Allied invasion from England, which Hitler agreed now was not likely to occur. These troops were at various stages of transit to Normandy, but as yet none had arrived. In considering his options of response to the American breakthrough, Hitler looked first at the vulnerability of the American army rather than at any threat they represented to his own forces. He was thinking in terms of attack, not defense. He reasoned that by attacking the American columns moving south toward Avranches, he could split them in two and turn imminent defeat into victory by destroying the American army piece by piece.

As this strategy became known to von Kluge, it is clear that he must have considered parts of it illogical, unreasonable, and impractical. On the other hand, there was that promise of reinforcement from seven divisions (most from the Calais area), which he had been urging on the Führer for some time. That most of them did not arrive in time to do any good could only have been a matter of conjecture at the time. At least in this very early stage, von Kluge appears to have accepted these strategic directions from his Führer without the objections and arguments that were to mark their relations over the next several weeks. While stemming the tide of American successes and building the best defense possible under the circumstances may have been a major challenge and a full-time job for von Kluge, he now began directing his attention also to the vulnerability of the American Third Army as it streamed southward, and the intriguing possibility of a counteroffensive that might cut it in two. Even if it did not result in the crowning victory the Führer had in mind, a semisuccess might be very useful in buying time badly needed to stabilize a rapidly deteriorating front. But how to find the troops? What Panzer divisions were available to spearhead the attack? Could the Luftwaffe supply enough planes to even begin to challenge the Allied mastery of the air over Normandy? How about organization and command of the attack? Difficult questions for a commander who was largely out of touch with his subordinates and whose troops were fighting for their lives.

Without a doubt, the happiest man in France was Lt. Gen. George S. Patton, Jr. His year in purgatory was over. He was again where he knew his destiny intended him to be—in command of a large army locked in a battle of major consequence, a battle in which decisive victory would establish him among the ranks of the great military leaders—Hannibal, Caesar, Alexander. By God, it felt good.

Almost a year had gone by since he led the Seventh Army into Messina to conclude the Sicilian campaign. A campaign that in less than a month had driven the Italian and German troops out of Sicily and provided a sound base for the upcoming invasion of Italy. A campaign made doubly satisfying by his winning the well-publicized race to Messina against the British Eighth Army of General Montgomery. A campaign which Eisenhower described as "sure to be a model of 'swift conquest' for future students at the Army War College."[13] President Roosevelt had wired: "All of us are thrilled. . . . My thanks and enthusiastic approbation."[14]

And then the bottom fell out. Within a matter of days Patton received his first "very nasty letter from Ike"[15] concerning his harsh treatment of two hospitalized soldiers—known more widely as the "slapping incidents." These unfortunate incidents, combined with Patton's exuberant nature and often uncontrolled tongue, had caused Eisenhower to write General Marshall that Patton continued "to exhibit those unfortunate personal traits which you and I have always known."[16] Within a month, Patton saw the two most important commands in the European theater go to generals he considered to be his juniors both in terms of experience and ability: Mark

Clark to command the Italian campaign and Omar Bradley the European invasion. His star was clearly on the decline.

A long sustained period of inactivity and routine or ceremonial duties was very difficult for one who had become used to being in the limelight, and who loved it. He wrote to his wife in January 1944: "My present status is so confused as to be unexplainable—it is confusion doubly confounded and no one has told me a thing."[17] And later on in the month: "I am sure that the 'incident' was far harder on you than me as I simply did the ostrich act and would neither see nor hear any evil though I did a hell of a lot of thinking."[18]

Patton's inactivity was put to use by the Allied High Command, but hardly in a way that he would have approved of or that satisfied his all-consuming ambition and belief in his destiny. Since his military abilities were highly regarded by the German High Command, his disappearance from the scene was used by intelligence sources to suggest a number of possible military operations that might be under his command. A decoy, if you will. The most significant of these was put in place after Patton reached England in late January 1944. He was at the center of a plan called FORTITUDE— a complex intelligence operation whose purpose was to convince the German High Command that the Allied invasion of the Continent would occur in the Pas-de-Calais area of northwestern France. The plan was even continued after June 6 by implying that the Normandy landing was a feint to disguise the real invasion to take place at Pas-de-Calais under the leadership of Patton. Even after he took official command of the Third Army in France, no public announcement was made for some time in an effort to prolong the deception. Although he certainly appreciated the value of FORTITUDE, he did not like the role he played in it. But if that was his ticket back to active command of troops in the field, he was by then more than willing to pay the price.

And now he was back. Had he been given the choice, he could not have picked a more propitious moment. The Third Army's war had become one of movement, speed, and daring—his kind of war. The VIII Corps under Middleton was now into Brittany and moving at such a pace that it was impossible to keep track of its location and movements. The XV Corps under Haislip was operational and advancing down the Normandy peninsula ready to move wherever needed. Patton's two other corps (XX and XII) were not far behind. It was a time for audacity. As the general said in his diary: "Do not take counsel of your fears."[19]

It was midafternoon when Bradley arrived at the Third Army command post a few miles south of Coutances. He had just come from First Army headquarters. The main purpose there as well as here was to outline the new army boundaries; the rapid pace of events caused frequent changes. While there Bradley expressed concern to Patton about the possibility of an attack on the left flank of the southward-moving Third Army, coming from the Mortain area. Patton was much more interested in pushing his attack into Brittany than worrying about his flank. But he agreed to send one of Haislip's divisions—the 90th Infantry—into the area to cover the flank.

As soon as Bradley left, Patton took off for the VIII Corps CP a few miles down the road towards Avranches. Middleton faced a difficult problem. He had two armored divisions— the 4th and 6th—taking off into the Brittany peninsula in different directions and already beyond effective radio communication range. He was concerned about his own lack of information and the increasingly exposed position of his forces.

But Patton would have none of that. He criticized Middleton for slowness in getting infantry follow-up to his two armored divisions and directed him to send the 8th Infantry to back up the 4th Armored moving south towards Rennes and the 79th to back up the 6th Armored moving west towards Brest, the major port in Brittany. He urged Middleton to develop speed and aggressiveness among his troops—not caution and concern. No matter that it was almost 200 miles to Brest through country presumably occupied by the enemy. He wanted Brest taken—and he wanted it in days, not weeks.

As he rode back to his own CP in the evening, Patton could feel the exhilaration of the day's activities. He wrote in his diary that evening, "Compared to war, all other human activities are futile, if you like war as I do."[20]

By God, it was good to be back.

As reports of Bradley's and Patton's successes poured into the Twenty-first Army Group headquarters located in the garden of the chateau at Creuilly near Caen, General Montgomery had reason to be pleased. It was "his" plan coming to fruition. He had seen it months ago in reviewing the early plans for OVERLORD. In his capacity as commander of all ground forces in Normandy, until superseded by Eisenhower (which would occur on September 1), his job had been to put the practical finishing touches on the OVERLORD plan. The strategy he decided on was to use the troops on the left—the British Second Army—as the hinge of a large turning movement involving the Americans on the right. The British and Canadians were to keep the enemy occupied, to draw the attention of their major forces so that the Americans could break through at the other end of the line.

As Montgomery saw it, that is exactly what had happened. In late July at the time of the American breakthrough, there were by his count six Panzer divisions (645 tanks) facing the Second Army and only two divisions (190 tanks) facing the Americans.[21] While the British and Canadian forces had gained very little ground in the almost two months since D day, they had kept the Germans occupied. They had absorbed most of the enemy's manpower (particularly its armored manpower) in a series of hard-fought battles in and around the vicinity of Caen. Operation GOODWOOD in the middle of July was quite similar to the later American COBRA operation involving an attack in depth on a narrow front with massive air support. In spite of some early success, it had ground to a halt after encountering heavy opposition, particularly from Panzer divisions. A disappointment in one sense, but it kept the German forces heavily engaged. Indeed, if there was any real reason for disappointment, it was rather the length of time required for the Americans to achieve their breakthrough, considering the balance of enemy opposition on the two fronts.

Although behind schedule, the plan had worked, providing vindication for Montgomery's strategic choices and some recompense for the heavy human costs of putting them into effect. But as evidence of strategic success mounted, the general saw storm clouds elsewhere on the horizon. There was growing dissatisfaction on the home front in England. The lack of any visible progress in the fighting during July was hard to take. The English people needed good news from the front to buoy their spirits and help them endure the terrible buzz-bomb attacks, which had risen to levels that outdid the blitz of 1940. Then, when the battle success finally had come, all they heard about were the Americans. What happened to "our" boys? Why weren't they ripping apart the Germans as the Americans were? Did Montgomery know what he was doing?

Civilian criticism was a cross that generals had borne for centuries. Montgomery knew that and could understand it. However, other sources of criticism disturbed him more. He had been told about a dinner meeting several days earlier between Eisenhower and Churchill at which Eisenhower had been critical of the lack of aggressiveness and vigor with which the British had pressed their attacks. This feeling had been growing at SHAEF, not only among American officers, who might be expected to be jealous and critical of the testy, flamboyant British commander, but among many British members of the staff as well. A leader among these was Air Chief Marshal Arthur Tedder, chief air officer in the Mediterranean during the period of Montgomery's Africa campaign and now Eisenhower's deputy commander. Lieutenant General Frederick Morgan, leader of the group that developed the original plans for OVERLORD and now a member of the SHAEF staff, was another. Most British Air Force generals were also highly critical—mainly because of their impatience to reach the flat terrain in the Caen area, badly needed for the establishment of airfields on the Continent. Indeed, Montgomery's conceited, imperious, and often abrasive nature had left him with more enemies than friends among the ranks of the British senior commanders.

This criticism and grumbling naturally did not sit well with Montgomery, but most galling was what emanated from Eisenhower. Montgomery had a rather low opinion of Eisenhower's strategic abilities. "It was always very clear to me that Ike and I were poles apart when it came to the conduct of the war," he wrote.[22] To Montgomery, Eisenhower was a politician, not a military man. To the hero of El Alamein, the conqueror of Rommel's Africa Corps, the chief architect of the now-successful breakout strategy in Normandy, it seemed hardly appropriate that an American with limited and dubious military credentials should be exercising judgements on his performance in battle. "I do not think that this great and good man, now one of my greatest friends, had any idea of the trouble he was starting," wrote Montgomery after the war. "From that time onward there were always 'feelings' between the British and American forces till the war ended."[23]

On balance, however, in spite of all the carping and criticism, Montgomery still had reason to be pleased today. His strategy was working. On top of that, he had a lot of other ideas on the best way to follow up these Normandy successes. If those "arm-chair strategists" would just leave him alone and give him the support he needed, he could end this war in a hurry.

Wednesday, AUGUST 2

Troy Middleton was a tried and tested soldier. He had enlisted in the army as a private thirty-five years ago. His performance during World War I had been outstanding. As commander of two different infantry regiments in France, he had become the youngest regimental commander in the army. Later he attended the Command and General Staff School at Fort Leavenworth. One of his classmates was George Patton. He retired from the army in 1937 to become administrative dean of Louisiana State University but was recalled to active duty in 1942.

He assumed command of the 45th Division, a National Guard unit from Texas, Oklahoma, Colorado, and New Mexico known as the Thunderbirds, and took them to the Mediterranean just in time to make the landing in Sicily. A risky business—sending a newly arrived, inexperienced division into a beachhead landing as its first combat experience. But the 45th had the reputation of being one of the best trained divisions ever to leave the U.S. for duty overseas, and their performance in Sicily proved the point. The first division to reach the north shore, they participated in the famous race to Messina under the watchful eyes of Bradley, their corps commander, and Patton, commander of the Seventh Army. Patton told Eisenhower that he was "very much pleased"[1] with Middleton.

After participating in the Salerno landing in Italy, an old knee injury caught up with Major General Middleton, and he was forced to enter a hospital in Naples and then return to Walter Reed Hospital in Washington, D.C. His recovery was facilitated by the knowledge that Eisenhower wanted him for an important corps command in Normandy. When General Marshall questioned the choice because of Middleton's disability, Eisenhower replied, "I don't give a damn about his knees. I want his head and his heart. And I'll take him into battle on a litter if we have to."[2]

No litter was required as the VIII Corps became operational in the middle of June and took part in the Cherbourg campaign, COBRA, and then led the breakthrough into Brittany. Middleton had indeed earned his stars, and few generals in the European theater could boast of a better combat record. He had every reason to be self-assured and confident as he went about his duties as VIII Corps commander.

This morning, however, in his command post at Sartilly, a few miles north of Avranches, he was experiencing pangs of doubt and confusion. Late the previous afternoon he had received a "dressing down" from Patton for being overly cautious and not sufficiently aggressive. But at the moment he had two armored divisions (the 4th and the 6th) speeding into the Brittany peninsula. They were widely separated, moving in diverging directions, without any protection on their flanks, rapidly getting beyond the range of effective radio communications with VIII Corps headquarters, and, worst of all, with their rear facing the enemy. Did this display caution and lack of aggressiveness? Or was it just plain stupidity and recklessness?

While he was pondering these questions, a most welcome visitor pulled into his CP—Omar Bradley. Middleton wasted no time in telling the general about his concerns. "I hate to attack with so much of the enemy at my rear, especially when it's exposed. If the other fellow were to break through at Avranches to the coast, I'd be cut off way out here in Brittany," he said.

He found a willing listener. Bradley had already warned Patton about the need to build up a strong shoulder of defense to the south and east of Avranches to protect the movement into Brittany. Now it seemed that these orders were being ignored, and that made him angry. "Dammit," he said, "George seems more interested in making headlines with the capture of Brest than in using his head on tactics. . . . We can't take a chance on an open flank. That's why I ordered George to block the peninsula neck."

After trying unsuccessfully to reach Patton, Bradley did something he did not ordinarily like to do; he countermanded an order of one of his subordinates. "Order the 79th down to Fougères, and we'll build up there as George was told to do," he instructed Middleton. "We can't afford to waste any more time. If the Germans were to bust in with a couple of divisions on that open flank, we'd all look kinda silly."[3]

The 79th Division had been ordered by Patton to support the 6th Armored Division in their advance toward Brest and were at that moment just starting their move into Brittany. It was, therefore, a relatively simple matter to reverse the division's direction toward Fougères, some twenty-five miles southeast of Avranches.

However, Patton had not been quite as unmindful of the protection of his flanks as Bradley had thought. At about the same time as the Middleton-Bradley exchange, he had issued an order for the 5th Armored Division to occupy Fougères. The 5th was a part of Patton's XV Corps, which was just now coming on to the scene. One of its divisions—the 90th Infantry—was already establishing a position at Saint-Hilaire, just north of Fougères.

With the shift in orders, the 5th Armored was held in the Avranches area, and the 79th Infantry was transferred from the VIII to the XV Corps. With two infantry divisions backed up by an armored division (all part of the XV Corps) facing southeast, the protection for the VIII Corps rear would at least get past the crisis stage as soon as the movements could be completed, hopefully by the following morning.

Bradley's change in the orders did create some confusion, as the 79th Division was required to shift from the VIII to the XV Corps. It also created some ruffled feathers. Although Patton accepted the change with outward good humor, his diary records, "I did not agree with him and feared he was getting the British complex of over-caution. It is noteworthy that just about a year ago to the day I had to force him to conduct an attack in Sicily."[4]

The change in orders did have one positive effect. By virtue of its position beyond Avranches, the 79th Division could be moved to Fougères without having to pass through that city. The same was not true of the 5th Armored. And Avranches was a traffic nightmare. It was a very small neck to a very large bottle with everything—tanks, trucks, infantry, artillery, supplies, ammunition—trying to squeeze through to the south side of the Sée River. Patton himself had spent most of the morning as a sort of super traffic manager trying to expedite the passage of the 90th Division on its way to Saint-Hilaire. Until the neck of the bottle could be considerably widened, only the tightest control and strictest discipline could keep utter chaos from taking over.

The effort to widen the gap was at this stage primarily defensive maneuver. Its purpose was to enable men and materiel to get through both to expedite the VIII Corps attacks into Brittany and to establish a defensive screen protecting the corps rear areas from enemy attack. As the troops of the XV Corps moved into the area over the next day or two, new and exciting opportunities began to unfold. What started out as a defensive tactic was rapidly changing into something entirely different.

At three o'clock in the afternoon, Lt. Gen. Courtney Hodges arrived at his new command post. His staff had made the move that morning. The CP was located on the grounds of the chateau of the Count of Marigny in the countryside a few miles southwest of Saint-Lô. The general's van was situated near a lake and some fifty yards from the chateau itself, which provided excellent working quarters for his staff. It was, all in all, a very satisfactory CP and a vast improvement over the staff's previous quarters.[5]

Hodges, however, was not all that concerned with the facilities offered by this new location other than to issue some sharp orders about a number of trucks that had been lined up near the chateau and were a dead giveaway to any enemy observation activity. What concerned him more was the fact that the new CP was no more than ten miles south of its predecessor, which had been headquarters for the First Army since before the fall of Saint-Lô. Even though the troops of the First Army had been responsible for the successful

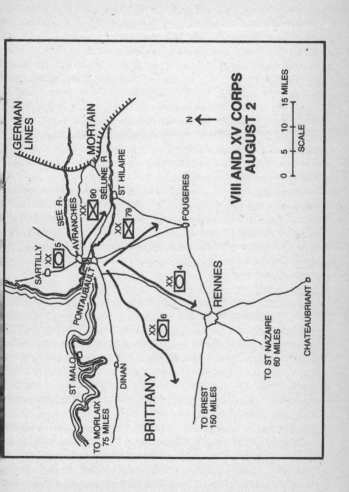

COBRA operation and subsequent breakout, the follow-up had fallen to the lot of the Third Army. The three corps of the First Army (V, VII, and XIX) were left facing heavy resistance from an undefeated opponent. After a few sharp gains made during the last few days of July, the fighting had settled back into that all-too-familiar pattern of determined resistance and grudgingly small advances. There was no need for rapid changes of CP location to keep up with the troops, as was the case with the Third Army.

Hodges had officially taken over command of the First Army from Bradley just the day before. Not much transition was required, however, as Hodges had been deputy commander under Bradley since the preinvasion days in England and was intimately familiar with all phases of First Army operations and personnel.

A military man all his life, Hodges enlisted in the Regular Army as a private following an unsuccessful stint at West Point. In spite of his failure at the Academy, he still managed to earn a second lieutenant's commission by being promoted from the ranks. He received his commission only one year later than his fellow classmates at West Point. He first saw service under Pershing in Mexico and fought in France during World War I as a battalion and regimental commander. He held various posts between the wars including the position of commandant of the Infantry School at Fort Benning, Georgia. After several stateside training and command posts during the early years of the war (including a brief stint as commander of the Third Army before it left for Europe), he was sent to England as deputy commander of the First Army in March 1944.

A spare, quiet, self-effacing person, Hodges was the absolute opposite of his fellow army commander General Patton. Yet in the eyes of his superiors, he took a second seat to no one. According to Bradley, "He was essentially a military technician whose faultless techniques and tactical knowledge made him one of the most skilled craftsmen of my entire command. . . . Because he was unostentatious and retiring, Hodges occupied an almost-anonymous role in the war. Yet as a general's general his stature among our U.S. commanders was rivaled only by that of Simpson. For Hodges successfully blended dexterity and common sense in such equal proportions as to produce a magnificently balanced command. I had implicit faith in his judgement, in his skill and restraint. Of all my army commanders he required the least supervision.''[6]

No sooner had Hodges arrived at his new CP than he went into conference with his two aides—Maj. Gen. Bill Kean, his chief of staff, and Col. Stubby Thorson, his operations officer. The rapid advances of the Third Army had formed the First Army front into a large arc. On the left and adjoining the British Second Army was Maj. Gen. Leonard Gerow's V Corps, facing south, with the important crossroads town of Vire as its main objective some five to ten miles away. On Gerow's right, facing in a southeastern direction, was Maj. Gen. Pete Corlett's XIX Corps. On the far right was the VII Corps of Joe Collins facing southeast to east. The mission of these three corps was twofold. First, they were to put all the pressure possible on the German *Seventh Army* to make it impossible for troops to be transferred to the U.S. Third Army area of operations. Second, they were to push the enemy back in order to widen the corridor through which the Third Army was moving and deny the Germans the use of important towns and roads that represented a threat to the Third Army advance.

But the German *Seventh Army* was rapidly recovering from the shocks it had received during the past week. Aided by hilly terrain and their interior lines of communication resulting from the shape of the front lines, they were effectively challenging the heavy pressure from the three corps of the First Army. The withdrawal of the German *LXXXIV Corps* to the southeast may have cost them the city of Avranches (as von Kluge had predicted), but it had enabled a more solid front to be built to resist the First Army advances.

Hodges and his staff were aware that only on the far right did there appear to be opportunity for any significant movement. The terrain there was more favorable, and the enemy less well established. In this part of the line, one of the problems had been not so much the Germans but rather the U.S. Third Army, which was crowding the VII Corps off the limited road network in the corridor to Avranches. The pressure naturally forced the corps toward the east. This plus the recognized need to widen the corridor had led Hodges to

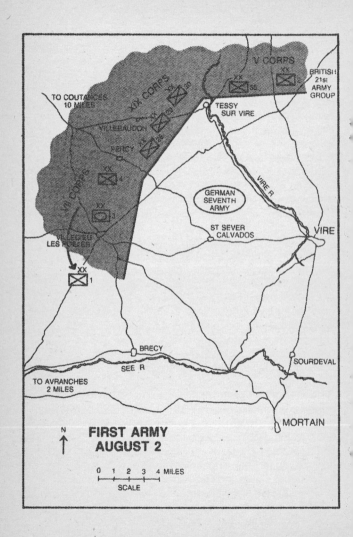

TO COUTANCES
10 MILES

XX
XIX CORPS

VILLEBAUDON

PERCY

XIX CORPS

VILLEDIEU
LES POELES

XX
VII CORPS

V CORPS

BRITISH
21st
ARMY
GROUP

TESSY
SUR VIRE

VIRE R.

GERMAN
SEVENTH
ARMY

ST SEVER
CALVADOS

VIRE

SOURDEVAL

BRECY

SEE R.

TO AVRANCHES
2 MILES

MORTAIN

N

**FIRST ARMY
AUGUST 2**

0 1 2 3 4 MILES
SCALE

order Collins earlier in the day to turn his corps in a more eastwardly direction.

As a preliminary move toward implementing this change of direction, Collins ordered Major General Huebner, commander of the 1st Infantry Division (the Big Red One) on the corps' right, "to envelop the enemy left flank and exploit the breakthrough of his defenses."[7] The objective of this movement was a series of hills that extended between the Sée and Sélune rivers some twenty miles to the east of Avranches. Nestled in these hills on the road back to Avranches was an ancient town of 2,000 inhabitants, which boasted a medieval parish church and a twelfth century convent. It was also an important road center, with seven roads radiating out from the "centre ville." This town would soon be spelled in capital letters on the First Army situation maps, and would give Hodges and Collins more than a little cause for concern. The name of the town was Mortain.

As von Kluge wrestled with his problem of organizing effective countermeasures to the Allied breakthrough, he became less and less confident as the day wore on. To launch any kind of counterattack would require troops, and where were they to come from? Realignment of the forces currently in Normandy seemed out of the question. The Allies were applying heavy pressure all along the line—from the British zone around Caen all the way to Avranches. True, his line was holding in all areas except his left flank, but the pressure was severe.

Then there was that troublesome problem of air cover. To organize a counteroffensive, the utmost in security was required. Without air cover, troop movements were an open book to the enemy unless done at night—and that certainly had its problems. Air cover had been promised, but von Kluge had for some time discounted these promises. Seeing was believing as far as the German air force was concerned.

Of course, there were the promises of additional troops. A total of seven divisions had been ordered to the Normandy front—six infantry and one armored. A substantial force indeed. One infantry division was already in the *Seventh Army* rear area. Four more infantry divisions were coming from the north—the *Fifteenth Army* area. One was already across the Seine River and a second was in the process of making the crossing. One infantry and one armored division were coming from the south.

For any countermeasures to be effective, time was of the essence. Delay would only result in the widening of the Avranches corridor and an increase in the pressure along the entire front. Could these additional troops arrive in time to do any good? By all odds, three of the divisions should be on hand by the end of the week. As for the rest, it was questionable. Constant harassment by Allied planes and the French resistance had made any kind of troop movement difficult and unpredictable. There was also the question of the quality of the reinforcements. The one division that could provide the most help was the *9th Panzer Division*, but its timely arrival from south of the Loire River was the most questionable.

As these problems were being considered, toward evening a visitor arrived at the Chateau La Roche Guyon. Lieutenant General Walter Warlimont had been present at the meeting with Hitler two days earlier and had been sent to the front to explain and assure compliance with the decisions reached that day—a sign of the level of distrust that had crept into the Führer's relations with his field officers. Warlimont's instructions from Hitler were very clear: "You tell Field Marshal von Kluge to keep on looking to his front, to keep his eyes on the enemy and not to look over his shoulder."[8]

While these discussions were under way, a message was being decoded in the message room nearby. A top-priority communication—from the Führer himself. It was brought to von Kluge around 10 P.M. The message contained orders which read, "*Army Group B* together with all its main armored units will prepare a counteroffensive aiming to break through to Avranches with the objective of isolating the enemy forces and ensuring their destruction."[9]

"Isolating the enemy forces and ensuring their destruction." This did not sound like a limited offensive for the purpose of covering a longer-term withdrawal. It was clearly an order to go on the offensive, regardless of enemy strength, troop dispositions, or any other tactical considerations. It was, according to von Kluge, "an operation of extreme boldness. But . . . impossible to realize in practice."

Obviously, the time for consideration of options, selection of strategy, analysis of alternatives was past. As the clock moved on toward midnight this Wednesday evening, von Kluge was left with no choice but to figure a way to do the impossible.

The SHAEF main headquarters was located in Bushy Park, on the outskirts of London beyond the Richmond Park area. Across the road was Hampton Court, that sixteenth century palace of splendor built for Cardinal Wolsey, occupied by Henry VIII (and said to house the ghosts of two of his wives), embellished by Christopher Wren, and now one of London's leading tourist attractions. When General Eisenhower first arrived in England, his headquarters was located on Grosvenor Square in the heart of London. It was not so much the crowded conditions as it was the distractions to his staff that caused him to look elsewhere. He found what he was looking for in an American air force headquarters in Bushy Park (hence the code name of Widewing). A more military setting complete with Nissen huts, PXs, and mess halls, it provided the atmosphere the general preferred. It was also conveniently close to Telegraph Cottage, a small house in Kingston that he had first used as a residence during his English tour of duty in 1942. In early March 1944, the SHAEF headquarters was established at Widewing.

General Eisenhower's naval aide was Comdr. Harry Butcher—a friend, confidant, an unfailing diarist throughout the war. As Butcher was walking down the hall at Widewing shortly before lunch, he ran into the general wreathed in smiles. "If the intercepts are right," he told Butcher, "we are to hell and gone in Brittany and slicing 'em up in Normandy."[10]

Eisenhower had reason to be happy about the news from France, of course. He had received enough bad news over the previous two months not to respond eagerly to the good news of the past week. But he also was feeling relieved, as he had just come from putting the finishing touches on a long-overdue report to his superior in Washington, General Marshall. "I am sorry that I have not kept you more fully abreast of future plans as I did in North Africa," his "eyes only" message began. "My excuse is that in my anxiety to push events the matter had merely slipped my mind. Hereafter I will have the staff draw up a suitable weekly appreciation for the Combined Chiefs of Staff. My current and personal appreciation follows.''

From here, he went on to give a review of recent events before moving on to his assessment of the major strategy decisions he faced. Considering that the basic OVERLORD strategy had always considered the move into Brittany as the primary objective of this phase of the operation, he had some rather surprising things to say:

> We are attacking viciously in an effort to accomplish our purpose before the enemy can be successful in establishing new and strong lines. Future prospects must therefore be gauged by the varying degrees of success that we may achieve in the battle now raging. The first and most favorable prospect is that both our major attacks will enjoy a great degree of success. Should [British] Second Army succeed in getting firm hold of Vire while Bradley makes good his seizure of the Avranches area and then both forces operate toward the rear of that portion of the enemy now heavily engaged between those two attacks, we should not only gain a real tactical victory but should destroy so many of his troops west of Vire that we will have created practically an open flank. In this event I would consider it unnecessary to detach any large forces for the conquest of Brittany and would devote the great bulk of the forces to the task of completing the destruction of the German Army, at least that portion west of the Orne, and exploiting beyond that as far as we possibly could.

''I would consider it unnecessary to detach any large forces for the conquest of Brittany''—a major change, indeed. An entire new direction and set of objectives for his rapidly growing military force in Normandy. An idea that led the general to conclude his report on a very optimistic vein:

> Personally, I am very hopeful as to immediate results, and believe that within the next two or three days

we will so manhandle the western flank of the enemy's forces that we will secure for ourselves freedom of action through destruction of a considerable portion of the forces facing us.[11]

An idea was born. Now for the execution.

Thursday, AUGUST 3

In the plethora of fast-moving events and constant demand for tactical decisions, it was difficult to keep one's eye on the big picture—to adequately examine the longer-term strategic issues that any commanding general worth his salt must deal with. General Bradley reflected on yesterday's activities with those thoughts in mind. After a day spent with the VIII Corps and the Third Army realigning divisions and mediating between his subordinate generals, he had returned to his CP only to get involved in another spat between generals.

This time it was Maj. Gen. Freddy de Guingand, chief of staff to General Montgomery, and Maj. Gen. Bedell Smith, chief of staff to General Eisenhower, both evening visitors to Bradley's CP. According to Bradley's aide, Chester Hansen, ''Smith was furious over something De Guingand had done and he stormed over, gave De Guingand hell for it. Reputedly hates the British guts and makes no pretense in telling it. Dreadfully suspicious of them.''[1] Hardly an atmosphere for quiet contemplation of long-term decision making.

Things were a little quieter this morning, and Bradley decided to take advantage of that. Eisenhower was coming over in the afternoon, so he could profitably spend some time before he arrived thinking about the strategic issues confronting him.

Quite frankly, he was worried and puzzled. The Germans were not reacting to the situation they faced in a fashion that made sense from a military point of view—at least the way the general saw it. Their left wing had become unhinged. Their major source of reinforcements—the troops of the *Fifteenth Army*—lay north of the Seine River. All military logic said that their forces in Normandy should be in the process of an orderly withdrawal to the north bank of the Seine, where in concert with the *Fifteenth Army* they could establish a truly effective line of defense.

But clearly that was not happening. Reports from Montgomery's Twenty-first Army Group and the U.S. First Army showed without a doubt that they were putting up a furious defense, and there was no evidence whatsoever of withdrawal anywhere along that front. Understanding of the enemy's intentions is one of the essentials of sound strategy, and the confused signals that the general was now receiving did suggest the need for some caution in considering his own course of action.

On the other hand, he had the position of his own troops to think about, particularly the troops of the Third Army. In his effort to widen the Avranches corridor to expedite the movement of forces into Brittany, he now had one whole corps—the XVth—facing in an easterly direction, toward Paris and the Seine, and presumably toward the enemy flank and rear. In addition, there were two more Third Army corps (the XX and XII) coming into action. Both were positioned to sweep into Brittany to expedite the conquest of the peninsula and the capture of its major ports.

But was early capture of the Brittany ports all that important? Or, given the Germans' capabilities for destruction, would the ports be usable in any reasonable period of time after capture? These questions challenged the basic premises of OVERLORD strategy and as such were not to be taken lightly. But the glimmer of opportunity in the general's eyes was much too bright to be put aside.

The enemy's left flank was unquestionably "in the air." Bradley had troops (the XV Corps) on the very ground best-suited to take advantage of the situation. On top of that, the XX and XII Corps could just as easily swing to the east toward the enemy flank and rear as to the west toward Brittany. The glittering possibility offered by such a change in strategy was obvious—the defeat and destruction of the German forces in Normandy south of the Seine. If this could be accomplished, certainly the road to the Rhine—and perhaps even to Berlin—would be open.

The general's doubts about the Germans' intentions paled in the face of this opportunity. The time to act was now, before the enemy could realize what was happening. Delay would be costly.

So into his letters of instruction for the day went one for General Patton. His Third Army was to clear Brittany with "a minimum of forces"[2] and exert its major effort in a move to the east to establish a strong position on the enemy's flank.

It was a gutsy decision. It had been made with dispatch, and now he was ready to meet his boss. He felt confident that Ike would approve what he had done.

Field Marshal von Kluge arose in the morning with the words still ringing in his ears: "*Army Group B* together with all its main army units will prepare a counteroffensive aiming to break through to Avranches with the objective of isolating the enemy forces and ensuring their destruction."

The words of the Führer's order were unequivocal and peremptory. It was to be a major, all-out effort. But how it was to be accomplished was, of course, up to von Kluge. He had little reason to be at all hopeful that anything positive could be accomplished by such an assault. However, in his order the evening before, Hitler had opened one very small crack in his previous directive that his armies in Normandy were not to give ground or retreat. He authorized a slight withdrawal to a somewhat shorter line of defense in the western sector north and west of the town of Vire.

To von Kluge, this minor concession was significant. Because of the interior nature of his defensive lines, a withdrawal automatically meant a shorter line to defend. In spite of the heavy pressure being applied by the British, Canadians, and American First Army all along the front, a shorter line offered the possibility of withdrawing Panzer divisions now playing a defensive role and using them to mount an effective counteroffensive. Then, in addition, there were those seven divisions he had been promised. Certainly all of them could not be counted on to arrive in time to do any good, but those that did could be put into the line to plug the gap created by the withdrawal of Panzer divisions.

There was really no question about where to launch the attack. The shortest route to Avranches lay across the Sée-Sélune Plain from Mortain. In addition, the hilly terrain behind Mortain provided reasonable cover to assemble a major attack group without revealing its presence to the enemy. Obviously, Mortain was the proper launching point.

The selection of the attacking force was another matter. Von Kluge currently had eight Panzer divisions in his line plus remnants from two others that had been badly mauled during COBRA. He felt that four divisions was the minimum force required for a counterattack to have any chance of success.

Von Kluge's army in Normandy was made up of two major components—the *Seventh Army* under Hausser and *Panzer Group West* under a newly appointed commander from the Russian front, Gen. Heinrich Eberbach, who was considered to be one of Germany's most outstanding armored officers. The *Seventh Army* held the western portion of the line, facing the U.S. First Army and nearest to the Mortain area. *Panzer Group West* faced north, opposing the British and Canadians.

Five of the eight Panzer divisions belonged to *Panzer Group West* and represented the class of the German armored strength in Normandy. They had held the British at bay in the Caen area since D day and accounted for the lack of forward progress at this end of the front. The temptation was strong to use these divisions in the attack. As a matter of fact, Hitler suggested it.

Von Kluge, however, knew it was not possible. The pressure from the British was too strong. On top of that, no withdrawal had been authorized for this portion of the line, and any troops removed would have to be replaced. Finally, these divisions were the farthest from Mortain, and transportation and logistical problems would be overwhelming. In spite of this, von Kluge knew he had to have one division from *Panzer Group West*. His only alternative was to count on the timely arrival of the *9th Panzer Division* coming up from the south. He knew that would be foolhardy.

The three remaining divisions would come from the *Sev-*

enth Army—the *2nd, 2nd SS*, and *116th Panzer Divisions*.
Removing them from the line would certainly not be easy,
but von Kluge had some comfort from the fact that these
divisions would be taken from that part of the line where
withdrawal had been authorized by Hitler. In addition, because of their proximity to the Mortain area, they did not
have to be withdrawn at the same time. A phased withdrawal
was possible over the next several nights and would still meet
the August 6 date von Kluge had in mind for assembling the
attacking force.

The planning took most of the morning, and the field marshal felt the pressure to get on the phone and get things started.
First on his calling list was General Eberbach. Even though
he was to supply only one Panzer division, von Kluge knew
he would be difficult. General Warlimont had already visited
Eberbach earlier that morning and received a stinging rebuke
to the idea of an Avranches offensive. He had cited reasons
why the whole idea was crazy: insufficient troop strength, air
inferiority, supply problems, and the fact that any gains made
could not be maintained.[3] Only one strategy made sense to
Eberbach—immediate withdrawal to the Seine. But orders
were orders. After airing his complaints, Eberbach reached
agreement with von Kluge that the *1st SS Panzer Division*
would leave its position in line south of Caen late that evening
and begin the fifty-mile trek to the hills just east of Mortain.

General Hausser was much easier to convince. He was in
favor of the Avranches attack; he had been pushing the idea
for several days and complained only that it was taking so
long to get organized. But the cooler-headed von Kluge
calmed him down. Together they worked out the timing of
the movement of the three divisions involved. They agreed
that the attack would be commanded by Lt. Gen. Hans Freiherr von Funk, commander of the *XLVII Panzer Corps* under
Hausser. They also agreed that the attack should be launched
at night, without any artillery preparation, to achieve maximum surprise. The night of August 6 was selected as the
earliest possible launching time.

At 5:45 P.M. von Kluge finally called General Jodl with
his plans for the attack. Jodl approved.[4] The plan was now
set, but von Kluge felt little sense of satisfaction or accom-
plishment as a result of his day's work. He was left only with

a feeling of grim foreboding—a sense that it was all wrong and may very well be the beginning of the end.

The 6th Armored Division had bivouacked the previous night about halfway between Rennes and Saint-Malo—fifty miles into Brittany on the way to Brest. The members of Major General Grow's staff were still reeling from the announcement he had made at the previous night's meeting. For the first time, Grow revealed to them the substance of his discussion with Patton two days earlier.

"Take Brest—by Saturday night."[5] The idea was breathtaking. It changed their whole concept of the campaign. Racing unprotected through several hundred miles of enemy territory was an idea that took some getting used to. A whole new set of objectives, opportunities, and problems were presented. And all in just three days!

But the men of the 6th Armored should not have been too surprised at the previous night's announcement. After all, their commander was, like Patton, a cavalryman. He was used to thinking in terms of wide-ranging, high-speed campaigns. As a matter of fact, Grow had been Patton's operations officer in the prewar days. This Brittany campaign was the type of operation that "we spent years studying and training for,"[6] he was to recall. Now, they had a spectacular opportunity to put the training to use.

In spite of all the pressures to move and move quickly, General Grow had to take a few hours this morning to rest and reorganize his command. It was only six days since they had pushed off from the Saint-Lô-Periers highway to inaugurate the final phase of the break-through of the German *Seventh Army*. They had been constantly on the move since then. They had covered 100 miles—more than 15 miles a day—a distance record soon to be greatly surpassed, but at this point in time a notable achievement. The last two days had been particularly difficult. They had fought their way through the narrow corridor of the Avranches-Pontaubault sector, scrambling to get across the important bridges over the Sée and Sélune rivers before they could be destroyed. The congestion had been unbelievable, and for one of the few times during the campaign the German air force had been active, adding to the confusion and supporting the various last-ditch defenses organized by the enemy to stop the Allied move into Brittany.

Many of the troops as well as their officers were asleep on their feet. The various units of the division had become disoriented over the last several days, and time was needed for reorganization and realignment. The staff needed some time to revise plans and think through the changes in tactics required by the expanded scope of the campaign. Grow ordered the advance to be resumed at noon.

While the 6th Armored rested and refitted, an event was taking place 100 miles to the west that was crucial to the success of their campaign. The harbor facilities at Brest were, of course, the key objective of the 6th Armored advance. But equally significant was the railroad that crossed the entire peninsula from Brest to Rennes. This double-track railroad ran close to the north shore of Brittany during much of its length; a number of important bridges crossed the numerous rivers and ravines along the shore. None was more important than the high bridge at Morlaix, fifty miles east of Brest. Destruction of the bridge would cause extensive delay in the use of this valuable transportation link. It was time for the French resistance to make its presence felt.

Throughout their history, the Bretons have been a fiercely independent people. Nowhere in France were the German occupiers more intensely hated or more severely resisted. The French Forces of the Interior (FFI), the paramilitary branch of the French resistance, had at least 20,000 (some thought many more) fighters active in the Brittany peninsula. In recognition of this, the Allies made every effort to assist, encourage, and organize this large group of maquisards (freedom fighters). The Special Air Service (SAS) organized a small group of highly specialized parachutists (known as the "Battalion of Heaven") that could be used for sabotage or small paramilitary operations. Many such units had been dropped into Brittany. Their overall commander there was Henri Bourgoin—better known as "La Manchot" as he had only one arm. (Later in August, he would lead his "Battalion of Heaven" down the Champs-Elysées on liberation day.)

The Allies also organized the Jedburghs, small highly trained teams consisting of one Frenchman, one Briton, and one American. They were to be dropped into France to work with the local maquisards. While they were to supply specialized equipment and training, their main purpose was to organize the maquisards into more effective military units and coordinate their activities with Allied military operations.

While the 6th Armored Division was getting ready for their drive to Brest this Thursday morning, Jedburgh Team Giles was busy. Its leader was an American, Capt. Bernard Knox, a Greek scholar who had studied at Cambridge and would later become director of Hellenic Studies at Harvard. The Giles team had been in Brittany since July 6, operating in the province of Finistère, a hilly region at the western end of the peninsula.[7]

Knox was aware that a 100-man team of the "Battalion of Heaven" had dropped the day before and successfully seized and secured the bridge at Morlaix after a fierce battle with its German defenders. He also knew that the Germans would retaliate quickly to recapture this vital bridge, and that in all likelihood the rescuers would move through his territory on their way to Morlaix. Team Giles had organized a group of 2,000 maquisards and had positioned them to take advantage of the hilly terrain along the portion of the Rennes-Brest highway that the German relief force was most likely to follow. Armed with bazookas, machine guns, grenades, and tire busters (small contact explosives laid on the roads), the group was ready and waiting.

True to Knox's prediction, a battalion of 1,000 German paratroopers were seen leaving the town of Chateaulin headed for Morlaix. The convoy moved directly into the trap. Within minutes, most of their vehicles were immobilized. In an effort to escape the trap, the paratroops ran for the countryside where the maquisards were waiting. Those Germans who were not killed or captured filtered back into Chateaulin and other small towns in the area. For the moment, any thought of mounting another relief operation for Morlaix was dead.

In the scale of military operations that were taking place daily across all western France, this action at Chateaulin was minuscule. Its consequences, however, were considerable. Within two days, General Grow's 6th Armored would pass within a few miles of Morlaix on the way to Brest. Within four days, the town itself would be entered by other American units. They would be greeted by a bridge intact and in friendly hands. Had they found a destroyed bridge and a battalion of German paratroops, the course of events certainly would have been different.

The action at Morlaix and Chateaulin was a signal for the FFI to go on the attack all across the Brittany peninsula. They heard their rallying cry from Gen. Pierre Koenig, the Free French representative at SHAEF. ''French people of Brittany, the hour of your liberation has come. . . . The time has come for you to take part, with or without weapons, in the last battle. . . . The whole of France will follow you in the national insurrection.''[8]

To the proud, resourceful Bretons went the honor of leading the way. General Grow and his 6th Armored Division knew that while they were heading into a vast area still heavily garrisoned with German troops, the French maquisards were there also—behind every hill, around every bend in the road—ready to do what they could to speed the day when the ''boches'' would be eliminated from their beloved peninsula.

Friday, AUGUST 4

The 6th Armored Division was not the only force pushing its way into Brittany. There was also the 4th Armored, which had participated with the 6th in the breakthrough and struggle through the Avranches bottleneck. Rather than turning to the west, the 4th Armored had been ordered south toward Rennes with the ultimate goal of crossing the base of the peninsula, thus effectively sealing off all the German forces in Brittany.

Under the command of Maj. Gen. John Wood, the 4th had made rapid progress, covering the forty miles from Pontaubault to Rennes on the afternoon of August 1. Finding the city too heavily defended to warrant an attack by his division alone, Wood decided to wait until units of the 8th Infantry Division, following in his division rear, could reach the city and join in the attack. In the meantime, he would swing his 4th Armored Division around to the west and south of the city, thus sealing off some of the many roads that converged on this important center.

By this morning things were well in hand. Troops of the 8th Infantry Division were in the city, which the enemy had apparently abandoned during the night, heading eastward (the only direction open to them). Wood's division was by now in the vicinity of Chateaubriant—more than thirty miles southeast of Rennes. The city of Angers in the Loire Valley was only forty miles to the east. Ever since the previous morning, when he was swinging his troops around to the west and south of Rennes, Wood had become intrigued by the possibility of a continuing movement to the east rather than south to Lorient and Saint-Nazaire at the southern hinge of Brittany. Wood saw nothing very exciting or productive about being stuck in Brittany, which he considered likely to become the backwater of the campaign. Toward the Loire Valley, Chartres, and Paris—that is where the important battles would be fought, and Wood wanted to be a part of that. He was now far closer to these prizes than any other Allied force in the field, and as far as he could determine, there was nothing to stop him, at least until he got to the Loire Valley. With luck, he could be in Chartres in a couple of days.

After all, the 8th Infantry could secure Rennes, and if necessary Wood could leave a small part of his troops to block the roads to the south shore of Brittany and thus effectively seal it off. Having done that, had he not in essence fulfilled his original orders so he was free to take on a new assignment? He had tried all the day before to get some support for his plan from VIII Corps headquarters. By moving to Chateaubriant, he was already starting to put the plan into effect. But communications were difficult and messages confused, and he had been unable to convey to VIII Corps the significance of what he had in mind.

So Wood was delighted when Major General Middleton drove into his CP this morning—so delighted that he threw his arms around his superior. "What's the matter?" Middleton asked. "Have you lost your division?"

"No," replied Wood. "They [the Allied High Command] are winning the war the wrong way."[1]

Wood proceeded to work on Middleton, trying to persuade him to see things his way. He had some success. Middleton agreed that if he would block the roads, secure the bridges, and effectively seal off the area to the south with part of his command, the rest could cautiously test the waters to the east.

Shortly after this agreement had been reached, the VIII Corps sent its daily mission list into Third Army headquarters. Even though this was a routine report primarily for administrative purposes, the reaction was immediate. The sharp eyes of Maj. Gen. Hugh Gaffey, Patton's chief of staff, caught the change in the mission of the 4th Armored Division.

In the person of Brig. Gen. Hobart Gay, assistant chief of staff, word was dispatched to Wood. The 4th Armored was to continue its movement toward the south shore of the Brittany peninsula as originally ordered. No changes, no exceptions.

Wood was disappointed, disgusted, and angry. He was to say later, "I protested long, loud, and violently. But no, we were forced to adhere to the original plan—with the only armor available, and ready to cut the enemy to pieces. It was one of the colossally stupid decisions of the war."[2]

Wood was to get his wish by the middle of the month, when the 4th Armored was sent east to participate in the drive across the Seine. But that was different. In Wood's view, the once-in-a-lifetime opportunity had been passed by this Friday, August 4.

General Wood was bitter and disappointed about the denial of approval of his plan to swing his division toward the Loire Valley. But if he thought he was the only one thinking about this strategically important area, he was mistaken.

At Third Army Headquarters, located in the woods near Beauchamps on the Villedieu-Granville road, the staff was busy. They were now all aware of Bradley's decision of the previous day for the Third Army to clear Brittany with "a minimum of forces" and put its main effort to the east toward the flank of the German army. There was much to do to translate that general directive into specific orders for Third Army troops.

General Patton had left about 10 o'clock this morning in his jeep to see if he could locate the 6th Armored Division. He wanted to be absolutely certain that they were using maximum effort in their advance toward Brest. No one was quite sure how long he would be gone because no one knew the exact location of the division, but the general did plan to be back later in the day. He was expecting a visit from Bradley and his chief of staff, Lev Allen, who were coming down to review the Third Army plans to carry out its new directives. Then he would have to call in his two corps commanders, Haislip and Walker, to explain their part in the overall plan. On top of that, Lt. Gen. Carl "Tooey" Spaatz, commander of the U.S. Strategic Air Force, was also planning to drop by. These visits from the "brass" did not always come at the most convenient times.

So Hugh Gaffey and the rest of the staff had their work cut out for them: to put together a plan that could be reviewed, approved, and implemented before the day was over. One fact was clear—the XV Corps under Wade Haislip would be in the lead. The 90th and 79th Infantry and 5th Armored divisions were in the right place and facing in the right direction to implement the change in direction of attack. Furthermore, the recent movements of these divisions had not indicated any significant enemy strength in their front. Their immediate target would be the Mayenne River, which ran north to south. A sixty-mile stretch of that river from Mayenne on the north through Laval to Chateau-Gontier on the south looked like a reasonable area of operation for the corps. The river crossings were about thirty miles from the corps' present position.

Depending on the enemy resistance, this was a tall order for three divisions. A larger force was needed not only to add weight to the attack but also to provide a degree of protection to the right flank of the XV Corps.

The XX Corps under Walton Walker was the obvious candidate for this assignment. Originally scheduled to consist of one armored and two infantry divisions, the XX Corps would be dispatched toward Angers and the Loire Valley. It was understood that the XX Corps was at least a couple of days behind the XV. What was not known was the extent to which subsequent events would siphon off the divisions of the corps to other more urgent tasks.

As the generals gathered at Third Army headquarters later in the day, the plan was ready. After discussion and approval, the orders were written up. The key actor, Lt. Gen. Wade Haislip, was given his set of the orders in person at 7:00 P.M. They read in part: "XV Corps will move early 5 August 1944 initially to seize and secure crossings of Mayenne River from Mayenne to Laval both inclusive; attack with two infantry divisions abreast, one Regimental Combat Team in each division to be motorized and preceded by mechanized cavalry. 5th Armored Division echeloned to right rear prepared to (1) support attack of assaulting divisions, (2) extend front to

CHATEAU-GONTIER, or (3) extend front as far south as ANGERS."[3]

Not particularly dramatic—in fact, the orders sounded rather routine. They were not. The idea contained in Eisenhower's letter to Marshall and Bradley's response to the changing strategic situation as he understood it—these were the genesis of the order that Wade Haislip put in his pocket as he returned to his new CP that evening. OVERLORD had been changed. The entire campaign from this point forward would be influenced by that fact.

Change was definitely not the order of the day at First Army headquarters, twenty-five miles away. Courtney Hodges had just returned from a visit to Cormolain, headquarters of the British Second Army. His counterpart there was Lt. Gen. Miles Dempsey. A veteran, Dempsey had been at Dunkirk, had fought against Rommel in North Africa, had led a corps in the Sicilian and Italian campaigns, and was selected by Montgomery for command of the Second Army. In many ways he was like Hodges, although they were to have their differences as the campaign progressed. Modest and shy, an outstanding tactician, he lived under the shadow of his outspoken and flamboyant superior, General Montgomery.

Hodges and Dempsey had a great deal to discuss. The boundaries of their armies met generally along the Vire River in some of the most hotly contested territory in Normandy. The crossroad town of Vire had been a major objective of both armies for the past several days. British troops had come within a mile or so of the town two days before, only to be driven back by two Panzer divisions. Since then the Americans had assumed the responsibility for taking Vire. Many problems came up when two separate armies shared boundaries, and they could be best handled on a face-to-face basis.

Back in his CP, General Hodges was on the phone with his corps commanders seeing what could be done to speed up the campaign. Two corps with two divisions each were bearing down on Vire. On the left (adjacent to the British army) was the V Corps (Gerow) with the 2nd and 35th Infantry Divisions. On their right was the XIX Corps (Corlett) with the 28th and 29th Infantry.

Progress had been agonizingly slow. One good piece of news was that the 28th Division had today entered St. Sever-Calvados, several miles west of Vire, and the 29th was just to the northwest of the town. But the town was fiercely defended by elements of the *LXXXIV Corps* and *II Parachute Corps*, and this was still Norman bocage country, with two rivers aiding the defense. Vire itself was an ancient fortified town originally laid out with defense in mind. It was proving a very hard nut to crack.

Any actions that von Kluge and his generals may have taken to shorten their line in preparation for their counteroffensive at Mortain certainly were not yet apparent to General Hodges. Particularly in the V and XIX Corps areas and the vicinity of Vire, there was no evidence on August 4 of anything except determined, unremitting resistance to any First Army advance.

Saturday, AUGUST 5

Prime Minister Winston Churchill was not one to sit in his office when an opportunity presented itself to be where the action was. His plan to be with the invasion forces on D day was thwarted only when the king himself notified Churchill that if he went, then he (the king) would go also. Churchill's travels throughout the world during the war were legendary.

This morning he decided it was time to go to Normandy. Together with Adm. Sir Andrew Cunningham, First Sea Lord; Brigadier Hollis, secretary to the British Chiefs of Staff; and his naval aide, Comdr. Tommy Thompson, he took off for the continent. Today, however, the weather was against him. An earlier plane had crashed at their proposed landing site, killing all the occupants.[1] So it was back to England.

Churchill thought of the next best alternative: if he was unable to be brought up to date on the spot in Normandy, why not visit SHAEF Forward Headquarters near Portsmouth to see Eisenhower? The pilot was directed to land at Thorney Island, just a few miles from SHAEF Forward.

Commander Harry Butcher came off his chair in a hurry when he received the news by telephone. He rushed to the airfield with the general following close behind. Having met the party, they returned to headquarters, where a lunch was hastily improvised. Actually the surprise was not complete, as the prime minister had been expected for dinner that evening.

The subject matter to be discussed during the visit was also no surprise to General Eisenhower. It would be ANVIL, just as it had been at almost every meeting they had held over the past several months. The story of ANVIL—the Allied landing on the French Mediterranean coast scheduled to take place in ten days—was not a happy one. Since its inception, it had been perhaps the major source of contention between the American and British Allies.

The plan was originally discussed as early as the spring of 1943, more or less formally adopted at the Quebec Conference in August, and further confirmed at Teheran in November. But the British, and most particularly the prime minister, resisted the plan from the very beginning. At the heart of the dispute was the British Mediterranean (or so-called "soft underbelly") strategy. To the British, the most attractive opportunity lay in pressing the Italian campaign and using northern Italy as a springboard into the Balkans, hopefully before the Russians could arrive. Admittedly more political than military in its purpose, such an operation was, in the British view, militarily achievable provided sufficient resources were committed. ANVIL would take away (or perhaps waste) those resources.

The Americans, on the other hand, under the leadership of General Marshall, took a more purely military approach to the question. The British Balkans "adventure" was unsound militarily and strategically. The war would be won by defeating the German army in France and Germany. ANVIL would provide major port facilities (Marseilles and Toulon) through which to pour in men and supplies directly from America. The American high command, never fully sold on the Italian campaign, was unconcerned about slowing down progress in Italy to provide the strength necessary to make ANVIL a success.

The arguments had gone back and forth for months, and without the iron will of General Marshall, preparations for ANVIL might well have floundered. After a number of changes in date and much scrambling to provide sufficient landing craft, the August 15 date was now firm. Firm, that is, in everyone's mind except Churchill's.

Realizing that his Balkan plan was at least temporarily sidetracked, he had come up with another alternative to ANVIL. He proposed Bordeaux as a substitute for Marseilles and Toulon. He suggested that the troops committed for ANVIL be shipped through the Strait of Gibraltar and landed in Brittany instead, where presumably German forces would have been defeated or at least badly scattered by Patton's Third Army. Would not this be a preferred alternative to the uncertain prospects of landing on a beachhead defended by the enemy?

The discussion was launched after lunch. Joining the group were Maj. Gen. Bedell Smith; Adm. Bertram Ramsey, Eisenhower's British naval commander at SHAEF; and Ramsey's assistant, Rear Adm. William Tennent. Eisenhower's position was not an easy one. As an American general, he was clearly subordinate to General Marshall, whose views on the subject were well known and unequivocal. As commander of SHAEF, however, he was required to accommodate American and British views into workable solutions. His own opinion on ANVIL had wavered, but he was now fully committed. He had been through previous sessions with the prime minister and knew he was in for a long and difficult afternoon.

Two of the three other important participants each supported their own superior—Cunningham with the prime minister and Ramsey with Eisenhower. It came as somewhat of a surprise, however, that Smith appeared to be attracted to the prime minister's proposal and tended to support it. That said something about Eisenhower's style of command. He had always encouraged free exchange of ideas among his subordinates and had the patience necessary to consider all reasonable proposals.

But the burden of the argument was assumed by Churchill himself with all the forcefulness and rhetoric that have become legend. To Eisenhower, the change of plans proposed by the prime minister was no longer possible. It was too late. Certainly, the assumption about the ease of a Brittany landing was premature. Furthermore, Brittany was farther from the German border than Marseilles. Eisenhower was also impressed by the fact that ANVIL represented another front that the Germans would have to defend and offered some possibility of trapping German troops in southwestern France.

The prime minister was indefatigable in his arguments, and according to Butcher, ''Ike said no, continued saying no all afternoon, and ended saying no in every form of the English language at his command.''[2] After about six hours of discussion, ANVIL had survived. The session left Eisenhower feeling limp, and he commented to Butcher that Churchill would undoubtedly return to the subject in a few days, regarding the issue as being still unsettled. The prime minister, indeed, continued the debate by transatlantic cable with President Roosevelt and Harry Hopkins but met unified resistance to his proposals.[3] Convincing Eisenhower had really been his only hope for success, and ANVIL's survival had been assured this Saturday afternoon under the canopy outside the general's office tent at SHAEF Forward.

Sunday, AUGUST 6

It was Ray McLain's chance to prove what his division could do. His position was an unusual one—an Army National Guard officer in command of a division, a job usually reserved for Regular Army officers. On top of that, he had the 90th Infantry Division, whose past performance had been suspect under two Regular Army commanders over a period of two months. When General Haislip laid out the 90th Division's part in the XV Corps advance, McLain was eager to get started.

Part of his division, which had been highly motorized, had reached the west bank of the Mayenne River by noon of the previous day—having covered almost thirty miles in half a day. With the bridge at Mayenne still intact but well defended, McLain launched a two-pronged attack—one to outflank the town and the other directly across the bridge. Resolute action had paid off. The speed of the attack prevented the enemy from destroying the bridge, which had been mined.

So by this morning, elements of the division were across the Mayenne River in strength. While part of the division encountered stiff resistance within a few miles, another group, by slipping south, found little opposition and managed to advance another twenty-two miles in the direction of Le Mans.

An advance of more than fifty miles in two days, crossing

a river, occupying a town, and leading the XV Corps advance—those were accomplishments of which any infantry division could be justly proud. Perhaps the 90th was on the way back.

Meanwhile, the 79th Infantry Division to the right was also making progress. By late the previous night, they had reached the river near the town of Laval. But unlike the 90th, they had found the bridges thoroughly destroyed. Today they set about finding ways to cross the river: footbridges were laid, rafts were built, and one battalion aided by French policemen found a dam they could cross. Once across the river, they found that the enemy had left. The town of Laval was now theirs. While they were somewhat behind their compatriots on their left, the way was now open for the 79th to advance on Le Mans as well.

On the far right, the 5th Armored Division made somewhat less progress. In their advance of yesterday and today, they did manage to reach the Mayenne River at Chateau-Gontier —the southern limit of the XV Corps objective. For an armored division facing little enemy resistance, this was not an impressive advance. Their problem was gasoline. Having given up the valuable fuel to help motorize the two infantry divisions, and facing delivery problems through the Avranches bottleneck, Major General Oliver had to put the brakes on his division's advance until sufficient fuel could be obtained. It now appeared that this would occur either tonight or early tomorfow morning. The advance could then be speeded up.

Obviously, the divisions of the XV Corps had outstripped the boundaries of the order Haislip had received two nights earlier. Patton had recognized this late the day before, following the fall of Mayenne, and received permission to make Le Mans the new corps objective. A major communication center with a population of 75,000 and for some time location of the headquarters of the German *Seventh Army*, Le Mans was an important prize. Perhaps equally significant, with Le Mans as their objective, the direction of the XV Corps advance again shifted from a southeastward to an eastward direction. The threat to the flank and rear of the German army was becoming more clear with every mile of the XV Corps advance.

* * *

Forty miles north of Le Mans as the crow flies is Mont Pinçon. The highest point in Normandy, it is in the heart of the "Norman Suisse" or Normandy Alps—a hilly region traversed by the Orne River as it runs north to Caen and the sea. Its advantages as a defensive position were well recognized by Lieutenant General Eberbach, commander of the *Fifth Panzer Army*, and he had made it a key point in the front line of his defense.

Facing him was the British XXX Corps, part of Dempsey's British Second Army. XXX Corps had a new commander— Lt. Gen. Brian Horrocks—another veteran of the North African campaign under Montgomery. He had been wounded in an air raid in Bizerte and spent a year in the hospital. At the end of July, when Montgomery became dissatisfied with XXX Corps' performance and dismissed its principal commanders, Horrocks was called back to rejuvenate the corps. Fiery, spirited, and vocal, he "moved among his troops more like a prophet than a general."[1]

Mont Pinçon was to be captured now—no delays. This was the word sent to Gen. G. I. Thomas and his 43rd Division. The job fell to the 129th Brigade with the 13/18th Hussar tanks in support. The brigade, made up of the 4th and 5th Wiltshire Regiments, was at the foot of the western slope of the mountain—the steepest slope but also the most accessible.

The weather was hot and dry. Throughout the day numerous unsuccessful attempts were made to get a foothold on the western slope. Late in the day some progress had been made and the Hussars located an unguarded track that led to the summit. At 6:00 P.M. the tanks headed up the narrow path with a bank on one side and a sheer drop on the other. Although several tanks were lost during the ascent, the rest made it to the summit.

Although exhausted from the day's fighting, the Wiltshires, encouraged by the success of the Hussars, made one more attempt in the fading light. This time they were successful. Through darkness and fog, they found their way to the tanks on the summit. Mont Pinçon was in British hands.

A company commander described the battle as "not a battle against Germans, so much as against the burning sun, the

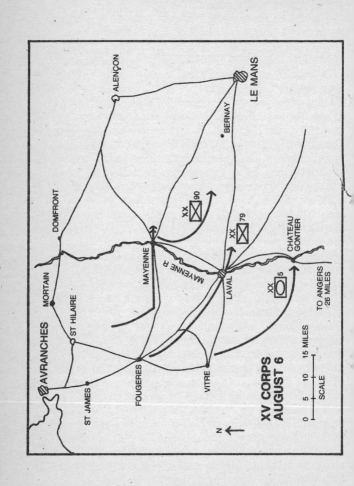

XV CORPS
AUGUST 6

SCALE

0   5   10   15 MILES

N

AVRANCHES

ST JAMES

MORTAIN

ST HILAIRE

DOMFRONT

FOUGERES

MAYENNE

MAYENNE R

VITRE

LAVAL

CHATEAU
GONTIER

TO ANGERS
26 MILES

ALENÇON

BERNAY

LE MANS

XX 90

XX 79

XX 5

choking dust, our parched throats and empty bellies, the craggy slopes and tangled thickets, the rocky earth and above all our utterly weary bodies."[2]

The fall of Mont Pinçon was the first significant crack in the northern defensive line established by the Germans. Other cracks were coming.

Colonel Hammond Birks had arrived in Mortain last night ahead of his troops, who were due this morning. His 120th Infantry Regiment (30th Infantry Division) had been ordered to Mortain to relieve troops of the 1st Division who had been in the town for several days. General Hodges needed the 1st Division farther around on the First Army right to fill the growing gap in the lines caused by the eastward movement of the XV Corps.

The 1st Division people had told Birks that things were quiet in Mortain, and indeed they seemed to be so. It was rare to be in a town in Normandy that was actually functioning, but that appeared to be the case in Mortain. Even the hotels were open. Though it was night, Birks could still see the large hill rising on the eastern outskirts of the town. It dominated the entire vicinity and was obviously a strong point for positioning his regiment.

The troops arrived at 10:00 A.M. after a forty-six-mile trip from Tessy-sur-Vire and immediately began relieving the 1st Division troops. Just north of town, the colonel had discovered another important defensive position. At the little hamlet of Abbay Blanche, four roads converged into one, which in turn wound through the hills into Mortain. Just to the west of Abbay Blanche was another hill, which dominated the road crossing. It was designated Hill 285.

Birks sent his 1st Battalion to occupy Hill 285 as soon as they arrived. The large hill to the east of town (designated Hill 317) was to be the responsibility of his 2nd Battalion under the command of Lt. Col. Eads Hardaway. Hardaway also drew responsibility for establishing the roadblock at Abbay Blanche.

Hardaway set up his CP in a hotel in the town. He dispatched four companies of the 2nd Battalion up Hill 317 to establish control over that obviously important position. Along with them went two forward observers of the 230th

Field Artillery Battalion—a most fortunate addition, as events would prove. Then he ordered several platoons from several companies to set up the roadblock at Abbay Blanche.

By evening, Hardaway was satisfied that he had gotten his men into position at the critical locations around the town. They had not yet had time to establish strong defensive positions, but things were quiet. They could get started on strengthening their defenses in the morning.

Despite his pessimistic view of several days ago concerning the planned counterattack at Mortain, von Kluge had to admit that things had not gone too badly these past two days. General Hausser had been able to pull the *2nd* and *2nd SS Panzer Divisions* out of the line near Vire without any disastrous consequences. They were now in position to attack. He had not been quite so fortunate with the *116th Panzer*—it was literally defending the line with part of the division while withdrawing the other. But it looked as if the unit would be able to be in position by sometime this evening. The *1st SS Panzer*, which was coming down from the Caen area, was also a little behind schedule. It was late starting because of the delayed arrival of the *89th Infantry*, which was to take its place in line. Movement to the Mortain area was delayed by the usual problems of traffic congestion and air attacks, compounded by the need to travel at night as well as during the day. But the *1st SS* was not scheduled to lead the attack. It was to be used to exploit the initial breakthrough of the other divisions, and it looked now as if the division would arrive in time to fulfill that role.

Von Kluge had his fingers crossed. He could not take four first-class armored divisions out of his line without making it extremely vulnerable. The Allied attacks were increasing in intensity. He was thankful indeed that he had established tonight as the time to launch the attack—he was sure his defenses could not hold out much longer. He was counting on this success at Mortain to force the Allies to reduce their pressure elsewhere. And how much longer could he maintain the element of surprise on which he was counting so heavily to provide at least initial success to the attack?

There was another reason for the field marshal's somewhat brighter view of the situation. For two days now, he had had no calls or instructions from the Führer. He had been able to work things out his own way without interference and as a result felt that things were now under much better control.

That ended abruptly late in the afternoon: a phone call from Jodl informed von Kluge that Hitler wanted some changes in the plan. First of all, he wanted to change commanders. He wanted Eberbach instead of von Funk. Second, he would make available 140 additional tanks now being held in reserve. Von Kluge was to wait until those reinforcements were on hand before launching the attack.[3] How long would that be? At least twenty-four hours—probably longer.

Von Kluge was dismayed. The attack was to start in a matter of hours. The risks of delay were unacceptable; indeed, they were suicidal. It was still another indication that Hitler's view of the purpose and scope of the counteroffensive was far different from von Kluge's.

The phones were busy for the next several hours, and by 7:00 P.M. von Kluge had worked out the best compromise he could achieve. The attack could start as planned. However, once Avranches was captured, Eberbach would take command and swing to the northeast to attack the flank and rear of the U.S. First Army. It was to be a "grand offensive"— not a limited attack to protect the movement of the army to improved defensive positions along the Seine, as von Kluge had always envisaged.

Hitler's trust of von Kluge had not improved. Again he sent a member of the OKW Staff to the front by plane. This time it was Gen. Walter Buhle. He was to make certain that the expanded operation was to be vigorously pursued. However, this grand offensive was an operation that von Kluge and most of his commanders in the field believed was ill-conceived and had not even the remotest chance of success. Thus, as the night wore on, four of Germany's finest Panzer divisions assumed their positions to launch a major attack, the purposes of which were conflicting, ill-defined, and out of touch with reality.

Major Melvin Helfers[4] felt somewhat like a fish out of water. He had been assigned to the Third Army headquarters as their ULTRA officer. ULTRA was the code name given to intelligence gained through the deciphering of German secret messages using a system developed by British intelligence. It proved to be invaluable to the Allies throughout the war, and its secrecy was so well kept that it was not until thirty years after the war that its use became public knowledge.

The British were particularly sensitive about maintaining ULTRA security, with the result that all transmissions of ULTRA information were under the control of a small group of British intelligence officers. Such a group was attached to the Third Army, and all ULTRA dispatches were received and decoded by them. Major Helfer's job was to accumulate the data received by the ULTRA group and organize it for presentation to Third Army headquarters.

So far, little interest had been displayed in the material collected. Col. Oscar Koch (Patton's G-2 officer) could not really see why the Third Army needed British intelligence officers on the staff. His people were perfectly capable of providing adequate intelligence, and furthermore he was not at all sure how much trust he could put in information from the British. On the other hand, Captain Hutchinson, the British intelligence officer, felt very protective toward the information he was receiving and passed it along to the Americans only because he had been ordered to do so.

Melvin Helfers was caught in the middle. Mistrusted by the British and ignored by the Americans, he was left to shift for himself around Third Army headquarters. He generally had to acquire whatever supplies or equipment he needed by some sort of devious methods. Whenever headquarters moved, he had to hitch a ride for himself and his equipment; he had no transport of his own. He was generally the forgotten man.

The major's anonymity was about to come to an end, however. Today's ULTRA dispatches contained some startling information about a German armored buildup just east of the town of Mortain. At about 8:00 P.M. Helfers had received the information from the British, and he took it immediately to Colonel Koch's tent. The colonel was on his bunk suffering from his usual bout with ulcers. His normal reservations about ULTRA information were forgotten when he read the dispatches. This must be seen by the general.

It was 9:00 P.M. when Koch and Helfers reached General

Patton's office van. He had just returned from another visit to VIII Corps to push the advance into Brittany. When Koch showed him the dispatches, Patton asked, "How much of this have you been getting? How long has this officer been with us?" When Helfers's position was explained, Patton told Koch he wanted an ULTRA briefing every morning at 7:00 A.M. Major Helfers's period of isolation was at an end.

The general's diary recorded the incident. "We got a rumor last night from a secret source that several Panzer divisions will attack west from . . . Mortain . . . on Avranches. Personally, I think it is a German bluff to cover a withdrawal, but I stopped the 80th, French 2nd Armored, and 35th [Divisions] in the vicinity of Saint-Hilaire just in case something might happen."[5]

The usually rash Patton was showing an uncharacteristic bit of caution. Saint-Hilaire was nine miles down the road between Mortain and Avranches. The three divisions were those assigned to XX Corps for their sweep to the Loire. It was not easy for an aggressive general like Patton to stop three entire divisions in their tracks and wait for something to happen. In spite of his comments about a "German bluff," he took the ULTRA information seriously. After this experience, he would listen to Major Helfers with renewed respect.

Lieutenant General Hans von Funk was furious. The apparent absolute refusal of Lt. Gen. Gerhard Graf von Schwerin to attack with his *116th Panzer Division*, as he had been repeatedly ordered to do, was putting the whole Mortain counteroffensive into jeopardy. This attitude of von Schwerin had been an important factor in the necessity to postpone the attack from 10:00 P.M. last night until after midnight. His continued failure to advance throughout the night was exposing the northern flank of the attack. Schwerin's stated reason for withholding his division was that attacks from the north by the U.S. First Army threatened him with encirclement. But von Funk was also aware that Schwerin was active in the July 20 conspiracy against Hitler; had lost all hope of victory; and, in fact, had literally given up.

Regardless of the reasons, it was rank insubordination and something had to be done. It was particularly infuriating to von Funk because, in all other respects, the attack had gone rather well. The weather had been kind. Fog covered the area, which enhanced the element of surprise that clearly had been achieved. The two attacking divisions (the *2nd Panzer* on the north and the *2nd SS Panzer* on the south) had both made good advances during the night. The right-hand column of the *2nd Panzer*, attacking on the most direct route to Avranches along the south side of the Sée River, had ad-

vanced more than five miles, reaching the small hamlet of
Le Mesnil-Adilee. The left-hand column was slower to jump
off and had not had as much success. Von Funk was getting
ready to commit the *1st SS Panzer* to their support and was
confident that this additional strength would speed the advance.

On the left, the *2nd SS Panzer* had burst through the town
of Mortain against little opposition. True, they had left a few
pockets of resistance in their rear—that hill just to the east
of the town and a road junction at Abbay Blanche. But the
division was now moving rapidly down the road to Saint-
Hilaire. There was reason to be encouraged that the left flank
of the attack was on, or perhaps even ahead of, schedule.

Von Funk was concerned, however, about what daylight
would bring. With the lifting of the fog, the factor of air
support would become important. Von Funk was aware that
General Hausser had been promised strong air support on
numerous occasions. As recently as the day before, he had
been reassured by the Luftwaffe that 300 planes were available to provide support. So, as the skies cleared during the
morning, the eyes of the German commanders turned towards
the sky. Instead of ME-109s, they saw British Hurricanes
and Typhoons—hundreds of them moving in to attack the
advancing German columns. The German airfields around
Paris, from which the Luftwaffe had planned to provide the
support, were well known to the Allies. The few German
planes that did take off this morning were shot down literally
within sight of their bases. Not a single plane made it to the
Mortain area during the day. Allied air superiority was an
all-too-familiar pattern to the German ground forces in Normandy and led the tank commanders to start thinking more
about cover than about continued attack.

As the morning progressed, von Funk found he had another
equally severe problem—American artillery. Failure of the
116th Panzer to attack left an open flank on his right just
across the Sée River, and the Americans were quick to take
advantage of that as soon as daylight appeared. Well positioned on the heights above the river and within easy range,
they began an intensive barrage on the tanks of the *2nd Panzer*. Artillery also began to find the *2nd SS Panzer* on the
road to Saint-Hilaire. Hill 317 offered ideal vision down the

road from Mortain to Saint-Hilaire, and the forces that von Funk's troops had bypassed on the hill included two well-trained forward artillery observers who were able to call in artillery barrages with accuracy and precision.

When the addition of the *1st SS Panzer* to the attack in the center failed to produce the expected results, von Funk decided he had had enough. He could no longer afford the serious and growing loss of tanks. Around noon, he ordered his forces to dig in. The advance was halted.

During the afternoon, the question became what to do now. Von Funk relieved Schwerin from command of the *116th Panzer*. The division started to move late in the afternoon, but the opportunity had passed. It made little progress. Von Funk had done what he could. Two Panzer divisions had advanced about six miles down two separate routes toward Avranches—less than one third the total distance. However, the American line had been broken; surprise had been achieved. At this point, it was up to his superiors to decide what action was called for.

To von Kluge, the answer was simple: the attack had failed. The troops were dangerously exposed. Another very important indication to von Kluge was that he noticed no letup in Allied aggressiveness on the other fronts during the day—a clear sign that the major purpose of the attack (at least, in von Kluge's mind) had not been accomplished. Withdrawal was clearly the proper course to follow.

To Hitler, a different answer was called for as, once again, the confusion of purpose with respect to the attack became apparent. "I command that the attack be prosecuted daringly and recklessly to the sea,"[1] he ordered. He also ordered further weakening of the German lines elsewhere to commit greater strength to the attack. He criticized von Kluge for starting the attack too soon with too little force. He also made another criticism that military analysts have subsequently judged to be an important mistake in the conduct of the attack—the failure to commit the *1st SS Panzer Division* in support of the *2nd SS* down the road to Saint-Hilaire instead of in the center where no real progress had been made. The Saint-Hilaire road was the one point of the attack that offered potential for a real breakthrough. The military axiom that

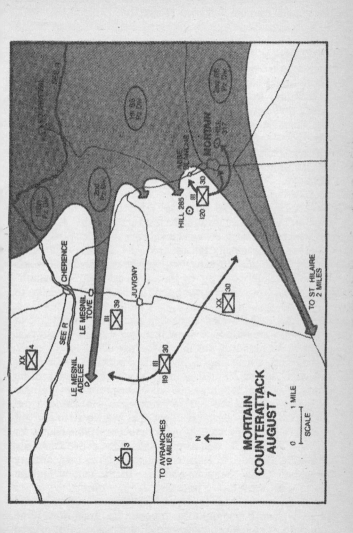

MORTAIN
COUNTERATTACK
AUGUST 7

SCALE

0   1 MILE

reserves should be used to reinforce success rather than protect against failure had been ignored.

The additional strength for Hitler's renewed attack was to come in the form of two more Panzer divisions from Eberbach, whose forces faced the British to the north. These divisions were to be turned over to Hausser's *Seventh Army* so the attack could begin within a couple of days. Meanwhile, von Funk's troops were to hold their positions at all costs.

By now, even Hausser realized the futility of continuing the attack. Among the three men—von Kluge, Eberbach, and Hausser—a growing sense of impending doom was developing, a feeling that they were launching on a course of action whose only consequences could be failure and perhaps even disaster.

Lieutenant Colonel Hardaway never got the chance to improve the defensive position of his troops on Hill 317. It was all over before he knew what had happened. He and his small staff were completely cut off from the battalion and hiding out in the center of town, which in the past hour or two had been completely overrun by the Germans. Hardaway and his staff had no way of knowing the fate of their own troops on the hill.

Actually, the troops had taken their fate into their own hands. By morning they knew that they were completely cut off and surrounded, but they were not about to surrender. The group, consisting of three rifle companies and a heavy weapons company, realized the importance of their position and set up the best possible defense against heavy attacks from elements of the *2nd SS Panzer Division*. Meanwhile, the two forward observers of the 230th Field Artillery Battalion set up to provide firing coordinates of the enemy assaulting the hill, as well as any other units visible from their dominant hill position. There were slightly less than 700 men on the hill. If the Germans wanted to take it, they were going to have to pay a heavy price.

By morning, Major General Collins, VII Corps commander, was beginning to understand the dimensions of his problem. The entire attack occurred within the boundaries assigned to his corps. First, he turned his attention to the northern prong of the attack and the *2nd Panzer Division*.

Although the attack had successfully penetrated and cut off the 39th regiment of the 9th infantry division and parts of the 30th division as well, he did have several options available to him. First and foremost was the 4th Infantry Division located just across the Sée River and on the right flank of the *2nd Panzer* advance. Without waiting for any direction from VII Corps, its commander, Ray Barton, who had led the division when it landed at Utah Beach on D day, launched a heavy artillery barrage on the advancing Germans. He also assembled his division in defensive positions to prevent a crossing of the river, which could threaten the rear of the entire First Army. Collins had reason to be proud of this fine example of initiative shown by one of his division commanders.

He was also fortunate in that part of the 3rd Armored Division was also in the area, having been just released from temporary attachment to the 4th Division. It was on its way to join the rest of the division south of Mortain when Collins had it stopped and turned over to Major General Hobbs, 30th Division commander, for use in strengthening his defenses against the *2nd Panzer* attack.

On the road to Saint-Hilaire, the southern prong of the attack, Collins was less fortunate. No troops under his command were in an advantageous position to counter the *2nd SS Panzer* attack. Third Army troops were in the area, however—the troops that Patton had halted the night before. Bradley arranged to transfer the 35th Infantry from Patton's XX Corps to Collins. It would be evening before the 35th could be on its way to the Saint-Hilaire road, but at least Collins knew that the way to Saint-Hilaire was no longer wide open.

The combination of these hastily assembled defensive dispositions and an apparent slowdown in the advance of the two major German attacks made Collins feel by evening that he had the situation under reasonable control. Although Collins had sensed the possibility of such an attack, its magnitude and aggressiveness did come as a surprise. It was clear to him that, although the threat had been contained, it was still very real.

The person who had the most cause to be concerned about the threat was General Bradley. He now had twelve divisions south of Avranches. These were the divisions most obviously

threatened by a successful counterattack at Mortain. They
would be cut off from their sources of supply as well as from
the First Army on their left. Conservatism argued strongly
for returning a number of these divisions to the Mortain area
to make absolutely certain that the German offensive could
be stopped.

Yet Bradley had released only the 35th Division to Collins
as part of his effort to shore up defenses. The remaining
eleven divisions were left free to pursue the offensive strategy
laid out for them over the past several days. It was a difficult
decision—certainly a risky one. But by taking it, Bradley
had effectively changed the Mortain counteroffensive from a
threat into an opportunity—an enhanced opportunity for the
new strategy of encirclement that was taking form in his mind.
He was just about ready now, and, with Ike coming to see
him tomorrow, perhaps they could tie the whole idea together.

"Take Brest—by Saturday." That was the startling challenge given by Major General Grow to his 6th Armored
Division the previous Thursday morning as they refitted and
reorganized for the continuation of their advance at noon.

Well, they had not made it. For a while they thought they
might. Patton had visited them on Friday and was pleased
and surprised at their progress. He made arrangements with
Grow for delivery of adequate gasoline and other supplies to
keep the division moving. By Saturday morning they were
within forty miles of Brest, and it looked as if the challenge
that had seemed so impossible might really be achieved. That
afternoon, however, they struck the first of several delaying
actions that began to slow their progress. None of these involved significant numbers of troops, but the terrain was
becoming hilly and wooded, and the Germans made good
use of this advantage.

Progress on Saturday afternoon and Sunday was somewhat
slower than it had been on the previous two days, but by
Monday morning they were in the Brest area. Now they were
faced with the critical question: Could the city be taken by
a single armored division without support?

Grow thought the chances were good. Their advance had
been so rapid that they must have arrived before the Germans
expected them. Enemy communications surely had been dis-

rupted by the 6th Armored advance and the element of surprise was in their favor. Finally, although Grow had no way of knowing exactly how many troops were defending the city, he did know that many German troops had been moved from Brittany to Normandy. He expected that the figure might be no more than 3,000.

Grow was certain of one thing. If he was to take the city, it had to be done quickly while the element of surprise was still in his favor. In spite of fatigue, he pushed his division toward the city during the afternoon. They were coming down on Brest from the north and northeast, and when they got within about four miles of the center of the city, they had their answer. Heavy artillery fire and strong resistance from well-defended outposts stopped them cold. The element of surprise was gone. There would be no ''cheap'' way to capture Brest. This was a job for infantry and artillery. The 6th Armored needed help.

Tuesday, AUGUST 8

As von Kluge moved Panzer divisions westward to launch the Mortain counteroffensive, it became increasingly clear to General Montgomery that it was time for another major assault by his forces around Caen to break through the northern sector of the German defenses. The town of Falaise, twenty miles to the south of Caen, would be the objective.

The task was given to the II Corps of the Canadian First Army. The man in charge of developing and carrying out the attack was its commander, Lt. Gen. G. G. Simonds. A forty-one-year-old veteran of the Sicilian and Italian campaigns, he was a quiet but tough commander who was both feared and respected by his troops. He had some rather different ideas about the best way to break through the enemy lines.

Simonds was not in favor of the saturation bombing techniques used during the previous month both in the successful U.S. COBRA operation as well as the unsuccessful British GOODWOOD attack. He felt that the damage done to the terrain made it impossible for the attacking forces to move fast enough to prevent the enemy from establishing an effective second line of defense. He was not opposed to using air bombardment, however. What Simonds had in mind was to create a corridor down which his forces would attack and to have the air attack concentrate outside of both flanks of the corridor. By this technique he hoped to neutralize the strong German artillery positions as well as seal the corridor off from support and reinforcement from the outside.

In order to speed the attack, he had several other ideas. He planned to align the attack in six long, narrow columns of tanks, antitank guns, and the chassis of self-propelled artillery from which the guns had been removed. In these chassis would ride the infantry. The attack would be launched at night in order to achieve surprise. To avoid confusion and loss of direction in the darkness, he planned to use radio directional beams, green flares fired along the line of attack, bursts of tracers along the flanks, and high-powered searchlights. After the column had penetrated two or three miles, the troops would then leave their transport to deal with whatever second line of defense the enemy had been able to establish. It was an original and unique form of attack. It was given the code name TOTALIZE.

The attack was launched shortly after midnight, and during the hours of darkness things had gone rather well. True, there had been a great deal of confusion. Heavy dust from the concentration of vehicles and smoke screens laid by the enemy made visibility extremely poor in spite of all the directional aids. Collisions were common and many vehicles strayed completely off course. But generally, the direction of the attack was maintained. Individual resourcefulness often saved the day. Some officers led their columns on foot, periodically firing Very pistols to keep the column on track.

If there was confusion among the attackers, that among the German defenders was often worse. They had no idea of the magnitude of the attack, and forward elements were surrounded or bypassed before they were aware of what was going on. In spite of an early morning ground fog that created further problems, the Canadians had penetrated more than three miles inside the German lines by midmorning, and the way seemed clear for a complete breakthrough.

Simonds had two armored divisions poised to exploit the breakthrough—the Canadian 4th and the Polish 1st. Unfortunately, they were both inexperienced—going into action for the first time—and this was to cost him dearly. Failure to bypass enemy strong points and particularly to press the attack as evening approached caused the momentum gained by the earlier assaults to gradually fade away. Simonds's

elaborate plan to deal with the enemy's second line of defense
appeared to be falling short.

At least in part, this was the result of the caliber of the
German defense. The heaviest defensive responsibility fell
on the *12th SS Panzer Division*, one of Germany's elite armored divisions. Led by their young and very able commander, Maj. Gen. Kurt Meyer, they recovered rapidly from
their initial confusion to set up effective defensive positions.
Meyer himself had driven up the Caen-Falaise road before
dawn to rally his confused troops and organize the defenses.
While his forces were hardly sufficient to stop an attack of
such magnitude, they were able to gain time for the Germans
to organize a stronger defense behind the Laison River, a
mile or two to the south.

By nightfall, Simonds faced the disappointing prospect that
his plan had not fully succeeded. However, both he and
Montgomery could be cheered by the fact that definite progress had been made down the road to Falaise. Perhaps with
more aggressive follow-up the next day, momentum could
be regained and the way to Falaise opened.

General Bradley knew what he wanted to do. He had made
up his mind. But reasonable precaution dictated one final
check. He called Courtney Hodges to receive the latest news
on the situation west of Mortain. The news was reassuring.
Hodges advised Bradley that the German counterattack appeared to have run its course. No progress had been made
since the previous afternoon. Collins was confident that the
defensive steps taken the day before would hold the Germans
in check. While no ground had yet been retaken and the
Germans could certainly be expected to continue to press the
attack, Hodges felt that any real threat of a breakthrough was
unlikely.[1]

Thus reassured, Bradley's next call was to George Patton.
It was 10:00 A.M. Patton's XV Corps was close to Le Mans
and could be expected to be in the city later in the day after
its rapid three-day advance of almost eighty miles.[2] With the
center of gravity of the German army shifted to the west as
a result of the Mortain attack, Haislip's XV Corps was now
obviously well to the east of the enemy's main forces. The

opportunity was all too clear, and Bradley intended to seize it.

First, he told Patton that he was releasing to the XV Corps the three divisions he had withheld the day before to protect against the German attack. The 35th and 80th Infantry and 2nd French Armored Divisions were to join the one armored and two infantry divisions already near Le Mans as quickly as possible. The combined force was to change direction ninety degrees and attack to the north. The line of attack was to be from Le Mans to Alençon to Sées, the town situated on the current boundary line between the British and American armies. Bradley did not have to explain to Patton the reasoning behind this change in direction. The latter expressed it well at the conclusion of his own order written later in the day: "The purpose of the operation is to surround and destroy the German Army west of the Seine."[3] That is exactly what Bradley had in mind.

With that accomplished, Bradley rushed off to his rendezvous with General Eisenhower. Ike had moved his headquarters to France just the day before. It covered about two acres in the hedgerow and apple orchard country, halfway between Montgomery's headquarters near Caen and Bradley's near Coutances. Being that much closer to the front gave Eisenhower a greater opportunity to become more closely involved in the day-to-day events, and the first thing he wanted was a tour of some of the scenes of recent American military successes.

Bradley met him a few miles west of the new SHAEF headquarters. Ike arrived in his Packard Clipper driven by Kay Summersby and accompanied by Col. Jim Gault, his British military assistant. The group headed south across the Marigny-Saint-Lô road used as the COBRA line of departure. They turned west to Coutances—a city largely destroyed and deserted except for the cathedral, which miraculously had escaped destruction. It was then south to Roncey, where they saw huge piles of destroyed German equipment shoved aside by bulldozers as the town attempted to return to some semblance of order. All along the roads, Ike was greeted by scenes of destruction—from derelict German tanks to shattered trees to dead cattle—the horrible aftermath of the sweep of battle through the Norman countryside. On the more cheerful side were the waves of recognition and cheers for "Ike" from the American GIs along the road.

The entourage stopped for lunch at the side of the road. K rations and GI bread wrapped in an old copy of the *Chicago Times* was the bill of fare.[4] After lunch, it was back to Bradley's CP and down to business. Bradley explained his plan. Ike asked a number of questions, particularly about the Mortain situation. Once assured on that front, he gave his whole-hearted support to Bradley's plan. After all, just six days before that he had written General Marshall to inform him that he "would consider it unnecessary to detach any large forces for the conquest of Brittany and would devote the great bulk of the forces to the task of completing the destruction of the German Army. . . ." Bradley's plan represented the fulfillment of his own ideas of how to best exploit the Allied successes of the past several weeks.

With Montgomery's TOTALIZE operation moving down from the north and XV Corps moving up from the south, the jaws of a giant trap were beginning to form. Ike planned to head for Montgomery's headquarters late in the afternoon to make sure that the Twenty-first Army Group was being sufficiently aggressive in carrying out their part of the plan. Before he left, however, the two generals phoned Montgomery and Patton to make sure everyone was "on board" and fully understood their part in the larger opportunity now emerging.

After Ike left, Bradley had to take care of some details related to a planned visit the following day from Treasury Secretary Henry Morganthau. He certainly did not look forward to it—a retinue of twelve people taking up his time and that of his senior officers. But VIP visitations were apparently an unavoidable part of his job, so he might as well make the most of it.

Neither VIP visits nor any of the other problems and annoyances he faced could take away Bradley's good feeling about today's events. A major change of strategy had been put into motion. He was confident that his decision was the correct one and the results would be fruitful.

Wednesday, AUGUST 9

The distinguished visitor arrived at Bradley's headquarters at 8:45 A.M., half an hour early. Secretary of the Treasury Henry Morganthau and his entourage of eleven people were in fine spirits. It had been a good trip so far. The secretary was particularly pleased about his visit two days before with General Eisenhower at SHAEF Forward in Portsmouth, England. While the stated purpose of his visit was to investigate currency problems in France, he had drawn Eisenhower into a long discussion about the proper treatment of Germany after the war. He felt that Eisenhower's views were quite similar to his own—that Germany should be heavily punished, reduced to a pastoral state, and her industry destroyed. (Morganthau was to later claim that much of his "Morganthau Plan," which was widely discredited, came from his discussion with Eisenhower. This led to a break in relations between the two men, and Eisenhower would never forgive the secretary for what he considered a gross misrepresentation of his views and an unforgivable breach of privacy.) And now Morganthau was going to get to see the war at close range.

There was considerably less enthusiasm over the visit among the members of Bradley's staff, who were further aggravated by the group's early arrival. Bradley had already expressed his views about such VIP visits, but his aide, Chester Hansen, knew that he, not the general, would bear the brunt of the "entertaining."[1] Bradley did take the group in tow as soon as they arrived and gave them a briefing on the current military situation. Fresh from his discussion with Ike the day before and excited about the decisions they had reached, he was upbeat. "This is an opportunity that comes to a commander not once in a century," Bradley told the group. "We are about to destroy an entire hostile army. If the other fellow will only press his attack here at Mortain for another 48 hours," he said, pointing to the situation map, "he'll give us time to close at Argentan and there completely destroy him. . . . We'll go all the way from here to the German border."[2]

While Bradley was effusive in his briefing for Morganthau and his group, he had no intention of accompanying them on their tour of the front. The pressure of directing the battle was the excuse he gave to the group. Privately to Hansen, he said, "I don't care to follow screaming sirens half a day."[3]

So, as Hansen fully expected, it was his duty to conduct the tour. The best he could get from the motor pool was a worn-out Packard sedan, and the group took off for their next destination—First Army headquarters. Following much the same route that Bradley and Eisenhower had followed the day before, they passed through Coutances, on to Roncey, and another fifteen miles southeast to the new First Army CP outside of Montbray.

If there was little enthusiasm for the secretary's visit at Bradley's headquarters, there was considerably less at Hodges's. With the Mortain counteroffensive still very much on his mind, Courtney Hodges did not need a VIP visit at this time. In the words of Major Sylvan, Hodges's aid, "Without too much difficulty, the party was safely engineered out of the way by eleven o'clock."[4] In true military fashion, this was accomplished by passing the group along to the 28th Division, whose CP was four miles farther down the road near Saint-Sever Calvados. Here Morganthau got his wish to see the war "close up." Against a background of 105mm guns firing in preparation for an infantry attack, Pete Corlett, commander of the XIX Corps, gave a vivid description of the attack plans of the 28th Division.

It was then time to leave in order to be back at Bradley's headquarters in time for lunch. The group got only as far as

Roncey, however, when the Packard broke down, joining the hundreds of destroyed German vehicles already lining the streets of the town. They had to requisition a jeep from a second lieutenant to complete the journey, but arrived just ten minutes late for lunch.

Hansen's day was not over. The tour continued in the afternoon, this time in the opposite direction. After a tour of the battlefields near Saint-Lô, the group went on to Omaha Beach and the American cemetery on the heights above the beach. Following this tour, the entourage attended a dinner that had been arranged nearby for the secretary and his son, Lt. Henry Morganthau, Jr., who was stationed in the area. The party then left for England.

It was 9:45 P.M. when Hansen finally arrived back at head-quarters. He may have had some questions in his mind as to what his activities of the day had contributed to the war effort. On the other hand, Morganthau was indeed an important person and a longtime confidant of the president. Perhaps it was worth all the time and effort. Hansen probably would have felt better if he could have taken a peek at the entry in the secretary's diary for that day: "We were at Bradley's headquarters. He makes an excellent impression. . . . Very quiet, complete self-control, complete balance. . . . He planned our trip. They let me go down within 5,000 yards of the Germans . . . but they wouldn't let me go any further because the thing is so fluid. . . . We were west of Avranches and east of Villedieu and due south of St. Lo . . . where the fighting was most severe and they have five German Divisions right opposite there. Three were SS Divisions."[5]

If his general received good press from someone that close to the White House, then perhaps Hansen really had earned his pay.

Generals Eisenhower and Bradley may have been satisfied that the German counteroffensive at Mortain had lost its momentum, but it would have been very difficult to convince Capt. Reynold Erichson. Having heard nothing from his battalion commander, Lieutenant Colonel Hardaway, he had taken over command of the 700 men who were now surrounded on Hill 317. He had under his command a heavy weapons company under Capt. Delmont Byrn and three rifle companies commanded by First Lieutenants Ralph Kerley, Joseph Resider, and Ronald Woody, Jr. In addition, there were the two forward observers from the 230th Field Artillery Battalion, Lieutenants Barts and Weiss, whose presence was critical to the use of this dominant position as an artillery spotting location.

There was no question about the extreme importance of Hill 317 to the outcome of the battle. Erichson and his men could see it clearly and, although surrounded by vastly superior forces, they had made the decision to hold out rather than surrender. To the Germans and the *2nd SS Panzer Division*, it was even more obvious that the hill must be taken if their attack was to stand any chance of success. It was unacceptable for such a dominating position in the rear of their attacking forces to be in enemy hands. The frequency and force of the German attacks demonstrated their concern.

For two days now, Captain Erichson and his men had held out. They were helped immeasurably by heavy artillery fire called in by their two observers. The lines of battle were so close and confused that they were calling fire almost into their own positions, but so far it had been effective. Although their own losses were heavy, those inflicted on the enemy were heavier, and they had succeeded in taking a number of prisoners. An SS officer brought within the lines with a surrender proposal was given a curt refusal by Captain Byrn. No one on Hill 317 was thinking in those terms.

The small force defending the hill did have its problems. Food was one. There were a number of small farms on the hilltop within their lines, and the farmers had shared their meager supplies, but this source of food was just about used up. Of greater concern were items that the farmers could not supply—ammunition, medical supplies, and, most critical, radio batteries to keep the artillery spotters in business.

To the 30th Division headquarters, only one avenue of supply seemed to be open—by air—and that presented a difficult problem. The battalion perimeter was small, so it was necessary to fly low and slow over the area to make an accurate drop. This made the planes easy targets for German antiaircraft guns. A supply officer from the First Army had been shot down this morning while making a reconnaissance flight—he was forced to parachute from his light plane and was taken prisoner. Getting close to the hilltop position by air was a very risky proposition. Nevertheless, the attempts to drop supplies continued during the day, with little if any success.

Although the efforts so far had produced little in the way of supplies, they did show the troops on the hill that they were not forgotten. Their resolve to hold on to the position was strengthened by this knowledge and the hope that a way would be found to get them what they needed. Captain Erichson and his men had no thoughts of giving up. They would hang on somehow until supplies and reinforcements could arrive.

Most professional military officers would consider it an honor and good news indeed to be notified that the size of their command would be doubled to the level of an army group. Even more so if the group were to bear their name. But to Gen. Heinrich Eberbach, it was the worst possible news. He objected strenuously when he received the order from his superior, Field Marshal von Kluge.

It was all part of Hitler's unbreakable resolve to renew the Mortain offensive. When the attack bogged down on Monday afternoon, Hitler's first words were, "I command that the attack be prosecuted daringly and recklessly to the sea." To Hitler, the attack had been unsuccessful because of von Kluge's tactical errors and for no other reason. These errors were now to be corrected.

He would establish *Panzer Group Eberbach*. The general would have under his command not only the four Panzer divisions used in the first attack but also two additional Panzer divisions plus one battalion to be taken from the northern sector of the German defenses. They were to be organized and regrouped in order to renew the attack by August 11 over approximately the same ground as the original attack.

Eberbach had several reasons for objecting to this assignment, not the least of which was turning over command of his *Fifth Panzer Army* to Col. Gen. Josef "Sepp" Dietrich, currently commander of the *I SS Panzer Corps*. Dietrich's rise up the military ladder was the result of his friendship with Hitler, whom he had served as chief of his personal bodyguards during the violent early years of the Nazi regime.

This close connection to Hitler aroused suspicions among the professional military officers. A tough, rough-and-ready type, Dietrich was considered by Eberbach (and others) to be unfit for higher command. As a political officer, he had none of the military background and training expected to be part of the credentials of a high-level commander in the Germany army. While his courage could not be questioned, his grasp of military strategy and his general level of intelligence certainly could.

However, Eberbach's main objection to his assignment was his view that renewal of the Mortain offensive (or, for that matter, the original offensive itself) was ill-conceived and offered not even the slightest chance of success. Ever since his assignment to the western front in July, he had been urging the necessity of withdrawal behind the Seine as the only means of organizing an effective defense against the power of the Allied armies.[6] It seemed that everything he had done since then was in direct contradiction to his own view of what constituted sound military strategy.

Be that as it may, he had his orders, and he gloomily set about developing a plan. To help him in this, he set up a small staff consisting of Lt. Col. Guenther von Kluge, the field marshal's son, as his chief of staff, and Major Eckesparre, formerly of Rommel's staff, as operations officer. The first shock came when it was discovered that only about 125 tanks would be available for the attack. Eberbach needed many more and they would have to be brought in from the outside, a process that would certainly take time.

One clear lesson learned from the first offensive at Mortain was that it was suicidal to attack during daytime hours because of the overwhelming Allied air advantage. Eberbach calculated that all attacks would have to be concluded by 10:00 A.M., when the morning fog and mist had risen. This limitation on the duration of the attacks increased the need for tanks—a large number would be required to have any chance of success. Furthermore, to attack at night required some moonlight, and it was determined that proper conditions would not prevail until August 20. Therefore, if there was to be an attack at all, August 20 appeared to be the earliest possible date—a delay of eleven days.

If Hitler's plan for an August 11 attack was beyond the

realm of possibility, Eberbach must have realized that his own plan to delay until August 20 was equally unrealistic. To expect the front to remain stable for that length of time was pure nonsense. The signs were everywhere. The first Mortain attack just two days before had done little, if anything, to relieve the Allied pressure everywhere else along the line. The Mortain offensive had been followed the very next day by a major drive by the Canadians south from Caen—the heaviest action in that sector for weeks. The pressure could be expected to continue, and, to make matters worse, this was the area that was to supply most of the additional Panzer troops for the renewed Mortain offensive.

In addition, the pressure on the western end of the front, north of Mortain, continued to mount. General Hodges's First Army was driving toward Sourdeval and Vire. No German troop withdrawals from this front were possible, or the whole attacking force at Mortain would be jeopardized by the collapse of its northern shoulder.

Then there was the most serious threat of all—the Americans were now in Le Mans. It took no great knowledge of military strategy to appreciate the dangers inherent in this situation. While there was yet no indication of the direction the American forces might take from there, the possibilities were clear and included a turn to the north as well as continuing their drive eastward in a race to the Seine. In either case, failure to stop them would offer grim forebodings for the bulk of the German forces still fighting some eighty to ninety miles to the north and west of Le Mans.

It was a Catch-22 situation. To attack now assured failure and probably destruction of whatever armored strength the Germans still had in Normandy. To wait until prospects for success could be improved was to expect the impossible—namely, that the status quo over the entire front could be maintained for a week or more. The dilemma was crystal clear to Eberbach. He was certain it was to von Kluge as well. But could Hitler be made to understand? Well, that was von Kluge's job. All he could do was outline the choices and define the alternatives. He picked up the phone to call von Kluge.

Thursday, AUGUST 10

Duty officer Ralph Bennett reported to Hut 3 at midnight. He had the graveyard shift as he had had so many times since he came to Bletchley Park more than two years ago.

Bletchley Park was the headquarters of the supersecret ULTRA project. A rather ugly red-brick country estate, it was chosen not for its architectural charm but rather for its location—fifty miles north of London near both Oxford and Cambridge; the universities there would be the source of many of the scientists whose contributions to ULTRA were critically important. It was in Hut 3 that the enemy dispatches were decoded using the system developed by the British early in the war.

ULTRA had proven itself with such dramatic intelligence coups as the discovery of Rommel's intentions in Africa, which contributed to Montgomery's victory at El Alamein; advance warning of the targets of many German air raids over England; and information that led Churchill to warn the Russians about BARBAROSSA, the German invasion of Russia (information that, unfortunately for the Russians, was ignored). Senior American military commanders were developing a high degree of confidence in ULTRA intelligence because of the valuable and accurate information it had produced about D day, the battle of Saint-Lô, the breakout in the Normandy peninsula, and numerous other engagements.

Even the skeptical Patton now made it a regular practice to listen to his ULTRA officer, Major Helfers.

For Bennett, however, service at Bletchley Park had been a two-year grind of man-killing working hours and tremendous pressures. There had been a number of suicides among ULTRA people for whom the tensions had become unbearable. Tonight seemed different, however. "Excitement at the significance of the intelligence we were providing at the moment which might be decisive for the whole campaign was already intense in Hut 3 at midnight," he later wrote, "and I can still vividly recall the exhilaration of the next few hours."[1] The performance of the ULTRA group had by now reached a certain peak level both in terms of the amount and value of the material it was decoding, as well as the speed with which it was making this information available to the military commanders in a position to use it effectively.

The past few days had already produced a treasure trove of information. A dispatch decoded and sent out at midnight August 6 announced the German decision to counterattack at Mortain, listing the four armored divisions involved and the direction of the attack. While this information was disseminated too late to give advance notice of the attack, it did outline its scope and objectives very clearly. The decisions made and actions taken by Bradley and his commanders had the benefit of unusually precise information about the intentions of the enemy.

But the biggest prize of all had come in just a few hours before Bennett reported for his midnight shift. As the subject of the intercepted dispatch began to emerge, the pressure on Bennett and the others in Hut 3 to decipher and disseminate the entire message became intense. The intercept was an order from von Kluge calling for renewal of the Mortain offensive—the order that von Kluge had issued following Hitler's command that "the attack be prosecuted daringly and recklessly to the sea." As decoding work continued, both the intended date for the attack and the troops to be employed were spelled out. It listed the four Panzer divisions that had participated in the first attack (*1 SS, 2 Pz, 2 SS,* and *116 Pz*) plus the *10 SS* and *9 Pz* as the troops to be engaged. August 11 was established as the kick-off date, although there was some discussion of a possible postponement for twelve to twenty-four hours. The order also authorized Gen. Sepp Dietrich to assume command of the *Fifth Panzer Army*, freeing Eberbach to take charge of this renewed offensive.

Here was news of extreme significance to the Allied High Command. Less than forty-eight hours previously, Bradley had issued his command for Patton's XV Corps to swing north from Le Mans toward Alençon and Argentan while the British and Canadians were driving south toward Falaise. This action had been taken at least in part in response to the initial Mortain offensive, which had shifted the center of gravity of the German forces to the west, making encirclement a very real prospect. Now ULTRA was advising that, in spite of the failure of the first attack, another one was planned, which would continue to shift von Kluge's troops in a westerly direction. Clearly the chances of a successful encirclement on the Argentan-Falaise axis had been greatly advanced. Omar Bradley certainly would enjoy a comfortable feeling when this ULTRA intercept reached his command caravan.

Additional intercepts for decoding arrived at Hut 3 as night turned into day this Thursday morning. Information that a number of German fighter groups were being moved back to Germany for refitting, the location of two German divisions on their way to reinforce the *Seventh Army*, establishment of the location of General Eberbach's headquarters, information that the German *First Army* headquarters was to be moved from southwest France to Fontainebleau by rail—all this vital intelligence came pouring out of Hut 3 to the limited group of Allied commanders who were authorized to receive ULTRA intelligence. Never before had ULTRA produced such a volume of critical intelligence data in such a short period of time.

When Bennett was relieved from duty to return to his quarters, he was as limp as a rag. The exhilaration and excitement had vanished. He was exhausted. But it was a day he would never forget. He had been in the middle of history in the making.

"In consonance with this plan, you will advance along the axis LE MANS-ALENÇON-SÉES with the purpose of initially securing the line SÉES-CARROUGES, both inclusive, prepared for further advance, utilizing the 5th Armored Division, the 79th and 90th Infantry Divisions, and the 2nd French Armored Division which is hereby attached to your Corps. . . ."[2]

General Hobart Gay had brought up the order in person from Third Army headquarters early the previous morning. This gave Wade Haislip a chance to look it over before Patton arrived at noon. He was excited. His XV Corps had been given an assignment that was daring as well as crucial to the success of the entire Allied plan in Normandy. The dash to Le Mans had proved to him that his troops were ready to tackle tough jobs, and the job coming up had all the earmarks of being the toughest one yet.

The meeting with Patton had cleared up Haislip's questions about the attack and ironed out the details. The attack was to be made with the two armored divisions leading the way, followed by the infantry. The French and the 90th Infantry were to be on the left and the 5th Armored and the 79th on the right. It was to be a rapid penetration on a narrow front. Speed was the key, as there was no indication that the area to the north of Le Mans was as yet heavily defended. Some concern had been expressed about the exposed flanks that would result from this kind of attack. Patton had agreed to mitigate the situation by sending the 80th Infantry Division into the twenty-five-mile gap between the XV Corps and the VII Corps troops on its left at Mayenne. But basically Haislip was to be more concerned about speeding his advance than protecting his flanks.

The 2nd French Armored Division had arrived in the Le Mans area the day before, following a one-day delay because of the German attack at Mortain. To Haislip, who was familiar with the rest of his troops, the French division was an unknown element. He had every right to be optimistic, as the division was experienced in combat and certainly had ample incentive provided by the opportunity to liberate their homeland from four years of German occupation. They had fought in Africa; been sent to England, where they had received American equipment; and then been sent on to Normandy in early August. They were the only organized French military unit now fighting in France.

Their commander was Maj. Gen. Philippe Leclerc, a genuine French hero. A member of the French nobility, his real

name was Philippe, Vicomte de Hauteclocque. He had assumed a "nom de guerre" to protect his family from German
reprisals. Captured during the German invasion in June 1940,
he had escaped from the chateau in which he was imprisoned
and reached London. He was immediately sent by General
de Gaulle to French Equatorial Africa to take command of
the Free French forces there. A dramatic 1,500-mile march
through enemy-held territory brought his forces to Tripoli and
junction with Montgomery's Eighth Army in time to participate in the Tunisian campaign.[3]

The general was well aware that he and his forces would
be special objects of attention in an otherwise exclusively
American army, and he was anxious to demonstrate the fighting qualities of his troops. He was also aware that his American superiors might have doubts about the reliability of their
French division and as a result use it only for assignments of
secondary importance. He would have to be vocal and insis-
tent that his forces be given a leading role in the liberation
of their country.

Wade Haislip had no compunctions (and, for that matter,
no choice) about giving the 2nd Armored a leading role in
the upcoming attack. His 5th Armored Division had spent
the previous day clearing the departure lines and providing
adequate assembly areas for the arriving French forces. This
morning, the two divisions had jumped off right on schedule.

Little, if any, intelligence was available to XV Corps headquarters about the extent of enemy resistance that the two
divisions were likely to encounter. It was not known what,
if any, German troops were in the area. As the morning
progressed, however, Haislip's forces were delayed by some
sharp tank skirmishes and troublesome artillery fire from the
German *9th Panzer* and *352nd Infantry Divisions*. This enemy
harassment was compounded by considerable traffic congestion as the two Allied armored divisions attempted to organize
their forward movements.

The German forces were insufficient to cause any serious
delay, however. Once the Allied forces were able to overcome
their own traffic problems, they were able to outflank their
enemy opposition, who were quickly forced to withdraw to
the north. By day's end, the leading elements of the 2nd
French and 5th Armored Divisions had advanced about fifteen

miles, halfway to their first objective—Alençon. With the two infantry divisions bringing up the rear, Haislip's XV Corps was off to a good start. The first round in Bradley's battle to encircle the German forces in Normandy was clearly a success.

Friday, AUGUST 11

When he had first heard the day before about the movement of the American XV Corps north from Le Mans, von Kluge knew that Eberbach was right. Something had to be done to get the Führer to abandon his fixation on renewal of the Mortain offensive. Eberbach had suggested that earlier when it became obvious that it would take days to organize any effective attack. Still he hesitated. Getting approval for such a change from the Führer could be a very difficult and humiliating experience. Finally, late the day before, he had called Jodl. Would he ask the Führer to consider "whether the spearheads of the enemy columns driving north should not be smashed by a . . . swiftly executed Panzer thrust?"[1] In other words, forget Mortain and use the Panzer divisions to stop the XV Corps advance.

As expected, the request produced an avalanche of questions from Hitler's headquarters in East Prussia. Why could the renewed Mortain offensive not be launched sooner? When could an attack toward Le Mans be instituted? Was recapture of Le Mans a part of the plan? How about the *11th Panzer Division* in southern France? Could it not be brought north quickly so that both attacks could be carried out?

In response to the questions, von Kluge carefully pointed out that he was representing the combined opinions of his two main subordinates—Eberbach and Hausser—as well as his own. He was well aware that his own reputation with the Führer was at a low ebb not only because of the failure of the Mortain counteroffensive but also because of suspicions that he had been a participant (or, at least, a sympathizer) in the July 20 assassination plot. He wanted to make certain that his own poor standing did not have an adverse effect on obtaining the desired approvals.

Von Kluge pointed out that all the commanders agreed that another attack at Mortain had no chance of success. He emphasized the threat of encirclement represented by the Canadian attacks toward Falaise and the American attacks toward Alençon. Alençon was of further importance as a major supply base for the army. There was no possibility that the *11th Panzer Division* could move from southern France in time to have any influence on the present situation. Von Kluge sidestepped the question about recapturing Le Mans by pointing out that the precise direction of the attack would depend on developments. He added, however, that he expected to launch the attack by August 13.

Discussion went back and forth all during the afternoon. By 6:00 P.M. von Kluge decided he could wait no longer. He issued an order that was destined to become known as the "Alençon Plan." Effective immediately, the *Seventh Army* was to abandon Mortain. The *XLVII* and *LXXXI Panzer Corps* would regroup in the Carrouges area with the *1st SS*, *2nd*, and *116th Panzer Divisions* in the lead. The force would be commanded by Eberbach, who had already reached Alençon during the afternoon. An attack on Alençon would be prepared for August 14 at 5:00 A.M. (He had already slipped one day from what he had previously proposed to the Führer.) The *V Panzer Corps* would retire in echelon behind the Orne River and then the Touques River in order to cover the northern flank. The *Seventh Army* would cover the southern flank from Domfront to Alençon, moving in an easterly direction.

The Alençon Plan had all the earmarks of being much more than simply a redirection of the focus of attack. It was the beginning of withdrawal—a recognition that entrapment of the entire German force was a distinct possibility and that something must be done about it.

Several hours later, Hitler's response arrived at von Kluge's headquarters. It did accept the fact that a new set of circumstances required some different responses. However, Hitler refused to give up completely on the Mortain offensive, merely accepting the fact that it must be delayed. Rather than seeing a movement to halt the American advance toward Alençon, Hitler envisioned an attack toward the deep left flank of the XV Corps with the expectation that it could be cut off and destroyed. He authorized "minor" withdrawals in the Mortain-Sourdeval area to free up the forces required for movement against the XV Corps.

The differences between the Alençon Plan and the response by Hitler were duly noted by von Kluge, but nothing was done to change his orders. Von Kluge was rapidly coming to the conclusion that his decisions and actions from now on would be controlled more by events than by directives from OKW. The realities of his situation could no longer be ignored, and events were moving too rapidly for him to be held hostage to delays and unrealistic orders emanating from the Führer's headquarters more than 1,000 miles away.

Montgomery called them his "General Operational Situation and Directives." Written periodically in a rather informal but usually dramatic style, they contained a review of the situation as he saw it, as well as general orders to the major armies under his control, including the Americans. Today he was issuing Directive M-518 and, as he affixed his signature to the document, General Montgomery was feeling particularly effusive and confident.

"It begins to look," the directive stated, "as if the enemy intends to fight it out between the Seine and the Loire. This will suit us very well. . . . Clearly our intention must be to destroy the enemy forces between the Seine and the Loire."[2] It went on to talk about the German failure at Mortain, the Canadian offensive toward Falaise, and the American position at Le Mans; it was generally upbeat in its analysis of the current situation.

Optimism was running high among the British generals. Several days before in an interview with the press, Major General de Guingand, Montgomery's chief of staff, and Lieutenant General Crerar, commander of the Canadian army, had made the startling statement that the war might be over in as little as three weeks.[3] Lieutenant General Dempsey had offered a wager to Bradley that the British would beat the Americans to Argentan.[4] Perhaps much of this talk was bravado, designed to encourage both the troops and the folks at home. But still, from a purely military point of view, there was much reason to be encouraged.

For Montgomery, the events of the past few days were further justification of his master plan for defeating the Germans in western Europe. His idea of using the British position around Caen as the hinge of a huge turning movement had already been proven sound. Now the second part of the plan—encirclement of the German army—appeared well within reach. True, his original thoughts envisioned a much wider turning movement along the Seine. However, when Bradley and Eisenhower had called several days ago with the proposal for a shorter encirclement on the Alençon-Falaise axis, Montgomery had to admit that it made a lot of sense. The Germans, in their puzzling refusal to retreat from the Mortain sector, had created the opportunity. With the Canadians north of Falaise and the Americans north of Le Mans, the jaws of the pincer were in place. To close the trap was the next order of business.

Montgomery still officially held the position as overall commander of the Allied ground forces in Normandy. As such, one of his major responsibilities was to define the boundary lines between the Allied armies. The responsibility he faced was particularly important, considering the fact that two major Allied forces were now heading directly toward one another. The II Corps of the Canadian First Army, under Lieutenant General Simonds, was heading south toward Falaise while Haislip's XV Corps was heading north from Le Mans. There had to be a clear understanding about the limits of advance of each force to avoid a confrontation. As General Bradley put it, "Any head-on juncture becomes a dangerous and uncontrollable maneuver unless each of the advancing forces is halted by prearranged plan on a terrain objective."[5]

At this moment, the Canadians were about six miles north of Falaise and twenty miles from Argentan, while the Americans were in the vicinity of Alençon, twenty-seven miles to the south of Argentan. The Canadians had made little progress in the previous two days since the launching of Operation TOTALIZE. The Germans had dug in along the Laison River, and efforts to outflank their position had been unsuccessful. However, Montgomery had put heavy pressure on the Canadians to take Falaise, and another major frontal attack was in the works.

By contrast, the XV Corps had made spectacular progress during the same period—thirty miles from their jumping-off place at Le Mans. Montgomery expected the Germans would now throw the bulk of their available forces against the American advance. He also noted that as they approached the Alençon-Argentan area, they would be returning to the bocage country, and difficult terrain would become a more serious problem. He expected the American advance to be dramatically slowed down in the face of these two obstacles.

Given these assessments of the likely progress of the two forces, Montgomery decided that the town of Argentan would remain, as it had been, the boundary line between the Twelfth and Twenty-first Army Groups. The advance of either of the two approaching forces was not to go beyond that point. This gave the Americans a slightly greater distance to cover, but it failed completely to consider the recent progress of the two approaching forces.

Few decisions during the campaign have been as heavily second-guessed as this one. To many critics, a line farther to the north would have been much more appropriate. Many American officers felt that the decision reflected long-standing reservations held by Montgomery concerning the fighting qualities of American troops. They felt also that "the British effort [to close on Argentan] . . . appears to have logged itself in timidity and succumbed to the legendary Montgomery vice of over caution."[6] However, these feelings did benefit from the clarity of hindsight and were fueled by the jealousy and divergence of strategic concepts that were a growing source of friction between British and American military leaders.

As Montgomery handed the signed directive to his aide, he was thinking more of the major victory that would be his if that gap of less than fifty miles somehow could be closed before the German forces could escape. Surely, there was plenty of glory to go around—enough for the British, Canadians, and Americans—if the two approaching Allied columns could reach their objectives, and reach them quickly.

Saturday, AUGUST 12

Shortly before noon they heard the noise of small-arms fire and what sounded like vehicles or tanks coming up the south slope of the hill. At first, Captain Erichson and the men still alive on Hill 317 refused to believe that this could be the relief they had been waiting for. They were now in their fifth day of isolation on the hill, during which time they had been under constant attack by forces many times their number. Then they saw them coming up the slope—men of the 35th Infantry Division. Their ordeal was over.

How much longer they could have held out would be anyone's guess. Their food and supply problems had become acute in spite of some ingenious efforts to come to their aid. When the earlier attempts at dropping supplies from the air proved unsuccessful, the commander of the 230th Field Artillery Battalion—the same battalion that had two of its observers, Lieutenants Barts and Weiss, on the hill—came up with an idea. He would take shell casings that had been originally designed to fire propaganda leaflets and fill them with supplies instead. The first attempts two days before had been successful. A day later, larger guns from other units had joined the effort. They found that it was possible to deliver a wide range of items, including medical supplies, with a degree of accuracy that kept them from falling into enemy hands. The one item that could not withstand the rigors of this method of delivery was blood plasma, which, of course, was badly needed by the many wounded men on the hill. However, those supplies that did arrive, and the ingenuity involved in delivering them, gave a huge boost to the morale of the troops, who were becoming increasingly concerned about the desperate nature of their situation. Indeed, relief had come none too soon.

The defense of Hill 317 by the 700 men of the 2nd Battalion, 120th Infantry Regiment, 30th Division, ranks as one of the outstanding achievements of the campaign in western Europe. Of the 700 men who were initially surrounded, more than 350 marched off under their own power. The remainder were killed or wounded. The four company commanders plus Captain Erichson, all of whom survived the battle, were awarded the Distinguished Service Cross for their heroic leadership during the five-day siege.

The effect of this battle on the outcome of the overall Mortain offensive is difficult to measure. Certainly, the overpowering effect of Allied artillery and airplanes, the rapid adjustment of Collins's VII Corps to the attack, Patton's halting the march of his XX Corps troops on the basis of intelligence reports, Ray Barton's effective use of his 4th Division artillery during the early hours of the attack—these are just some of the many tactical maneuvers that resulted in blunting the German attack. However, it can be claimed that only rarely has so large a battle been influenced so significantly by the actions of such a small group as the 700 men on Hill 317. Their commanding position in the rear of the advancing German forces was a constant threat. Accurate spotting by the men on top of the hill made it possible for American artillery to be an extremely important factor in turning the tide of the battle. After-battle inspection of damage to German vehicles indicated that more tanks were destroyed by artillery than any other cause, including aircraft. The unwillingness of the men on Hill 317 to surrender siphoned off German troops, tanks, and supporting equipment that might otherwise have supported the main attack.

As the men prepared to march off the hill, one final act in the drama was still to be played out. Other troops were now seen ascending the hill from the direction of the town of Mortain to the west. As they arrived at the crest, they were quickly identified as the remaining troops of their own 120th Regiment. With the added satisfaction of being relieved by their own regimental comrades, the survivors marched off the hill. They left behind a legacy not soon to be forgotten.

Between Alençon and Argentan looms the Forêt d'Ecouves. Lying in the foothills of the more hilly country to the north and west, it covers an area of sixty square miles. It is a dense forest dominated by large spruce and Norman pines, and its prominent terrain features could offer strong defensive positions.

Aware of its potential to delay his advance if occupied by the enemy, General Haislip decided to bypass the forest by sending the 5th Armored around to the right (east) and the 2nd French Armored to the left (west) of this natural strong point. The objectives were Argentan for the 5th and Ecouche, five miles to the west of Argentan, for the 2nd. These two towns were on (or actually a few miles beyond) the army boundaries that had been confirmed yesterday by General Montgomery. From the morning positions of the various combat units of these two divisions, this represented an advance of from twenty to thirty miles—a difficult objective through country in which the enemy strength was unknown.

This was the first big challenge for the 2nd French Armored Division, and Major General Leclerc intended to leave no stone unturned to assure that his troops were in Ecouche by nightfall. The one road to the west of the Forêt d'Ecouves was hardly sufficient to move his division fast enough to cover the twenty to thirty miles in one day. He decided to split his command. One group would proceed on the road to the west of the forest. He would send another on a road directly through the forest and still another on a road to the east. The three groups would then rejoin north of the forest and enter Ecouche. Although in direct contradiction to his XV Corps orders, he apparently felt that the need to reach his objective—to perform well in his first real attack as a part of the American army—overrode any necessity for strict adherence to orders.

Major General Oliver's 5th Armored had a somewhat better road network available than did the French and also were starting from a slightly more advanced position. However, bordering the forest to the northeast was the town of Sées, and here all roads on the eastern side of the forest converged. By the time the French troops who were sent to the east of the forest reached Sées, it had already been taken by Oliver's forces, and one of his combat commands had advanced down the Sées-Argentan road to within five miles of Argentan. Unfortunately, the tanks of this forward command had run out of gas.

By taking over the road through Sées, the French troops effectively blocked the gasoline trucks that were on their way to deliver the precious fuel to the stranded 5th Armored tanks. It was six hours before the trucks could be cleared through Sées and reach their objective—six hours during which the American tanks waited helplessly almost within sight of Argentan. Meanwhile, the troops of the 2nd French Armored moved on to within sight of the town of Ecouche by nightfall.

Leclerc had reached his objective, but the price was high. As the refueled 5th Armored tanks resumed their march toward Argentan, they met heavy resistance. During the time they were waiting for their gasoline, the first of the German forces sent east from Mortain arrived in the area. General Eberbach hurried a battalion of the *116th Panzer Division* down the road toward Sées. They arrived as the 5th Armored tanks were receiving their fuel and were in a position to block their further advance. Without the unfortunate delay, the important town of Argentan, which was not to fall into American hands for more than a week, might well have been taken this afternoon.

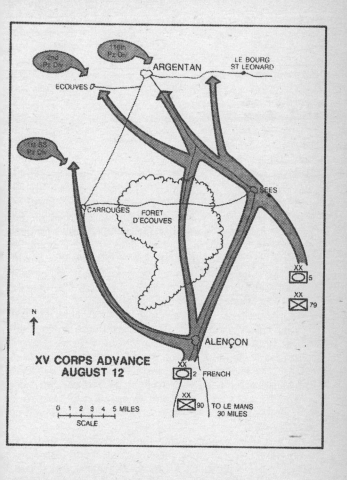

2nd Pz. Div.

116th Pz. Div.

ARGENTAN

LE BOURG ST LEONARD

ECOUVES

1st SS Pz. Div.

SEES

CARROUGES

FORET D'ECOUVES

N

XX
5

XX
79

ALENÇON

XV CORPS ADVANCE
AUGUST 12

XX
2 FRENCH

0 1 2 3 4 5 MILES
SCALE

XX
90

TO LE MANS
30 MILES

Sunday, AUGUST 13

From his command post in the little village of Chenedouit, twelve miles west of Argentan, General Eberbach and his small staff were doing everything they could to hurry the arriving Panzer troops toward the Ecouche-Argentan line. Eberbach had been in the area for two days now, trying to build up the vulnerable southern flank of the German defenses. For the first time, help was arriving. It was coming from the western sector around Mortain. But was it arriving soon enough? Eberbach was well aware that his time was running out. Today's events would be critical.[1]

The previous day had been close to catastrophic. The only force he had facing the American-French troops driving north was the under-strength *9th Panzer Division*. In its efforts to stem the advance of the French and American armored divisions, it had been almost destroyed—chewed up by attacks from all sides, particularly in the Forêt d'Ecouves. The Americans and French were to claim almost 100 tanks destroyed and 155 prisoners taken—numbers that Eberbach would not have disputed.

For a period of time during the afternoon, he had stood literally defenseless against the onrushing enemy. He did not see any way to prevent the loss of Argentan, a vital transportation center that also served as a major supply depot for the German forces. The Americans were only five miles away. But as the afternoon progressed, the American attack seemed to bog down and, at about that time, the first elements of the *116th Panzer* arrived in Argentan. Rushed down the road toward Sées as the day was drawing to a close, they were able to stem the American advance. It had been a very close call.

Eberbach's problems had been compounded the night before when he received orders from von Kluge. In spite of the fact that he realized von Kluge was under heavy pressure from Hitler and the OKW to take the offensive in the Argentan-Alençon area, he could not believe his eyes when he read the orders. They called for him to assemble the forces arriving from Mortain (in addition to the *116th Panzer*, the *1st SS* and the *2nd Panzers* were scheduled to arrive) and launch an attack across the southern boundary of the Forêt d'Ecouves. He was then to turn to the north and roll up the American forces approaching Argentan and Ecouche. It simply did not make sense. It completely ignored the realities of the situation. It could only be explained as another attempt by von Kluge to find some middle ground between the even wilder ideas of the Führer and that which was militarily feasible.

At any rate, Eberbach had decided this morning that he had no choice but to ignore von Kluge's orders. Even with the forces that were arriving on the scene, he saw no opportunity to do anything except stem the tide—to attempt to keep the enemy from overrunning both Argentan and Ecouche. Part of his problem lay in his uncertainty about the strength of the three arriving Panzer divisions. He was aware that their march from Mortain had been extremely difficult. Road congestion and fuel shortages alone would have been enough to cause severe problems. But, on top of that, the Allied air forces were now out in strength and having a field day attacking the long columns that were stalled or moving slowly down the few congested roads.

The first division to arrive, the *116th*, was immediately committed to the defense of Argentan. The *2nd* was sent to the Ecouche area, although the town itself had already been taken by the French 2nd Armored Division. The *1st SS* was committed to the Carrouges area, south of Ecouche near the western edge of the Forêt d'Ecouves. Three experienced Panzer divisions certainly seemed to be an adequate defense for any attack that the American XV Corps could mount. At full strength, they would have been. However, Eberbach estimated that all three divisions together had a total of only about seventy tanks—far less than the normal full complement of any of the individual divisions and certainly not a force that could be expected to hold the line against two armored and two infantry divisions, all at close to full strength.

In spite of this, during the morning the Germans were able to stop an attempt by the 5th Armored to bypass the town of Argentan to the east and reach the road north to Falaise. Artillery well positioned in the hills north of Argentan was effective in stopping the attack. Then in the afternoon, a patrol from the 2nd French Armored managed to penetrate to the very center of Argentan. The celebration of the town residents was short-lived, however, as the *116th Panzer* quickly forced the patrol back beyond the town limits.

Eberbach fully expected the frequency and strength of the attacks to escalate rapidly as the day wore on. But he was mistaken. As darkness set in, his three Panzer divisions held on to the same ground they had so hastily occupied that morning. While he was grateful that the line had held, he realized that their success was largely the result of the failure on the part of the XV Corps to fully apply all the pressure at their command. He could not help but wonder why.

Concern about his exposed left flank had been the first question Haislip raised with General Patton when he had received his orders to march north to Argentan. Patton, at that time, had promised to send the 80th Division into the large twenty-five-mile gap between the XV Corps and the VII Corps of the First Army at Mayenne. The 80th Division was now a part of the XX Corps but as yet had seen little action. The XX Corps orders called for the 80th on the right and the 7th Armored (another inexperienced unit) on the left to attack to the northeast into the gap on the left of the XV Corps. Since the 7th Armored had not yet reached the area, the 80th was to jump off in the morning by itself from its position southwest of Alençon.

By afternoon the division had become hopelessly entangled

with the XV Corps' 90th Division, whose mission was to protect the left flank of their corps' advance. Since the two divisions were moving in somewhat different directions, the entanglement became compounded and tempers flared. After much arguing, demands from the XV Corps that the 80th Division "get the hell of the road,"[2] and radio messages from regiment to division to corps and back, it was finally decided to countermand the orders of the 80th Division and have it pull back out of the area.

Largely a failure on the part of the Third Army headquarters to adequately research the road network in the area, this confrontation could have been costly. That it was not can be credited to Collins's VII Corps—more specifically his 1st Infantry and 3rd Armored Divisions. They too had an assignment to fill in the gap between their position at Mayenne and the XV Corps. Leaving Mayenne in the morning, the two divisions drove more than twenty miles in a northeastward direction until they reached the vicinity of Carrouges, where they ran into the newly arrived *1st SS Panzer Division*. At this point, resistance stiffened considerably. However, these two veteran divisions of the Normandy campaign had in one day of rapid movement joined forces with the left flank of the XV Corps, creating a solid line between the U.S. First and Third Armies.

A potential soft spot in the American lines had been eliminated. The Allies now held a solid front encircling the enemy. It was shaped like a giant horseshoe lying on its side, with the British Twenty-first Army Group on the northern and a portion of the western stretch of the line. Then came the American First Army on the western and southern portions to the point where the VII and XV Corps joined and the Third Army took over. The only opening in this otherwise solid line was the eighteen-mile stretch between Argentan and the Canadian forces north of Falaise. This stretch, known as the Falaise Gap, represented the only avenue of escape for the 100,000 to 150,000 German soldiers still within the pocket. The struggle was now under way: one side trying to keep the gap open, the other to snap it shut.

"The question why XV Corps halted on the east-west line through Argentan is certain to become of historical importance. I want a stenographic record of this conversation with General Allen included in the History of the Third Army."[3] These were George Patton's remarks to his chief of staff, Hugh Gaffey, at 2:15 on this Sunday afternoon. His conversation with Lev Allen, Bradley's chief of staff, had finally settled the issue beyond a doubt. The XV Corps would not advance beyond the previously established Argentan boundary, and any elements that might have gone beyond the line were to be recalled.

It had all started the night before around midnight. Haislip had called to inform Patton that his forces were almost in Argentan and to remind him that the XV Corps had been assigned no objective beyond that point. This prompted Patton to call Bradley in an effort to receive authorization for the XV Corps to continue its advance.

Bradley's answer was emphatic. "Nothing doing. You're not to go beyond Argentan. Just stop where you are and build up on that shoulder. Sibert [Bradley's G-2] tells me that the German is beginning to pull out. You'd better button up and get ready for him."[4]

In spite of this rather peremptory order, Patton was unwilling to let it go at that. He advised Haislip, "Upon capture of Argentan push on slowly direction of Falaise. . . . Upon arrive Falaise continue to push on slowly until you contact our allies."[5]

Any thoughts Patton may have had that Bradley would forget or reconsider his statement of the previous night were dashed this morning. A call from Lev Allen to Gaffey reiterated the orders, making it perfectly clear that Patton was to adhere to the established boundary restrictions. When informed by Gaffey, Patton was disturbed. He was convinced that it was Montgomery—not Bradley—who was behind this decision to put a stop to the XV Corps advance.

Patton called Bradley's headquarters to plead with him to convince Montgomery to remove these restrictions on his forces, but Bradley was reported to be visiting Eisenhower. A call to Ike's headquarters was equally unsuccessful in locating Bradley. In fact, both Bradley and Eisenhower were visiting Montgomery's headquarters, listening to Monty "unveil a grandiose strategic plan to carry the war beyond Normandy and the Seine."[6] They were not to be disturbed.

Since Patton was unable to reach Bradley, he had no choice but to press his arguments on Allen. But the chief of staff knew full well what his general wanted. He would not be cajoled, intimidated, or otherwise convinced. The order would stand; the boundary line would be observed.

Patton finally gave in. There was nothing more he could do but send word to Haislip to obey the boundary restrictions. Patton commented, "I believe that the order . . . emanated from the 21st Army Group, and was either due to [British] jealousy of the Americans or to utter ignorance of the situation or to a combination of the two. It is very regrettable that the XV Corps was ordered to halt, because it could have gone on to Falaise and made contact with the Canadians northwest of that point and definitely and positively closed the escape gap."[7]

Patton's assumption about the source of the unwelcome restrictions does not appear to have any basis in fact. Bradley was to emphasize on numerous occasions that the decision to adhere to the established boundary line was his and his alone and furthermore that he had never consulted Montgomery on the matter. In the face of substantial criticism of the decision from numerous sources and in spite of his growing antagonism toward Montgomery, Bradley never made any suggestion that might tend to shift responsibility for the decision in Montgomery's direction.

His reasons for the decision were concisely stated:

Although Patton might have spun a line across the narrow neck, I doubted his ability to hold it. Nineteen German divisions were now stampeding to escape the trap. Meanwhile, with four divisions, George was already blocking three principal escape routes through Alençon, Sées, and Argentan. Had he stretched the line to include Falaise, he would have extended his roadblock a distance of 40 miles. The enemy could not only have broken through, but he might have trampled Patton's position in the onrush. I much preferred a solid shoulder at Argentan to the possibility of a broken neck at Falaise. At the same time I was reluctant to chance a head-on meeting between two converging armies as we might have done had Patton continued on to Falaise.

* * *

Perhaps the most interesting aspect of Bradley's polemic lies in his reference to intelligence information that the Germans were in full retreat and that many were already outside of the pocket. The information was, of course, incorrect. No German forces were as yet retreating. The only eastward movement of German troops within the Falaise Gap was that of Eberbach's Panzer divisions, whose mission was to shore up the southern sector of the defenses.

ULTRA had given no information that would indicate a German withdrawal. As a matter of fact, output from Bletchley Park had been rather meager since that remarkable day (August 10) when record-breaking levels of information had been disseminated. It was not until the next day (August 14) that ULTRA intercepts gave any indication of a possible withdrawal. That came with a dispatch from Eberbach stating that another Mortain attack was not possible and urging immediate withdrawal instead. This was a clear indication that withdrawal not only had not begun but could hardly be expected to get under way for at least a day or two. Two days later, ULTRA intercepted von Kluge's order to begin withdrawal.

Furthermore, in spite of the concentrated area of the battle and the complete Allied air supremacy, Allied intelligence (and Twelfth Army G-2, in particular) apparently had been unable from their own sources to accurately assess enemy positions and movements within the pocket. They may have been influenced by an assumption that actions appearing logical to them must have been those actually taken by the enemy—a cardinal sin of intelligence analysis. For whatever the cause, this intelligence lapse was indeed costly, being, as it was, a major factor in Bradley's decision, which he himself was to later admit was a poor one—one that left him "torn with doubts about my own judgement."[8]

If faulty intelligence and a broader view of the battle had caused Bradley to become conservative, for Patton it was time to put his disappointment behind him and ask the question, "What next?" Having his battlewise XV Corps sitting on the Argentan boundary line was hardly his idea of effective use of his Third Army forces. On top of that, his XX and XII Corps (each with one infantry and one armored division) were now situated in the vicinity of Le Mans-Argentan and ready for movement in whatever direction the Third Army commander should decide. The answer to the question "What next?" was not long in coming.

Lieutenant General Lucian Truscott could hardly be described as a man who was easy to please. One of his first jobs on arrival in England in 1942 had been the establishment and training of the original American Ranger unit, an assignment that earned him a reputation of being "hard as hell."[9] Later, during the North African campaign, he had drilled his troops by gradually increasing their marching cadence, so his troop movements became known among his grumbling soldiers as the "Truscott Trots." He had established a well-deserved reputation as a stern taskmaster who considered thorough training and preparation as the hallmarks of effective leadership.

Truscott had commanded the 3rd Infantry Division during the Tunisian campaign and took it on into Sicily, where it was one of the main contributors to the success of Patton's campaign. From there the division went on to fight at Salerno and Anzio. Truscott was given corps command in February 1944 during the Anzio battle, and it was under his leadership that this disaster-laden campaign finally achieved the long-delayed breakout onto the road to Rome. His VI Corps was then selected to be taken out of the Italian campaign to provide the primary invasion force for ANVIL, the much-debated landing on the Mediterranean coast of France.

Truscott was sitting in his cabin aboard the headquarters ship *Catoctin* as it sailed out of the Bay of Naples on its way to join the invasion fleet. All in all, he felt rather pleased about the current state of affairs. This did not include the current weather, which was hot—insufferably hot. It had been particularly uncomfortable the night before as the ship lay in the harbor, and he had spent a mostly sleepless night. However, in the two months since the VI Corps had been assigned to ANVIL (now called DRAGOON because a breach in security had compromised the original name), preparations had gone well in spite of a number of troublesome problems.

He was particularly pleased to have kept in his corps the same three divisions that had fought with him at Anzio—the

36th Division under Maj. Gen. John Dahlquist, the 45th under Maj. Gen. William Eagles, and his own 3rd Division now under Maj. Gen. John O'Daniel. All three were invasion-tested divisions. On top of that, ample time had been found during the past two months to provide all three divisions with additional invasion training at several locations on the Italian coast. Truscott felt confident that there were no other divisions in the army better prepared for the task ahead.

The VI Corps was a part of the Seventh Army, which had overall responsibility for the invasion forces. The Seventh Army commander was Lt. Gen. Alexander Patch, a veteran of the Guadalcanal campaign in the Pacific.[10] Also reporting to Patch were the Free French forces under Gen. Jean de Lattre de Tassigny. The French were to land on D + 1 over the same beaches secured by the Americans the day before. This fact was a source of some injury to French pride and honor, which was to create problems for Truscott as he proceeded with his planning for the assault.

Early in July, Truscott had been visited by French Brigadier General Sudre, who led a Combat Command of the 1st French Armored Division. Agreement had been reached with the French to loan CC Sudre to the VI Corps since no U.S. armored unit was available for the invasion. In an effort to develop more effective cooperation with the American forces, Sudre and his immediate superior suggested that Truscott pay a visit to Sudre's headquarters near Oran in North Africa for several days of discussion and review. On hearing of this meeting, General de Lattre was furious that it should have taken place without his consent and approval. He invited Truscott to lunch, after which he launched into a furious tirade about violating protocol and slighting his honor and that of his country. In spite of prior agreement that CC Sudre would cooperate with the Americans, de Lattre now demanded to have prior notification and approval of all orders transmitted to Sudre, a condition that Truscott considered unacceptable.

Truscott immediately involved Patch in the controversy. Patch was angry with de Lattre and assured Truscott that he would be able to use CC Sudre without limitations. But Truscott was well aware that relations between French and U.S. forces were influenced more by political consideration than by military necessity. He was concerned that his control over the French armored troops would be very short-lived after they had landed on their native soil. Some more permanent arrangement had to be worked out.

Truscott was now satisfied that the solution he had reached was the best that could have been worked out under the circumstances. He had managed to gather together a corps cavalry squadron, a reconnaissance squadron, an armored field artillery battalion, one tank battalion, and one tank destroyer company, plus a number of support troops. This collection of units would be organized as an independent provisional armored group and commanded by his assistant corps commander, Maj. Gen. Fred Butler. It would be designated Task Force Butler and should provide the mobility and striking force required if he did lose control of the French troops. Truscott would have ample reason to be pleased with his decision within days after the landings took place.

Another big plus for the invasion prospects was the planned airborne assault. This also was a patched-together operation consisting of American and British paratroop and glider regiments and battalions under the leadership of Maj. Gen. Robert Frederick. The unit was organized late in the planning process under intensive time pressure and given concentrated training during July from airfields near Rome. The plan was to land the force directly behind the invasion beaches to cut roads, disrupt communications, and create diversions from the main landings. Truscott considered the plan to be sound and expected substantial help from the airborne operation.

True, it had been a difficult and often frustrating two months of planning and organizing, but the overall outcome had to be judged satisfactory—even to someone who was considered "hard as hell." So the general decided to flee his hot cabin and take a tour of the ship. The *Catoctin*[11] was the headquarters ship for Vice Admiral Hewitt, naval commander of the invasion forces. An unusual warship, it had hardly any guns or armor. It was a floating command center of communication equipment, radar, aircraft identification devices, weather-forecasting services—designed specifically for the task it was about to undertake. Being the invasion headquarters, it housed the commanding officers of all the various services involved in the invasion as well as any VIPs who may have come along. James Forrestal, U.S. Secretary of

the Navy, was the most distinguished visitor aboard on this
trip, which provided an opportunity for him to see in person
some of the results of his several years of effort in building
the United States Navy into the most powerful fleet ever
known.

The *Catoctin* was in control of a huge armada of 900 ships.
The invasion was quite different from Normandy in that the
invasion fleet had a great distance to cover to reach the
beaches. The ships were coming from all across the Mediterranean. With different departure points and ships of varying
speed, the departure times ranged from D − 6 to D − 2. In
addition to Naples, other Italian ports such as Taranto and
Salerno served as embarkation points. Some ships left from
Oran on the north coast of Africa. The islands of Malta,
Sardinia, Corsica, and Sicily were also used.[12] All ships had
to reach the assembly point off the west coast of Corsica in
time to fit into their proper place in the procession toward
the beaches. From that point, there were thirteen mine-swept
lanes down which the ships would proceed. Along these assigned lanes would pass all types of ships—from troop-laden
LSTs to the huge fire-support battleships—each in their
proper sequence depending on their mission.

Their goal—five beaches on a forty-five-mile stretch of
coast between Cavalaire and La Calanque d'Antheor, at one
time a playground of the wealthy but soon to become just
one more invasion beach for the three veteran divisions that
made up Lucian Truscott's VI Corps.

The German *Nineteenth Army* was responsible for the defense of the entire Mediterranean coast of France—from the
Spanish to the Italian border. When Lt. Gen. Friedrich Wiese
had assumed command in June, he felt relatively comfortable.
He had thirteen divisions to guard a front that was quiet and
showed little if any sign of becoming active.[13]

In two short months, the situation had changed considerably. Sitting in his headquarters in the historic Rhone River
city of Avignon, General Wiese no longer felt at ease. The
German losses in Normandy, even though several hundred
miles away, had taken their toll on the *Nineteenth Army*. Five
divisions had been shipped out to stem the losses in the north,
leaving Wiese with only eight. Four of these were spread

between the Rhone and the Spanish border. Two were in the Toulon-Marseilles area and one was along the coast of Provence. The eighth division was the *11th Panzer*, which while nominally a part of the *Nineteenth Army* was actually under the control of Hitler and the OKW. Not only was the division outside of Wiese's control, it was also currently in the Carcassone-Albi area—150 miles from Avignon and much farther from the Marseilles-Toulon-Provence area.

Wiese's problems were compounded by the fact that the caliber of his forces was well below average. Some of his divisions were at strength only by the addition of units that had suffered heavily in the Normandy fighting and had been sent south to a more quiet sector. In addition, mixed in with all the infantry divisions were many troops from eastern Europe—Poles, Armenians, Ukrainians, and others. Many of them were released prisoners of war, and hardly any of them spoke German. Low morale was a serious problem.

Only the *11th Panzer* was up to the standard of first-class German fighting units. Under its veteran commander, Wend von Wietersheim, it had earned the nickname "The Ghost Division" by its rapid mobility and outstanding use of firepower on the Russian front. It had been sent to the quiet area of southern France to refit. Both Wiese and his superiors at *Army Group G* had been trying for several weeks without success to convince OKW to release the division to their use. It was frustrating, to say the least, to have the only first-rate fighting unit so near—and yet so far.

Contributing further to Wiese's discomfort was his conviction that the quiet he had enjoyed on his front for the past two months was about to end. It was true that a report this morning from the *242nd Infantry Division* along the coast of Provence had indicated all was quiet, and many of the troops were escaping the heat by a trip to the region's famous beaches. However, reports had been filtering in for a number of weeks now from the Italian front about sizable Allied troop withdrawals. These troops could, of course, be sent in a number of different directions, but certainly the south coast of France was as good a bet as any. *Army Group G* had passed on intelligence from double agents in the French resistance that indicated August 15 as the likely invasion date. Then there was that report yesterday from two patrol planes of the Luftwaffe. They had sighted two large convoys with seventy-five to a hundred troop transports in the vicinity of Corsica.

It seemed clear to Wiese that something was about to happen—something big—and that it was likely to occur within the next couple of days. The big question was where. With more than 300 miles of shoreline to defend with troops of questionable quality, an adequate defense would be difficult to achieve even if he knew exactly where the landing was to occur.

Wiese's train of thought was interrupted by the entrance of his chief of staff, Maj. Gen. Walter Botsch. Botsch had just received a phone call from his counterpart at *Army Group G* with the good news that Hitler had finally approved the release of the *11th Panzer Division* to the *Nineteenth Army*. At last, the one truly reliable weapon that Wiese had in his arsenal was his to use. Nevertheless, it was hard to escape the conclusion that, good news though it may be, it was coming too late.

Monday, AUGUST 14

It had been six days since Lieutenant General Simonds sent his Canadian forces down from the road to Falaise in an effort to break through to this strategic northern hinge of the pocket that was to bear its name. That his TOTALIZE offensive had been something less than successful did not dampen his enthusiasm for trying new and unique tactics that might somehow succeed in breaking through the German defenses where other methods had failed. Although General Montgomery had done nothing to supplement the Canadian forces with additional troops, perhaps from the British Second Army, he had been putting heavy pressure on Simonds to renew the offensive. The Americans were, after all, only twenty miles away at Argentan, having covered more than fifty miles in the past six days.

New tactics took time to develop and organize, however, and it was not until today that Simonds felt ready to launch the attack. The code name this time was TRACTABLE. Not everything about TRACTABLE was new and different. As before, tanks would lead the attack. Heavy air strikes were also part of the plan.

Whereas the earlier TOTALIZE operation was launched at night, this attack was launched at noon. To replace the cover of darkness, Simonds used heavy smoke to protect his attacking tanks. Since it was a clear day, the sun was visible as a red disk through the haze and could be used as a directional guide by the attackers. The preponderance of the air attack was directed on the road to Falaise, and part of Simonds's force attacked directly down the road. This was to provide cover for the main attack, which was to swing to the east, cross the Laison River, and thereby flank the main German defenses in front of Falaise. The element of surprise that Simonds counted on had been lost last night, however, when a Canadian scout car containing conference notes describing the attack ran into the German lines by mistake.[1] General Meyer was thus given an opportunity to rearrange his *12th SS Panzer Division* defenses to meet the flanking attack.

As in the previous GOODWOOD and COBRA operations, "short bombings" again led to serious casualties—more than 300 killed and wounded. The casualties were made even more tragic by the fact that most of the pilots this time were Canadian.[2]

In spite of the disruption caused by the bombing shortfall, the loss of surprise, and considerable confusion caused by the smoke, the Canadians did make some progress. By dusk, they had succeeded in crossing the Laison River and were in places as close as three miles to Falaise. But the Germans still held the last ridge before the town and continued to direct heavy antitank fire on the Canadian columns. General Simonds was finding conquest of the town of Falaise very difficult indeed.

It was moving day for Omar Bradley. In order to keep up with the forward movements of his Twelfth Army Group forces, his headquarters was advancing some thirty-five miles from St Saveur Lendelin to the vicinity of Saint-James, a small town just southeast of Avranches. In spite of the confusion of moving, as well as a visit to Courtney Hodges, Bradley had spent most of the morning thinking about his options for deployment of the Third Army, now that he had stopped any further movement toward Falaise.

Three options came to his mind. One was to keep the XV Corps where it was and build its strength with additional Third Army forces. That was certainly the safe option, and perhaps most consistent with the reasoning behind his refusal to permit

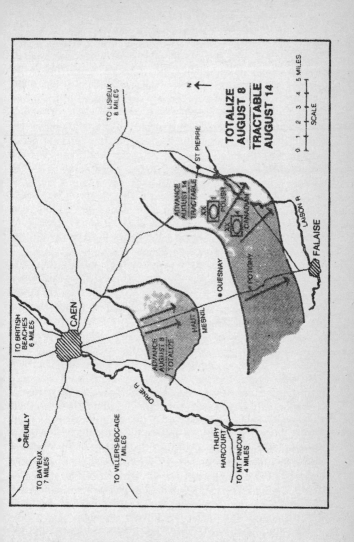

the XV Corps advance to continue. But it was a "do nothing" option and "offered no dividends whatsoever."[3]

The second was a somewhat more action-oriented choice. It involved a movement to the northeast toward the town of Chambois, about ten miles from Argentan. While this would not tend to close the gap, it would extend the neck of the gap and perhaps make the enemy escape more difficult and costly. It was worth consideration.

But there was another choice that, in Bradley's mind, offered potentially greater dividends, although with admittedly higher risk. This option would bring the First Army into the Argentan area, thereby freeing up the Third Army to launch a much more far-reaching encirclement to the north and east. This time the Seine River would be the target. The general was mulling these three options over in his mind when Patton flew in to the new Saint-James headquarters.

General Patton had been considering the "What next?" question as well, but unlike Bradley, his mind was made up. He proposed that the XX Corps, instead of supporting the XV Corps at Argentan, be sent on a wider swing to the Seine by way of Dreux, sixty miles to the northeast. The XII Corps would head for Chartres with the ultimate goal of reaching the Seine upriver from Paris.

Patton's support of what was basically option number three was enough to convince Bradley that this was the proper course to follow. Although the two generals would later dispute who originated the idea and who convinced whom to put it into effect, it was more than likely a case of strategies independently conceived, with each one supporting the other.

Bradley, however, went further. He offered an amendment to the Patton plan which the latter eagerly accepted. He would take two of the XV Corps divisions (the 5th Armored and the 79th Infantry) out of the Argentan line and send them to Dreux along with Haislip and the XV Corps headquarters team. The two remaining divisions (the 2nd French Armored and the 90th Infantry) would remain at Argentan and ultimately fall under First Army control. This would enable the XX Corps to strike out for Chartres, and the XII Corps to take an even wider arc by heading toward Orleans. In effect, the entire Third Army (excepting the VIII Corps in Brittany) was to strike out for the Seine with targets that ranged over a 100-mile stretch of the river both above and below the city of Paris. Paris was to be encircled and by-passed in an effort to trap more of the German forces now fighting in France.

Patton was delighted. His disappointment of Argentan was forgotten—the Third Army was off and moving again. His diary for the day records, "It is really a great plan, wholly my own, and I made Bradley think he thought of it. Oh, what a tangled web we weave, when first we practice to deceive.

"I am very happy and elated.

"I got all the corps moving by 2030 so that if Monty tries to be careful, it will be too late."[4]

He did indeed get his corps moving. Orders went out that day to Haislip as well as Walton Walker and Gilbert Cook, commanders of the XX and XII Corps, respectively. For Haislip, a quick start toward Dreux was possible by with-drawing his 5th Armored and 79th Infantry from the Argentan line. Their positions in line were taken over by the 2nd French Armored and the 80th and 90th Infantry, all of whom were in the area.

Major General Walker's XX Corps was somewhat more scattered. The 7th Armored was also in the Argentan area and could be rapidly deployed. The division was new, having landed at Omaha Beach less than a week before. His 5th Infantry Division was a veteran unit, having fought in the Saint-Lô and COBRA campaigns as part of General Hodges's First Army. Having been squeezed out of the line near Vire more than a week ago, the division was sent to join the Third Army and was currently in the Loire Valley near Angers but moving to the northeast.

Major General Cook just the day before had set up his XII Corps headquarters in Le Mans. While the corps organization was new, he had two veteran divisions assigned to him. The 35th Infantry, also veterans of Saint-Lô and COBRA, more recently had been involved in the battle at Mortain. They had been relieved of their duties in the Mortain area and were on the road to Le Mans. Finally, Cook had the 4th Armored Division—veterans of the Avranches breakthrough and the campaign in Brittany. Their commander, John Wood, was finally getting his wish to escape the backwater campaign in Brittany and move into the main arena—the drive across central France. The division was moving rapidly out of Brittany toward Le Mans and Orleans.

Upon returning to his CP that evening, Patton sent a letter to his wife, Beatrice: "This is better and much bigger than Sicily and, so far, all has gone better than I had a right to expect. L'audace, l'audace, toujours l'audace. . . . This is probably the fastest and biggest pursuit in history."[5]

Tuesday, AUGUST 15

It was 2:30 in the afternoon. From the deck of the *Catoctin*, Lieutenant General Truscott surveyed the panorama of an invasion that had gone like clockwork. To begin with, the predawn airborne operation had been successful. Although some elements of the drop had been badly scattered, a sufficient force had landed within the prescribed drop area to successfully carry out its assigned mission.

His own three divisions were all ashore now, having landed right on schedule. The casualties were minimal, and all three divisions were moving off the beaches toward their D-day objectives. Troops of the 3rd Division on the left had gone ashore virtually without opposition except from land mines and were about to enter Saint-Tropez along with the FFI and some of the airborne troops.

The 45th Division in the center had an equally easy time at the beach and was moving inland rapidly to make contact with the main elements of the airborne forces. Part of the 36th Division had landed to the west of San Raphael at the western end of the invasion beaches. Major General Dahlquist was on hand to lead the division, having been the first general officer to reach the beach before 10 o'clock this morning.

So far so good, but there was one very important landing yet to take place. The 142nd Regiment of Dahlquist's 36th Division was to land in the Gulf of Fréjus, between five and ten miles as the crow flies west of the landing area of the rest of the division. The regiment was to be followed immediately by CC Sudre, the French armored force that had been the cause of so much contention during the invasion planning period.

The importance of this part of the invasion plan had to do with geography. Immediately behind the invasion beaches lay two mountain ranges that dominate the area from Toulon to Cannes—the Massif des Muares to the west and the Estorel to the east. The two ranges are separated by the valley of the Argens River, which flows into the Mediterranean at the Gulf of Fréjus. The valley is served by major road networks to the west and north and was considered to be the ideal route for rapid movement inland.

Lucian Truscott was thinking well beyond merely getting off the beaches. He was looking for ways to speed his forces to the north while the French troops went west to liberate Toulon and Marseilles. Recognizing the Rhone valley as the obvious path of retreat for the German forces, he hoped to move his VI Corps north up the famous Route Napoleon to the east of the Rhone. Then by swinging to the west, perhaps he could trap the retreating Germans in one of the narrow defiles of the Rhone River valley. Speed was essential, and only the Argens valley promised a rapid beginning for the movements he had in mind.

It was well known, however, that the Gulf of Fréjus would be the most difficult of all the beaches to be assaulted. For that reason, the attack had been planned for 2 P.M. in order to allow a more thorough preparation. Mines were expected to be a serious problem, and mine-sweepers had been active in the gulf for several hours. The heaviest air and naval bombardment of the entire operation had been directed on the narrow stretch of beach. In spite of the intense level of attack, the German fire had been vigorous in response, and the men of the 142nd Regiment in their landing craft off the beach knew they were in for a far different reception than their fellow soldiers had received this morning.

The key decision to send the troops into the beach lay in the hands of Rear Adm. Spenser Lewis, naval commander of this eastern section of the invasion. A veteran of the Battle of Midway, Lewis was well aware of the value of aggressiveness and risk-taking as components of victory in battle, but this afternoon he was assailed by doubt. He wanted to talk to Dahlquist, but he was somewhere ashore and out of reach. The other landings had gone so well that he found it very difficult to launch the final assault into such an obviously strong position. In spite of a recommendation to proceed from his subordinate directly in charge of the assault, Lewis made the decision to cancel the landing in the gulf and send the 142nd Regiment in over the beaches where their division comrades had landed this morning. This landing was completed rapidly without incident.

General Truscott was furious. The change necessitated a new landing location for the armored troops of CC Sudre. He decided to send them in over the 45th Division beaches to the west during the night. The change also resulted in delay in securing the important airfields near Fréjus, which would make possible the necessary air support for rapid movement of his troops to the north. Even though all his troops were now ashore with fewer casualties than he had any right to expect, none of them was in the Argens valley, and he figured it would take at least a day to get them there. Considering the overall success of the landing, perhaps a delay of one day should not have been considered a significant problem, but Truscott was not thinking about today or tomorrow. Rather, his thoughts were on the day sometime in the next week or two when the German forces would be racing up the Rhone valley trying to escape the trap that he expected to lay for them. A day then could very possibly mean the difference between success and failure.

But enough of that. He had troops ashore and a battle to direct. It was time to go ashore, and he set off with his French liaison officer—Col. Jean Petit—for the beaches at Saint-Maxime, where his 45th Division had landed this morning. As he stepped ashore, he picked up a handful of sand and turning to Petit asked: "Well, Jean, how does the soil of France feel to an exile?" Petit was unable to answer. His eyes were filled with tears.[1]

Through the morning mist, Lieutenant General von Wietersheim could see the churches and towers of Avignon on the far side of the Rhone River. His *11th Panzer Division*

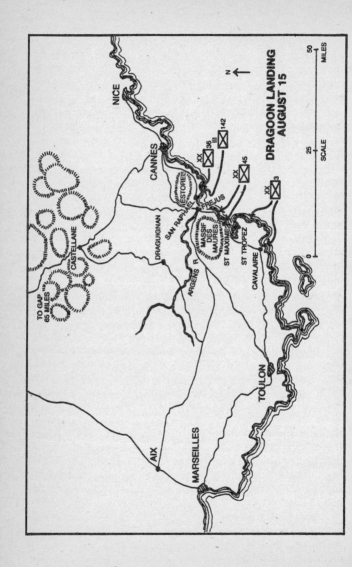

DRAGOON LANDING
AUGUST 15

SCALE

0   25   50
MILES

had been constantly on the move through the past two nights and a day just to cover the 150 miles from Carcassone to within sight of Avignon. Word of the invasion had reached him this morning. He felt increasing pressure to speed up the movement of his forces—especially his tanks, which were urgently needed if the American and French forces were to be contained.[2]

So far, the French resistance and the oppressive heat had been the main factors slowing the division's progress. But now another obstacle confronted von Wietersheim—the Rhone River. He understood that Allied air attacks had destroyed most of the bridges from north of Avignon all the way to the coast. He had heard, however, that one bridge, at Pont-Saint-Esprit, twenty-five miles to the north, was still intact. He ordered his tanks to turn north at maximum speed to force a crossing of the bridge.

The lead tanks were only a few miles up the road when an advance scout came back with the news that the bridge had been destroyed by Allied planes that very morning. If only Hitler's release had come twelve hours sooner! Then *11th Panzer* tanks would now be closing in on the Allied beachhead with a reasonable chance to have a major effect on the outcome.

As it was, von Wietersheim must now face the difficult task of getting his armor across the river by barge or whatever other means could be found. He knew it would have to be done under constant Allied air attack. It was not going to be easy, nor was it going to be quick.

As he rode into Eberbach's CP near Argentan, Field Marshal von Kluge had ample reason to feel angry and frustrated. It was approaching midnight, which meant that he was more than twelve hours late for his meeting with Hausser and Eberbach. The past twenty-four to thirty-six hours had been a succession of misfortunes, unpleasant decisions, and bad news.

It had all started the day before. In spite of the rapidly deteriorating situation in the Falaise Pocket, he had felt compelled to travel to his OB West headquarters in the Saint-Germain section of Paris. The reason for the visit was to discuss an order from Hitler concerning the defense of the city as well as the destruction of the city's bridges, public buildings, and important industrial plants and utilities. Present at the meeting were his chief of staff, General Blumentritt, and Lt. Gen. Dietrich von Choltitz, who had been commander of the *LXXXIV Corps* in Normandy when von Kluge had first come to the OB West. He had just recently been picked by Hitler as military commander of greater Paris. All present seemed to agree that Paris must be destroyed. The major issue at the meeting was one of timing. Blumentritt proposed immediate commencement of demolition activities, whereas von Choltitz proposed delay, fearing that the demolition work would hamper his ability to adequately defend the city. It was a question von Kluge had to decide and decide quickly.[3]

He left Paris in the late afternoon and, instead of returning to his headquarters at La Roche Guyon, he headed directly for Fontaine l'Abbe near the town of Bernay, just forty miles east of the Falaise-Argentan area. This was the headquarters of Sepp Dietrich, newly appointed commander of the *Fifth Panzer Army*, charged with the defense of Falaise and the northern flank of the pocket. While von Kluge enjoyed the relative comfort of spending the night in a castle built by Louis XIII, the news he had received on arrival was anything but comforting. Dietrich described the renewed Canadian attack on Falaise and pointed out that it was impossible for the *12th SS Panzer Division* to hold on by itself. It had been necessary to divert the *21st Panzer Division* to the northern defenses. The *21st* had been scheduled to participate in the attack to shore up the southern defenses as part of *Panzer Group Eberbach*. Even with this additional strength, however, Dietrich was not at all confident about his ability to hold Falaise or prevent a breakthrough elsewhere along the northern flank.

With this gloomy assessment still ringing in his ears, von Kluge took off early this morning for his scheduled meeting with Hausser and Eberbach at Nécy, four miles south of Falaise. The tangled road traffic slowed him down, and Allied planes made travel hazardous at best. After he had been on the road several hours, an Allied strafing attack on his party destroyed his radio equipment. Completely cut off from the outside world and forced into cover almost constantly by air attacks, von Kluge was making little progress toward Nécy.

Then when evening finally cleared the sky of planes, the party lost its way in the darkness and confusion of the night. Little did von Kluge realize the consternation and suspicions that his lack of contact with the outside world had caused during the day.

Both Eberbach and Hausser had reached Nécy close to the appointed time. After a wait of three hours, they decided that they must return to their CPs, which were quite near one another. As soon as Eberbach returned, the messages began coming in from Hitler's headquarters: "Ascertain whereabouts von Kluge. Report results hourly."[4]

It had not been a good day at the Wolf's Lair. The first thing that greeted the Führer this morning was news of the Allied Mediterranean invasion. Then when he had tried to reach his commanding general in the West, he was told no one could locate him. To Hitler, the conclusion was obvious. Convinced that von Kluge had been an active participant in the July 20 plot, he now decided that he was meeting in secret with the Allied High Command to arrange some sort of negotiated cessation of hostilities. Even if he should reappear, it was obvious he could no longer be trusted. It would be necessary to act immediately in order to maintain control of the rapidly deteriorating situation. He telephoned the two field marshals whom he considered to be his most reliable—Kesselring in Italy and Model on the Russian front—to obtain their advice on a permanent replacement for von Kluge. In the meantime, he sent orders for Hausser to take command temporarily.

While all this furious activity was taking place in the Wolf's Lair, von Kluge finally made his way to Eberbach's CP. The news he received from Eberbach and Hausser did nothing to brighten this dismal day. To the west, Hausser's *Seventh Army* was withdrawing slightly to avoid complete collapse of their defensive line. One of its Panzer divisions was unable to disengage not only because of First Army pressure but, more ominously, because it had no fuel. Eberbach's Panzer divisions defending the southern flank were being attacked relentlessly by troops from both the American First and Third Armies. Allied air and artillery attacks were increasing in intensity, and supply to the German forces was virtually nonexistent. Eberbach and Hausser agreed that their only recommendation could be to withdraw from the pocket as fast as possible. They urged von Kluge to issue the orders immediately.

Von Kluge was in complete agreement with their recommendation, but he was still unwilling to take such a major step without authorization from the Führer. Since communication facilities at Eberbach's CP were poor, von Kluge again took to the road and returned to Fontaine l'Abbe, where the facilities were much better. At 2 A.M. the message finally was sent to Jodl. After outlining the critical situation faced by his forces, von Kluge recommended immediate withdrawal of all troops through the narrow gap between Falaise and Argentan. He again made it abundantly clear that his recommendation had the unqualified support of Hausser, Eberbach, and Dietrich. Any hesitation in approval of this recommendation would result in "unforeseeable developments."[5]

Wednesday, AUGUST 16

For von Kluge at Fontaine l'Abbe, the morning seemed to drag on endlessly. Not a word had come from the Wolf's Lair. He had tried to make it absolutely clear in his message to Jodl the previous night that speed was essential. The situation was obviously getting worse by the hour, and the fate of all the German troops within the Falaise Pocket hung in the balance. This was not his first experience with the Führer's lack of sensitivity to the realities of the situation on the front lines, so perhaps he should be used to it by now.

But he could wait no longer. He had already talked to Lieutenant General Speidel at La Roche Guyon and General Blumentritt at Saint-Germain and discovered that nothing had been received from Hitler's headquarters at either place. Blumentritt also advised von Kluge of the landings in southern France and urged him to press for a free hand to proceed with the withdrawal. At 12:45 P.M., von Kluge called Jodl and forcefully reiterated his assessment of the current situation. Withdrawal was the only possible alternative, and even that choice would be foreclosed if action were not taken immediately. Jodl was sympathetic. He agreed that withdrawal was the proper course to take. He promised von Kluge that such an order from Hitler would be forthcoming in the shortest possible time.

An hour later, a call came to von Kluge from Speidel,

whose sources at the Wolf's Lair had advised him that a
withdrawal order from Hitler would arrive shortly, reportedly
giving von Kluge freedom of action. Von Kluge told Speidel
to start preparation of the withdrawal order immediately.

That was no easy task. The Falaise Pocket was currently
thirty-five miles long from west to east and between eleven
and fifteen miles wide from north to south. The western
extremity, held by the *Seventh Army*, was in the vicinity of
Flers. It was being squeezed hard by the British Second Army
from the north and the American First Army from the west
and south. The eastern extremity could now be best defined
by the Dives River, which ran southeast to northwest approximately five miles east of the Argentan-Falaise highway.
While the Dives was a small river, its steep banks made it
an important natural boundary.

About fifteen miles east of Flers (twenty miles west of the
Dives) was the Orne River, also running southeast to northwest. The Orne was a major river that entered the Atlantic
Ocean near Caen. Any withdrawal plan would have to be
built around the phased crossing of the two rivers. Von
Kluge's order as prepared by Speidel called for the *Seventh
Army* to withdraw across the Orne on two successive nights,
August 16 and 17. Part of the *Seventh Army* was to be dispatched to help defend the northern hinge of the pocket while
the remainder headed for the Dives. Meanwhile, Eberbach
was to use his Panzer divisions to hold the southern flank.

The problems faced by the withdrawing army were formidable. The crossing of two rivers was a problem in and of
itself. The difficulty was increased immeasurably by the fact
that the narrow width of the pocket brought almost the entire
area within the range of Allied artillery. This, in combination
with constant air attack, would make withdrawal dangerous
and costly. Much of the pocket was in the hilly country of
central Normandy, and the road network was poor—particularly in the east-west direction. Strict regulation of traffic
would be a necessity, and von Kluge assigned the headquarters of the *LVIII Panzer Corps*, which had been stripped
of its troops, to serve as traffic policemen.

The supply and transport problems further compounded the
difficulty. Fuel was a severe problem. Many motorized vehicles, including tanks, would have to be destroyed and left

behind for lack of fuel. Horsepower and manpower were to be used to extricate as much equipment as possible. Since delivery of supplies within the pocket had been almost impossible for days, food and ammunition would be rare commodities for the withdrawing troops.

On the other hand, it was expected that the various units could maintain their organization and that discipline within the units could be sustained. Most of the officers and many of the enlisted men were well aware that without organization and discipline their chances of getting out of the pocket alive were slim. Self-preservation should provide a powerful incentive to overcome the many difficulties faced by the withdrawing army.

By 2:30 P.M., von Kluge decided that he could wait no longer—with or without Hitler's permission. His concern about acting without authority was finally overcome by the disaster he was certain would result if action were further delayed. He told Speidel to proceed with the issuance of the withdrawal order. Two hours later, the long-awaited directive from the Führer finally arrived. It adhered generally to the outlines of the plan already disseminated by von Kluge but emphasized several points in particular, one of which was that Falaise must be held as a "corner pillar"[1] of the gateway out of the pocket. The symbolic nature of this part of the order must have caught von Kluge's attention; it was symbolic of the lack of realistic assessment of the battle situation, which permeated Hitler's headquarters. At about the time that the Führer's order arrived at Dietrich's headquarters at Fontaine l'Abbe, word came in that Falaise had fallen to the Canadians.

Hill 159 dominated the landscape north of Falaise. This position, one mile north of the city, had been carefully selected by Gen. Kurt Meyer for his final defense of this vital city on the northern shoulder of the Falaise Gap. General Simonds and his II Corps of the First Canadian Army had been on the attack constantly for the past week, and the *12th SS Panzer Division* had been cut to shreds. Only by anticipation of his enemy's maneuvers and clever use of the terrain had Meyer been able to keep the Canadians from entering Falaise days ago. He was well aware, however, that two of Simonds's armored divisions were now across the Laison

River to the west in a position to outflank his own troops and drive across the open end of the Falaise Gap.

Meyer's Panzer division had been so decimated during the past few days that he was forced to rely on a band of 500 Hitler Youth to man the defenses atop Hill 159. While the youths had all taken an oath to die for their Führer, Meyer realized that they were little more than children and not likely to be able to withstand a full-scale attack on their position. That such an attack was in the making was obvious. Masses of tanks were visibly forming for attack on all sides of the hill. The artillery barrage was intense. To make matters worse, the weather was clear, and constant dive-bombing by British Typhoons had been underway since sunup.

As the Canadians began to challenge the handful of Panzers still able to put up a fight, Meyer felt a sudden sensation of pain. His head had been wounded by a shell fragment and blood was pouring down over his face. His aides managed to get him back to an aid station, where several stitches were taken. As soon as the wound was bandaged, Meyer headed back toward his defensive positions on the hill. But it was already too late. The positions were being overrun as Simonds poured more and more of his tanks and troops from the Cameron Highlanders and South Saskatchewan regiments over the hill and down the road leading from Hill 159 into Falaise. For Meyer and the remnants of his once-proud *12th SS Panzer Division*, the only choice was retreat. By late afternoon, the Canadians entered the battered city of Falaise. An important step had been accomplished in the Allied drive to close the trap on the German army.

It had been one of the briefest periods of command that any general ever experienced. It was also one of the most confusing. Except for a short term as commander of the 2nd Armored Division in Sicily, Maj. Gen. Hugh Gaffey's wartime experience had been limited to being Patton's chief of staff. Then the night before came the opportunity to exercise line command at the corps commander level. This situation was the result of two separate chains of events.

When Bradley and Patton decided on Tuesday to swing two divisions of the XV Corps plus the corps headquarters north toward the Seine, they left behind three divisions in the Argentan area to maintain the line that had been established by the XV Corps advance. The 2nd French Armored and the 90th Infantry Divisions had been part of the XV Corps during their spectacular dash to Le Mans and then on to Argentan. In addition, the 80th Infantry Division, which had been involved in the mix-up with the 90th several days before, was also in the area. With the departure of the XV Corps headquarters, these three divisions were left without any control at the corps level.

Meanwhile, changes were taking place in the strategy to close the Falaise Gap. Montgomery had called Bradley the day before to advise him of his intention to close the gap along the Dives River line, somewhat to the east of the direct line from Falaise to Argentan. With the heavy pressure applied directly on Falaise by the Canadian attack, two armored divisions (the 4th Canadian and the 1st Polish) had been able to swing to the left, cross the Dives River, and be in a position to drive south on the east side of the Dives in an effort to close the gap. In order to cooperate with this new thrust, it was important for the Americans to take the town of Chambois on the Dives and then drive down the river to meet the Canadians and Poles and close the gap. The obvious force to make this attack would be the three orphan divisions, elements of which were within four miles of Chambois.

Bradley had informed Patton of this new strategy at 8:00 P.M. the previous evening. Patton had immediately ordered Gaffey to assume provisional corps command of the three divisions and organize an attack down the Dives. Gaffey left Third Army headquarters at 10:00 P.M. and headed for the site of the old XV Corps CP near Alençon. He took several Third Army staff members with him. He also arranged to have Generals Leclerc (2nd French Armored) and McLain (90th Infantry) meet him there.[1]

On arrival, Gaffey outlined his plan to the two generals.[2] The 2nd and 90th were to lead an attack, jumping off during the morning, with the 80th Infantry in reserve. He received an unexpected response: Leclerc announced that he refused to make the attack. His stated reason was that Gaffey's plan split up his division in a way with which he could not agree. A more likely reason was the strong desire on Leclerc's part to have his division join those elements of the American forces that were heading toward Paris rather than join an attack headed in the opposite direction. After calling in a stenographer, Gaffey repeated the order and asked Leclerc if he would or would not obey. Leclerc reluctantly agreed and the attack was scheduled for the morning.

While Gaffey was dealing with the reluctant Leclerc, other events were taking place at First Army headquarters, fifty miles to the west, which were to have an effect on Gaffey's command. After Bradley completed his conversation of the previous day with Montgomery, he had thought immediately of the V Corps and its commander, Leonard Gerow. The

V Corps had been pinched out of the First Army line as a result of the advances of the past several days, and its divisions were transferred to other corps. The V Corps was a natural to take responsibility for the three divisions at Argentan, which could then be transferred from the Third to the First Army. This, in turn, would free the Third Army from any responsibility for the Falaise Gap so that Patton could concentrate on his movements to the north and east. Bradley advised Patton of his decision, but the latter assumed it would be a matter of days before such a switch could take place.

Not so. Hodges had Gerow and his planning staff at First Army headquarters by 10:30 that evening, and, in spite of some uncertainty about the location of the troops he was to command, Gerow left for Alençon at 2:00 A.M. in the pouring rain with a party of seven jeeps.[3] By 7:00 A.M. this morning, the group arrived at the Hotel de France in Alençon, where Gerow set up his command post.

When the two generals got together, Gaffey was at a loss as to what he should do. With an attack planned to jump off shortly, he was reluctant to simply relinquish command to Gerow. A call to Patton, who talked to both Gaffey and Gerow, produced agreement that Gaffey would remain in command until he (Patton) could talk to Bradley. He was on his way at that moment to Twelfth Army Group headquarters. Gaffey's attack, originally scheduled for 10:00 A.M., was delayed, more as a result of aggressive action by the enemy near the town of Saint-Léonard than by the confusion of command. Then, at 2:30 P.M. Patton, who was still at Twelfth Army Group, sent word via the Third Army headquarters that Gerow was to take command.

In the several hours that Gerow had this morning to review the situation, he felt uneasy about the attack Gaffey had planned. Furthermore, he expected his V Corps artillery to arrive in the area the following day. He decided to postpone the attack.

Gaffey returned to Third Army headquarters, his brief period of command having been fraught with insubordination, uncertainties of command, and, most important, the failure to launch the attack he had planned. The last disappointment would pose a critical question to the American High Command. No one would ever know how successful Gaffey's attack might have been, but a day of grace to the Germans just as they began their withdrawal from the Falaise Pocket was indeed "a pearl of great price."

Friday, AUGUST 18

Relieved of any responsibilities in the Falaise Gap sector, Patton's Third Army headed off on a race through central France. Their opposition was generally light. With the developments in Normandy and the landings in southern France, the German troops in the Bordeaux area of southwestern France could see the handwriting on the wall. Approximately 100,000 men (most a part of the German *First Army*) were streaming to the northeast to avoid being trapped and to help provide some semblance of defense along the Seine. Harassed by the FFI and hindered by their lack of combat experience, progress was slow, and the rapidly changing situation in Normandy made difficult the establishment of any effective defense south of the Seine. Only at a few selected points were these troops able to supplement the badly outnumbered garrison troops scattered along the southern approaches to the river.

The southern prong of the Third Army advance was in the hands of Maj. Gen. Gilbert Cook's XII Corps. In two days, Cook's forces covered the ninety miles from Le Mans to Orleans, which had been secured the day before. Cook's major concern had been the German forces moving from the Bordeaux region, who were on his right flank across the Loire River. Most of the bridges over the Loire had been destroyed, some by Germans fearful of an attack by the XII Corps and some by Americans concerned about possible German attacks. Once in Orleans (forty miles from the Seine), Cook was halted by Patton, at least in part to save gasoline for his other advancing corps.

General Cook's first combat assignment had been a big success, but, unfortunately, it was to be his last. Crippled by a circulatory ailment, he was forced to enter a hospital. Patton came to see him with the news he feared. According to Patton: "His circulation was so bad that he has no feeling in his hands or legs below the elbows and knees. . . . I told him that in justice to himself and his men, I could not retain him in command. It was a great blow to us both."[1]

The major objective of Maj. Gen. Walton Walker's XX Corps on the left of the XIIth was the well-known cathedral city of Chartres. Elements of his 7th Armored Division covered the sixty miles from their positions near Argentan in one day, arriving on the evening of August 15. However, Chartres was one of the few points where the Germans were able to establish an effective defense. Regiments from two combat divisions, one from the southwest and one from northern France, were committed to Chartres. In addition, concern for the cathedral limited the use of artillery to reduce the defenses. However, with the arrival of the 5th Infantry Division the day before, the combined efforts of armor and infantry had been able to secure the town during the day. Chartres was an important prize. Just fifty miles from Paris, it contained a major German air force installation. In addition, the XX Corps was able to capture more than 2,000 German prisoners.

The left flank of Patton's army, the two divisions of the XV Corps, made equally satisfactory progress. Having reached their objective of Dreux the day before, they were ordered to advance twenty-five miles to the town of Mantes on the Seine, thirty miles downriver from Paris. By afternoon they had reached the Seine and began to place artillery fire on both sides of the river in an effort to hinder the German forces attempting to cross.

This was all good news for the Third Army commander, but Patton had other reasons for rejoicing as well. Just two days before, he had received two very welcome items of information. He had been appointed a major general, Regular

Army with a September 3, 1943, date of rank.* In addition, Eisenhower had decided that concealment of Patton's activities as part of the Allies' deception plan was no longer necessary. All the achievements of the Third Army for the past two weeks could now be revealed to the newspapers. Overnight, his name would become legend.

In spite of all his successes, Patton had learned the advantage of humility when applied in the proper places. Yesterday, he had written a thank-you note to General Marshall, which concluded:

> It is a great pleasure and privilege to work with General Bradley and General Hodges. . . .
> So far as I am concerned, I have made no statements or permitted any quotations, and I shall continue to follow this policy.
> Again thanking you for your many acts of forbearance and confidence.[2]

But lest anyone feel that the old Patton was dead, he dispelled that notion in his daily letter to his wife: "The family [Canadians] got Falaise. . . . I could have had it a week ago but modesty via destiny made me stop. . . . Courtney [Hodges] is really a moron. . . . Omar [Bradley] is OK but not daring. . . ."[3]

Patton's fine sense of his own worth remained a basic foundation of his character.

At age thirty-three, Maj. Gen. George Kitching was one of the youngest division commanders in the Allied armies. He had taken command of the 4th Canadian Armored Division in February. He compiled a fine record as a staff officer in the 1st Canadian Infantry Division in the Sicily campaign and later in charge of an armored brigade in the 5th Infantry

---

*The Regular Army grade of major general is different from Patton's temporary grade of lieutenant general (Army of the United States) which he held in August 1944. In this case, the temporary grade (AUS) is superior to the permanent grade (RA) but the distinction is unimportant for officers on active duty.

Division. His superior, Lieutenant General Simonds, was hopeful that his choice would be a good one in spite of the fact that the 4th Armored was not an experienced unit.

In fact, it was the youngest Canadian division, having been converted from an infantry division during 1942. While the division had spent eighteen months in England, its training had been limited due to shortages of equipment and the lack of experienced leadership at all levels. The division had arrived in France from England in late July, thus making it the last of the Canadian divisions to enter the line. Its performance during General Simonds's first major attack toward Falaise (TOTALIZE) in early August had been no better than one might expect from a green division. Failure on the part of the 4th Armored to follow up vigorously on the initial success of the attack was in large measure responsible for its inconclusive results.

During Simonds's second attack on Falaise (TRACTABLE), Kitching was more pleased with the performance of his division. While TRACTABLE did not result in the immediate capture of Falaise as expected, it did enable the Canadian forces to make a wide swing to the left, cross the Laison River, and put themselves in an advantageous position near the mouth of the Falaise Gap. Kitching's 4th Armored troops had been the vanguard of this wide-sweeping attack.

It was this favorable position, which had been reached by the 4th Armored and their sister division, the 1st Polish Armored, that had led Montgomery to call Bradley two days before to propose a new line of attack to close the Falaise Gap along the Dives River line. The 4th Armored Division was by then ten miles from Trun and fifteen miles from Chambois—the two key points along the Dives between which all German escape efforts were directed. With the Germans concentrating their defensive efforts at Falaise, the way to Trun and Chambois should be wide open for a rapid advance across open country. Montgomery had issued the orders two days before and confirmed them a day later with an official dispatch: "It is absolutely essential that both the Armd Divs of 2 Cdn Corps i.e. 4 Cdn Armd and 1 Pol Armd Div close the gap between First Cdn Army and Third U.S. Army . . . as quickly as possible."[4]

Here was a golden opportunity for Kitching and his division

to demonstrate the mobility and aggressiveness that had been lacking on the road to Falaise—a chance to spring the trap on a desperate German army trying to escape. However, things did not go quite as planned. The previous morning had been largely frittered away. Originally planning a straight dash for Trun on the southwest side of the Dives, the division ran into immediate trouble in crossing a small tributary of the river under harassing artillery fire from the German defenders around Falaise. With Montgomery's words "as quickly as possible" ringing in his ears, Simonds decided to change the mode of attack by having the 4th Armored cross the Dives and attack down the northeast bank instead, thus avoiding both the troublesome crossing as well as the artillery fire. This change of plan involved countermarching the division, which in turn caused difficult traffic-control problems. As a result, it was the midafternoon of the previous day before any elements of the division were able to start their dash toward Trun.

Once across the river, however, good progress was made. The leading element of the division, the Canadian Grenadier Guards, had arrived within a couple of miles of Trun by the previous evening. At this point, they halted to await the arrival of the Lake Superior Regiment. Together, they would make their attack on Trun.

This morning, the attack was slow getting underway as the Lake Superior Regiment was delayed in making their rendezvous with the Grenadiers. Meanwhile, other elements of the division to the north were moving in a southeasterly direction toward Chambois. By the end of the day, the Grenadier Guards and the Lake Superior Regiment had combined their forces and entered Trun. They found the town itself relatively free of German troops, although there appeared to be plenty of enemy activity in the hills around the town. Other forces of the 4th Armored were now scattered along the Dives River bank as far as the small hamlet of Saint-Lambert, three miles upstream from Trun.

In spite of false starts, indecision, confusion, and delays, Kitching's 4th Armored troops were the first Allied forces to reach this vital stretch of territory along the Dives. Their positions were scattered and lacking in strength. A more experienced division might have arrived somewhat sooner.

But if it was experience that Kitching's troops lacked, they would get plenty of it over the next several days.

Major General Gerow was ready to attack. His corps artillery had arrived and his plans had been made. They were somewhat different from those worked out yesterday by Hugh Gaffey. Gerow had brought up the 80th Division from reserve. He planned to have the 2nd French Armored screen the advance from the west while the 80th Division in the center and the 90th Division on the east made their attacks.

The 80th was to attack in a northward direction to the east of Argentan and then swing to the left and enter the town from the northeast. The 90th was to drive straight north for Chambois, three to four miles away.

The 80th Division, still looking for its first real baptism of fire, received it today "in spades." As described by one of the division's regimental commanders, "This was our first real fight and I had difficulty in getting the men to move forward. . . . When my tanks came up we lost the first four tanks with only eight shots from the Germans."[5] The division made little, if any, progress.

The 90th fared somewhat better. They covered about half the distance to Chambois before heavy enemy resistance halted their advance. Smoke from forest fires started by German phosphorous shells also hindered their progress. Although they failed to reach their objective, the men of the 90th fully expected to be in Chambois by the next day.

Meanwhile, from the north, the Canadians and Poles were making progress against lighter opposition. As night fell, the 4th Canadian Armored Division had entered Trun and a few of their tanks had even reached Saint-Lambert, more than two-thirds the distance from Trun to Chambois.

Three miles north of Chambois lies Mont Ormel, known on the Allies' military maps as Hill 262. It was a dominating position overlooking the Dives valley from Chambois to Trun. As darkness fell, up its slopes to the top of the ridge came men and tanks of the 1st Polish Armored Division. They had made a cross-country dash of about fifteen miles from the junction of the Dives and the Laison rivers during the past two days. At times lost and running out of fuel and supplies, they had nevertheless found a key position at the north end of the gap—a position that would put them in the very center of the final action of the Battle of the Falaise Gap.

In theory, the gap was now almost closed. Only a mile or two between Trun and Chambois had not been occupied at one time or another by some Allied forces. With the two sides of the neck of the gap being squeezed, the Polish position on Mont Ormel represented the cork in the bottle. But, practically, it was a different matter. German forces (mostly rear echelon) were moving regularly through the gap between Trun and Chambois, and the Allied forces in a position to block their way were as yet weak and unsupported. This five-mile stretch along the Dives would witness over the next several days some of the most desperate fighting of the entire campaign in western Europe.

Field Marshal Walter Model had arrived at La Roche Guyon the previous evening, less than forty-eight hours after receiving the first phone call from the Führer asking his opinion about a replacement for Field Marshal von Kluge. His own appointment to the command followed shortly thereafter and he left immediately from his headquarters in East Prussia.

Model was not a stranger to western Europe. He had served as chief of staff with the *Sixteenth Army* in the campaign of 1940 in France and the Low Countries. He moved to the Russian front in 1941 and served successively as corps, army, and army group commander. He was rewarded for his efforts with an appointment to general field marshal on March 1, 1944.

In an army whose generals' loyalties were often suspect, Model was an exception. He was unswervingly loyal to his Führer and was one of the first to congratulate him on surviving the July 20 plot. His new chief of staff, Lt. Gen. Hans Speidel, who also had served his two predecessors, von Kluge and Rommel, was strongly sympathetic to the July 20 conspirators and was undoubtedly somewhat prejudiced against Model. He gave this description of the field marshal:

> Model was short of stature, somewhat uncouth, extraordinarily active of mind and body. He hardly knew what sleep was and was fearless in the heat of battle. But his keen tactical eye was not balanced by an instinct

for the possible. He thought too highly of his own ability, was erratic, and lacked a sense of moderation. He was apt to score popularity with the troops at the expense of the officers. He was a one-sided soldier, unreflecting and original in his mannerisms and conversation. . . . His unstable temperament made him susceptible to the ideology of Hitler, often against his better knowledge.[6]

Model wasted little time in taking over his new command. At 6:00 A.M., he was off for a 9:00 A.M. meeting at Fontaine l'Abbe with Hausser and Eberbach. Hausser, however, decided that conditions would not permit him to leave his troops and sent his chief of staff, Rudolph von Gersdorff, instead. In spite of severe problems with artillery fire on the way, von Gersdorff did manage to arrive at Fontaine l'Abbe close to the appointed hour.[7] Eberbach, who had forty-five miles to travel, left his headquarters at 5:00 A.M. but was unable to reach the abbey before 11:00. The two generals gave their reports. The more pessimistic of the two was Eberbach. While both outlined the rapidly deteriorating situation within the Falaise Gap, Eberbach went on to describe the declining morale of the German troops. "Soldier's pride" and "fear of defeat"[8] were the only incentives left for the German soldier. Thoughts of victory or trust in his commanders were a thing of the past. Eberbach was plainspoken to his new commander about his pessimism concerning the course of future events.

After listening to the reports, Model stated that his plan was to withdraw behind the Seine. He put Hausser in complete charge of the withdrawal and gave Eberbach the responsibility, under Hausser, for keeping open both the northern and southern flanks of the gap until the *Seventh Army* could withdraw. When a report reached Fontaine l'Abbe that Allied tanks were threatening the village of Trun, the meeting broke up and Model returned to La Roche Guyon.

He immediately contacted Jodl to outline his plans and his needs. He hoped to have all his troops behind the Falaise-Argentan road by tonight, across the Dives by the following night, and across the Touques River (twenty miles farther

toward the Seine) by the night of August 20. He also hoped
to have released a number of Panzer units for assembly near
the Seine by that time. After withdrawal, he would assign
the *Seventh Army* to the northern part of the defensive line,
the *Fifth Panzer Army* under Eberbach to the center extending
to Paris, and the *First Army*, coming up from southwestern
France, to the upper Seine.

Model's troops were absolutely spent, and therefore he had
a long list of reinforcement needs to present to the Führer—
4 Panzer divisions, 10 infantry divisions, 15 engineer battalions, 270 tanks or assault guns, and a large number of
artillery and transportation requirements.[9] That Model would
have the temerity to even make such a request indicates his
confidence in the Führer's favorable attitude toward him. He
certainly must have known that there was no possibility of
supplying even a fraction of the items on his list. Perhaps he
felt that this was the best way to adequately convey the se-
riousness of the situation.

While Model's return from Fontaine l'Abbe was unevent-
ful, that was not the case with his two generals. It took
Eberbach six to seven hours to travel the twenty miles to the
headquarters of the *II Panzer Corps* near the northern hinge
of the pocket, only to be informed when he arrived of the
loss of Trun.[10] Von Gersdorff had even greater difficulties,
including being slightly wounded and having his car hit by
lightning near Chambois. It was late at night before he arrived
at *Seventh Army* headquarters in a stone quarry near Villedieu,
a small village two miles south of Trun.[11] His report to Hausser was not encouraging.

The courtyard at La Roche Guyon was alive with activity
and a picture of confusion. Allied mortar shells from across
the Seine had started falling in the vicinity early in the afternoon. The staff was getting ready to move the headquarters
of *Army Group B* to Margival, a village five miles north of
Soissons.

It had been more than six months since Field Marshal
Rommel had established his headquarters in this majestic
chateau overlooking the Seine. The tour of duty had been
long and pleasant for the members of the staff, and departure

was going to be difficult and unwelcome. Unpleasant or not, however, the Americans were at their doorstep and they could afford little time for reminiscence.

They did take the time, however, at 5:00 in the afternoon to bid farewell to their former commander, Guenther von Kluge. While the field marshal had been at La Roche Guyon for only a month, his departure was a sentimental occasion, and he "bade farewell with emotion to his small staff."[12]

As von Kluge left through the chateau's iron gates for the last time, he thought again of the long letter he had just sent to the Führer. It was a strange combination of criticism of Hitler's policies on the one hand and protestations of good faith and loyalty on the other. In light of subsequent events, it is hard to understand what purpose the letter was to serve, unless it was naively intended to provide some degree of protection to his family from the consequences of his own perceived disloyalty to the Führer.

My Führer

Your decision handed to me yesterday by Field Marshal Model relieves me of the command of the High Command West and Army Group B. The obvious reason for this is the failure of the Panzer thrust to Avranches which made it impossible to close the gap up to the sea. My "guilt" as the responsible commander is thereby confirmed.

[There follows a long exposition of the reasons for the failure of the Avranches offensive, as seen by von Kluge.]

I did my utmost to carry out your command. I also admit that it would have been better to have waited another day to begin the attack. But that would have altered nothing fundamentally. That is my unshakable conviction, which I am taking to the grave with me; for the position had developed much too far for anything to have been able to change it. . . .

By reason of these facts I stick to my assertion that there were no chances of success; on the contrary, the attacks ordered were bound to make the all-round position of the Army Group decisively worse. And that is what happened. . . .

My Führer, I think I may claim for myself that I did everything within my power to be equal to the situation. . . . Both Rommel and I . . . foresaw the present development. We were not listened to. Our appreciations were NOT dictated by pessimism, but from the sober knowledge of the facts. I do not know whether Field Marshal Model, who has been proved in every sphere, will still master the situation. From my heart I hope so. Should it not be so, however, and your new greatly desired weapons, especially of the air force, not succeed, then, my Führer, make up your mind to end the war. The German people have borne such untold suffering that it is time to put an end to this frightfulness. . . .

My Führer, I have always admired your greatness, your conduct in the gigantic struggle and your will to maintain yourself and National Socialism. If fate is stronger than your will and your genius so is Providence. You have fought an honorable and great fight. History will prove that for you. Show yourself now also great enough to put an end to a hopeless struggle when necessary.

I depart from you, my Führer, as one who stood nearer to you than you perhaps realized in the consciousness that I did my duty to the utmost.

> Heil,
> my Führer[13]

When von Kluge reached a point between Verdun and Metz, which was the site of a battle in the Franco-Prussian War of 1870, he stepped from his car, took out a vial of cyanide, and committed suicide.

Saturday, AUGUST 19

Generals do not ordinarily spend the night in foxholes, but Gen. Eugene Meindl was grateful for whatever protection could be provided in the maelstrom of the rapidly contracting Falaise pocket. For the past three days, his *II Parachute Corps* had served as the rear guard for the German troops attempting to escape. The experience had been one of unbelievable confusion, devastation, and terror. Enemy air raids and artillery attacks had made movement by day literally impossible, and the confusion during the hours of darkness was extreme. According to the general, "The chaos on the roads was already eloquent of the coming catastrophe. . . . It was the tank formations which were to blame for this—they took up all the available space on the roads without a thought for anybody else."[1] A common foot soldier's complaint, no doubt, but as the danger and destruction increased with every mile his troops moved to the east, his frustration and anger with the disorganization, fear, and panic that he saw all around him increased also.

They had managed to get across the Orne River two nights before in fairly good order and with little interference from the enemy ground forces facing them. However, as the size of the pocket decreased with their eastward movement, the air and artillery attacks became so concentrated as to be absolutely inescapable. Transport was collapsing as motorized vehicles either were destroyed by the enemy or ran out of fuel. As men became separated from their units, the problem of straggling increased, adding further to the confusion and crowding of the roads as well as the general feeling of despair and defeat. In spite of these appalling conditions, in the past two days Meindl had succeeded in leading the troops under his command—the *3rd Parachute* and *353rd Infantry Divisions*—the fifteen miles to their present position at La Londe, just a few miles south of Trun and the Dives River.

At dawn, the planes were out in strength and the results of their attacks were visible everywhere. At 7:00 A.M., Meindl saw his superior, General Hausser, approaching and he was concerned. "So early?! . . . A bad sign! . . . We were sitting or lying about still in our foxholes. One look at his face was enough to tell me what was wrong. . . . I greet him with the words 'Well . . . the lid's shut tight now! Which means, I suppose, that we'll have to try and shove it up again!' 'Yes . . . ,' he replies. . . . 'That's just what I've come to talk to you about. We've seen it coming for a long time.' 'Good . . . ,' I said. . . . 'We'll do it! But *how* we're to do it I shall decide, nobody's going to tell me how to do this. . . .'"[2] A rather insolent reply to the commander of the *Seventh Army*, but Hausser knew his man. He had confidence in this impertinent, egotistical general and that is why he had chosen Meindl to lead his *Seventh Army* out of the pocket.

Meindl was ready with a plan. He would concentrate his troops during the day in a large woods a mile or two west of La Londe. His remaining artillery would fire all their ammunition during the day and then be left behind. Late this evening, the movement of his forces out of the pocket would commence. They would cross the Dives at a point between Trun and Saint-Lambert where Meindl had been advised a gap existed in the enemy positions. Once across the river, they would head for the heights above Coudehard (the same Hill 262 at that time being occupied by the Poles). Having reached this position, he would then face his troops to the west and hold open the gap for the other escaping forces. His troops would march single file in two columns and absolute silence would be kept. No lights would be permitted and no guns would be fired. Resistance or obstacles were to be by-passed. Only when morning arrived and they had reached their goal on the Coudehard heights would fighting be permitted.

Hausser approved the plan and added that Meindl could expect help from two Panzer divisions (the *9th SS* and the *2nd SS*) that were already east of the Dives. They had been ordered to turn back to the west to help the *Seventh Army* escape. Meindl's normal disdain of any help from armored troops would have been further compounded had he known that, between them, these two divisions could muster no more than twenty to twenty-five tanks.

Hausser also advised that the Panzer units defending the southern flank near Chambois were to begin breaking through the gap that evening as well. The plan called for them to cross the Dives to the south between Saint-Lambert and Chambois. Their scheduled departure time was midnight. Meindl pleaded with Hausser to make absolutely certain that they left no sooner than the appointed hour. He was concerned that a premature attack might alert the enemy and destroy the element of secrecy that was crucial to the success of his plan.

Meindl spent the day visiting the units under his command to explain the escape plan and make certain that each understood his part. By 6:00 P.M., all the troops had reached the wooded assembly area. There was time to eat what little food was available and perhaps even snatch a few hours of sleep. Meindl was somewhat cheered by his visits among the troops during the day. They had given him more confidence than he had felt in several days. "The mood of the paratroopers was excellent, I had seen nothing but glowing eyes the whole day through; they knew what it was a matter of."[3]

The huge rectangular keep, quartered by four towers, rose 100 feet above the village of Chambois. Part of a twelfth-century military fortress, it was a highly visible landmark, useful to anyone who might be trying to reach the center of the village.

There were two such groups this afternoon. One was a detachment of the 1st Polish Armored Division, whose main body was occupied a few miles away attempting to secure a position on Hill 262. Second Lieutenant Karcz, a squadron leader in the 10th Dragoons, was cautiously entering the village from the west with a small group of men. They met

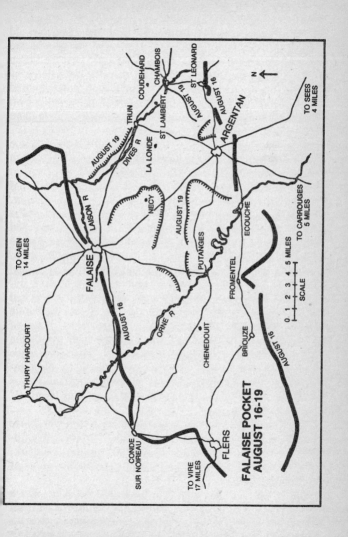

FALAISE POCKET
AUGUST 16-19

surprisingly little resistance as they approached the village center. Their progress was slowed rather by a grisly scene of burning German tanks, wounded soldiers, hundreds of corpses of both men and horses, and enemy soldiers by the hundreds giving themselves up as prisoners.

A second group was heading for the village center from the opposite direction. The U.S. 90th Division with help from tanks of the 2nd French Armored Division had been driving toward Chambois since dawn. By late afternoon, a company of the 359th Infantry Regiment led by Capt. L.E. Waters was working its way through the village, facing the same scenes of desolation and destruction that had greeted their Polish counterparts on the other side of the town.

Lieutenant Karcz called his Polish troops to a halt. Approaching from 800 yards away was a formation of troops headed in his direction. He deployed his men and opened fire. The formation scattered and soon white flags began to appear. Suddenly Karcz realized his mistake. "Feeling rather crestfallen I jumped onto the road and waved my hand. An American captain ran toward me and, still running, caught hold of me and lifted me in the air as if I had been a child. . . . That was the precise moment when the Falaise Pocket was closed. It was nearly 1800 hours and the American's name was L. E. Waters."[4]

The Poles and Americans immediately went to work to organize a common defense of Chambois. The Poles turned over 1,300 prisoners and all their own wounded to the Americans, as they had no facilities to care for them. They were, in effect, cut off from their own sources of supply and the rest of their forces.

The so-called "short envelopment" conceived by General Bradley early in the month was now officially accomplished. With the meeting of the Polish and American troops in Chambois, the German forces in the Falaise Pocket were completely surrounded.

But if the Germans were "in the bag," the bag was still full of holes. The three villages of Trun, Saint-Lambert, and Chambois were now in Allied hands, although the hold on the latter two was certainly tenuous. But along the four- to five-mile stretch of the Dives from Chambois to Trun, Allied strength (primarily in the form of Canadian armored forces) was still very spotty. As General Meindl had commented earlier in the day, the lid may be "shut tight," but it was certainly vulnerable to being "shoved up again."[5]

The three generals—Montgomery, Bradley, and Dempsey—offered a rather unusual picture standing in front of their map boards in the middle of a hay field. They had agreed to this meeting point, midway between their respective headquarters, in the interest of time so that they could conduct their business and be on their way.

Their business related to the next move of the American and British forces in their drive toward the Seine. Since the lower reaches of the river were in British territory, coordination of the movements of the two armies needed to be reviewed once again. To Bradley, the strategy was obvious. Whatever German forces had escaped from the Falaise Gap could be trapped again before crossing the Seine. With his XV Corps already having reached the south bank, what was needed now was a drive down the river to deny the crossings to the retreating German forces.

Bradley's first proposal was that Dempsey bring two British divisions around through Argentan so as to follow the XV Corps path to the Seine. These combined forces could then drive down the river to close the trap on the Germans. The answer he received from Dempsey was negative: "Oh, no thanks, Brad, we couldn't pull it off. I just can't spare two divisions for so wide an end run."

The answer was not unexpected, and Bradley was ready with another proposal. "If you can't do it, Bimbo," he said, "have you any objections to our giving it a try? It'll mean cutting across your front."[6]

There were no objections from either Dempsey or Montgomery. In spite of their ready agreement, Bradley knew he was asking for trouble by mixing up army boundary lines in this way, but the opportunity was too tempting to pass up. Besides, he had already made a good start in getting this movement under way. The XIX Corps of the First Army (like the V Corps several days earlier) had been pinched out of the line with the continued contraction of the Falaise Pocket. Bradley had already moved the corps most of the 100 miles required to put it in line alongside the XV Corps for a two-corps assault down the Seine. The XIX Corps under "Texas Pete" Corlett consisted of three first-rate, experienced divisions—the 2nd Armored and the 30th and 28th Infantry. To Bradley, it seemed a sufficiently promising opportunity to warrant the headaches he knew would result from this scrambling of army boundaries.

As he headed back to his CP at Saint-James, Bradley's thoughts drifted from this morning's discussion of short-term strategy to the longer-term issue of what strategy should be adopted once the Seine River had been crossed. Bradley was concerned about a discussion he had with Eisenhower yesterday at Saint-James. It all went back to the meeting a week ago at Montgomery's headquarters on the day Patton was trying so desperately to reach him for clearance to advance beyond Argentan. At that meeting, Montgomery had proposed to Eisenhower and Bradley that the major Allied drive should be through the Low Countries and then across northern Germany to Berlin. Most, if not all, of the Allied resources should be concentrated in this effort. It became known as the "single thrust" theory. It would withdraw resources from Patton's Third Army and assign Hodges's First Army to Montgomery's command. In Montgomery's view, this was a bold strategy designed to bring an early end to the war.

Bradley's view was different. He considered the Montgomery proposal entirely too risky. He felt that such a "single thrust" would be dangerously exposed to attacks on its flanks from reorganized German forces, particularly as it came closer to the "homeland." He also questioned that Montgomery's leadership style would encourage sufficient speed and aggressiveness to enable such a strategy to succeed. Bradley favored the "multiple thrust" approach, spreading the resources, and allowing Patton to continue his eastward drive toward the German border. It would also leave both U.S. armies under Bradley's control.

He had felt earlier that Eisenhower had favored this approach as well. His aide, Chester Hansen, had recorded in his diary, "Ike likewise favors Bradley's desire to drive eastward and violate the German border as quickly as possible."[7] However, after the previous day's meeting, Bradley was not so certain. Two targets along the northern coast of Europe were of great importance in Eisenhower's view—the V-2 rocket-launching sites and the port of Antwerp. While Ike clearly did not agree with the "single thrust" theory per se, he certainly was giving some consideration to the possibility of letting Montgomery have the First Army to expedite the capture of these two vital objectives.

"I believe Ike left my headquarters fully convinced that my plan was the sounder of the two," Bradley wrote.[8] Nevertheless, Montgomery had planted the seed and Bradley was worried. He must become more aggressive in promoting his own ideas if he was to prevent at least some portions of Montgomery's "single thrust" theory from becoming a part of the Allied grand strategy. Contention and disagreement were an inescapable part of life as an Army Group general, he thought.

Bradley could take some comfort in the fact that at least one issue had been agreed upon among the British and Americans. That issue was Paris. The plan was to bypass the city both to the east and west and then by joining forces to the north effectively force the Germans to withdraw. There were two basic reasons for this approach, one humane and the other based on cold, hard military necessities.

None of the Allies wanted a battle for the city of Paris. While it was uncertain what damage the Germans might inflict in an uncontested withdrawal from the city, there was no doubt whatsoever that a fight for the possession of the "City of Light" would cause untold destruction to this cradle of European civilization. No American or British general wanted to be remembered as the destroyer of Paris.

The more cold-blooded reason for bypassing Paris had to do with supplies. Allied supply officers had calculated that once Paris was liberated, the supplies that the population would require each day were equivalent to the supplies needed by the Allied armies for three days of mechanized march toward the German border.

Bradley was beginning to see dark storm clouds on the horizon as far as supplying his armies was concerned. Their rapid movements were outrunning their supplies—particularly their supply of gasoline. As an example of how serious the situation was becoming, this very afternoon twenty-one C-47s had started an emergency airlift to the Third Army, landing at airfields near Le Mans. These planes had been originally scheduled for use in a paratroop landing near Chartres, which the rapid movement of Walker's XX Corps had made unnecessary.

But airdrops and other emergency measures did not appear to be enough to ward off an upcoming supply problem that could conceivably stop Bradley's armies in their tracks. Further diversion of supplies to the city of Paris would, of course, greatly add to the severity of the problem. As Bradley stated, "If we could rush on to the Siegfried Line with tonnage that might otherwise be diverted to Paris, the city would be compensated for its additional week of occupation with an earlier end to the war."[9] A cruel assessment, perhaps, but one of the many hard choices dictated by military necessity.

Two hundred miles away, three men had choices of their own to make that were, in the end, to completely upset those coldly calculated plans of the Allied High Command to bypass the city of Paris. Theirs was a vastly different perspective located, as they were, in the city itself—vastly different, not only from that of the Allies, but also different one from the other.

Henri Tanguy (better known as Colonel Rol) was the leader of the Communist underground in Paris and effective leader of the FFI in the city as well. He had come up through the ranks of the Communist party as a union organizer before the war and had joined the resistance at its inception. He commanded the strongest force in the French capital.[10] His objectives were twofold—to force the Germans out of Paris and, once they were gone, to seize authority in the city (and, as a result, probably all of France as well) in the name of the Communist party. In order to accomplish this, he was prepared to commit all his forces in an all-out effort to seize the city. That the cost of such an effort would be severe both in damage to the city and casualties to its inhabitants was not a matter of prime importance to Rol. "Paris," he had observed, "is worth 200,000 dead."[11]

By midmorning, thousands of posters calling for "Mobilization generale" were on walls all over the city. German wiretapping equipment had been destroyed by sabotaging the city's telephone exchanges. Throughout Paris, isolated groups of German soldiers were attacked in an effort to increase the resistants' supply of arms at the expense of the German troops. These attacks became bolder as the day progressed. Colonel Rol had reason to be well pleased with the results on this first day of his insurrection, except for one fact. His people had not gained control of that bastion of authority within the city, the Prefecture of Police.

Alexandre Parodi was the leader of the Gaullist resistance forces in Paris. A high official in the prewar Ministry of Labor, he came from a different segment of French society than Colonel Rol, and he had a very different point of view toward resistance strategy as well. Under close control from the Gaullist leaders in Algiers and London, Parodi and his allies were strongly opposed to any sort of insurrection, seeing it only as an effort by the Communists to seize control of the government from its rightful heirs, the followers of Charles de Gaulle.[12]

However, Parodi faced a number of dilemmas. The Communists were more numerous and better organized than his Gaullist forces in Paris. In addition, insurrection was popular among many of the city's inhabitants after four years of German occupation. He saw that events would rapidly slip out of his control if he simply sat back and did nothing while Rol's forces took to the streets.

Limited in what he could do by the relative weakness of his forces, he struck upon a plan that was within the capabilities of his smaller organization but that could possibly maintain the rightful authority of the Gaullist forces in the city. As soon as he learned of Colonel Rol's plans, he organized a takeover of the Prefecture of Police—a key symbol of civil authority and the most important public building in the city.

With strong cooperation from the police themselves, the occupation of the prefecture had been highly successful. The building was effectively in control of Parodi's Gaullist forces by 8:00 A.M. But as German tanks began to appear in the square between the prefecture and the Cathedral of Notre Dame, the Gaullists realized that they faced a very unequal struggle. Their original plans to avoid fighting for control of the city were coming apart at the seams.

In his headquarters at the Hotel Meurice, Lt. Gen. Deitrich von Choltitz was confused and angry. He had been born, raised, and trained in the Prussian military tradition. His background and experience had been as a military man fighting in the field. From the invasion of the Low Countries in 1940 through the Russian campaign to the battles in Normandy just a month ago, he had never hesitated to make the necessary decisions regardless of the cost.[13] Now all that seemed to be changing.

Since taking over as commander in Paris ten days before, he had begun to experience an unfamiliar sense of doubt and uncertainty. His orders from above seemed clear enough. From Hitler, von Kluge, and now Model, it was the same—defend Paris to the last man regardless of the cost. The defense of Paris was an integral part of the defense of France as a whole, and the city must pay whatever price is necessary in supporting the German military strategy. Demolition experts had been in Paris for a week now mining all the bridges and important municipal buildings. It was clear that his orders were to supervise the defense and then the destruction of the city. For someone who had already been involved in the destruction of Rotterdam and later Sevastopol, this should have been a manageable assignment.

In the past several days, however, he had found himself procrastinating—putting off decisions and delaying actions that might irreversibly lead to the destruction that his superiors were demanding. He also found that, if things were quiet in Paris, his superiors tended to leave him alone, as they had other more pressing matters to attend to elsewhere. He had come to value the relative peace and tranquility that had prevailed since his arrival. He was anxious for it to continue.

Then this stupid uprising started this morning. Certainly these people were not so naive as to think they could prevail over his trained and well-equipped soldiers. He could not understand what they had in their minds. They had killed fifty and wounded a hundred of his soldiers during the day. They must realize that this would force him to take severe retaliatory measures, which would cause serious destruction to the city and large casualties among the population. If these senseless attacks continued, the situation could easily develop beyond his ability to control events.

Then, finally, toward the end of the day, a Swedish consul by the name of Nordling had shown up at his office proposing a cease-fire.[14] It was ridiculous! He had never requested or agreed to a cease-fire in his entire military career. And yet, on a moment's reflection, he found himself giving the proposal serious consideration. If it worked, it would do several things for him. It would restore quiet to the city and therefore keep his command out of the limelight. It would enable him to maintain control over events and keep his superiors off his back. His soldiers could return their attention to their major task of keeping open the lines of communication within the city so that the promised reinforcements could be easily moved into line to defend against the attack from the Allied armies, which von Choltitz realized was bound to occur within a matter of days. But, most of all, it would enable him to put off the bombing attack he had scheduled for the next day against the Prefecture of Police and other resistance strong points. From such an attack, there would be no turning back, and, for the first time in his life, he found himself reluctant to take such a step.

His acceptance of Nordling's proposal had just one condition: his name was not in any way to be associated with the cease-fire. He was anxious, at least at this point, that Field Marshal Model not find out what he was up to.

Sunday, AUGUST 20

"The enemy tanks now dominated the whole of the strip along which we hoped to make our attack, and I had been hoping a little while back that it was our tanks coming to the rescue from outside. Now we could clearly see that they were British tanks."[1]

These were General Meindl's words of bitter disappointment as early dawn gave him his first view through the rain of the heights above Coudehard. He had planned to use these heights as the strong point to rally his troops and keep the gap open as long as possible. He soon discovered his mistake in the nationality of the troops occupying the hill. They were not British but Polish.

It was a hard blow for troops already on the verge of exhaustion. They had headed out Indian-fashion at 10:30 the night before and had reached the Dives by 12:30 A.M. They had been under fire from enemy tanks a good part of the way. Fortunately, the tanks were firing mainly tracer shells. The light from these shells enabled Meindl and his troops to locate the tanks and steer a path between them as they worked their way toward the river. Once across, the tanks were even more numerous, at times getting as close as twenty to thirty yards to the silently moving columns of German soldiers. Some of the troops got lost and drifted off while others joined in the snakelike procession. It seemed as if the night would never end.

As it became lighter and the rain ended, the fire from Hill 262 increased in intensity, keeping the Germans pinned down in ditches or whatever other protection they could find. But there were a surprising number of German troops in the area as well. Meindl had to call a halt to one eager group that was about to charge straight up the hill in the face of the Polish tanks. He suggested instead that they work their way up north in an effort to circle in behind the Polish position.

Late in the morning, Meindl set out to find his commander, General Hausser. Having located him in a bomb crater a mile or so to the south, they discussed the situation. Hausser advised that the *2nd SS Panzer Division* was coming south and would be in a position to attack the northern end of the Polish position on Hill 262. Hausser told Meindl that he planned to join this division for the final breakout. He suggested that Meindl see what he could do to organize an attack on the southern perimeter of the Polish position.

By 5:00 P.M., the Poles were under heavy attack on all sides. The *2nd SS* from the north and Meindl's collection of assorted troops from the south had them literally surrounded. Neither attack was able to develop sufficient force to penetrate the fiercely defended Polish perimeter, but they did have one very beneficial effect from the German point of view. Fighting for their lives, the Poles were unable to concentrate the same level of firepower on the roads at the foot of the hill as they had been able to do earlier in the day. To the Germans, this meant the gap was still open, if only a crack.

"The news spread like wildfire inside the ring that there was a way through at Coudehard. A stream of stragglers now swept through the gap from nightfall until the morning of the 21 August."[2] Meindl sent officers on bicycles back to the Dives to round up any groups they could find and direct them toward Coudehard and the way out. As the troops struggled northward, they brought with them tales of indescribable death and destruction within the pocket. German troops, having given up any hope of escape, were surrendering by the thousands. And yet, they continued to come, mostly in isolated small groups—those who somehow or other had found a crack in the growing wall of Allied troops along the Dives. The organized resistance being shown by Meindl's patched-up force and the open road at Coudehard were a welcome sight to the German troops, who had experienced nothing but confusion and hopelessness for the past several days.

Another concern had been bothering Meindl all during the day. How would he get his wounded out? Most of them had been wounded fighting to keep a way open for all the troops now making their way out of the trap. Meindl felt a compelling obligation to see to it that these people were not left behind. He managed to locate several large Red Cross flags—white with a red cross—which he draped over whatever vehicles he could find. At 6:30 P.M. he stopped all traffic down the Coudehard road for thirty minutes. He then sent the column of wounded down the road, waited another thirty minutes, and then permitted the other traffic to move again. As he had hoped, the Poles recognized the gesture for what it was, and not a single round was fired as the convoy of wounded wound its way down the road.

Meindl was to comment later: "Not a shot was fired at them and I recognized, with thankfulness in my heart, the chivalrous attitude of the enemy. . . . After the ugly scenes I had witnessed that day, the nobility of our enemies made me forget for a moment the nastiness of it all and I offered thanks in my heart in the name of the wounded."[3]

The mile or two along the Dives River between Chambois and the small hamlet of Saint-Lambert was a scene of complete confusion and devastation. In theory, this portion of the mouth of the Falaise Gap had been closed by a combination of the American 90th Division coming downstream from Chambois and the Canadian 4th Armored Division coming from the opposite direction. In practice, it was anything but closed, as events of the early morning hours would soon demonstrate.

General Hausser had directed most of his remaining Panzer units into this narrow area of the Dives River crossing to make their effort to escape from the rapidly collapsing Falaise Pocket. On paper, it sounded like a formidable force—*1st SS*, *2nd Pz*, *12th SS*, and *116th Pz*, an aggregation of armored power that in earlier days would have been able to break out of any trap the Allies could devise. In fact, these divisions were by now reduced to mere skeletons with only a fraction of their former strength.

Their situation was made more difficult by the incredible desolation and disarray existing in the remaining area of the pocket, which must serve as the staging area for their escape effort. In spite of the small size of the area into which these forces had been concentrated, communication between units or groups was practically impossible. The whole area was littered with abandoned vehicles, destroyed equipment, and dead animals. Road travel was next to impossible. Thousands of soldiers, adrift from their units and without leadership, were desperately trying to find any means of escape from the certain capture or death that awaited them. Officers were separated from their units, and in many cases the only existing organization was that of small groups that had banded together for their own protection. Allied artillery made life within the pocket miserable—steady fire was directed into what had by now become a very concentrated target.

True to the word given by Hausser to Meindl the previous afternoon, none of the armored forces had made any effort to escape until after midnight. One of the first groups to attempt a breakthrough included elements of the *1st SS Panzer Division* under the leadership of Maj. Gen. Freiherr von Gersdorff, chief of staff of the *Seventh Army* under Hausser. Having crossed the Dives River between Chambois and Saint-Lambert, this small group ran into a position held by elements of the U.S. 90th Infantry Division. The Americans were taken by surprise and offered to surrender. They were disarmed and left where they were as von Gersdorff's group headed on to the east.

At approximately the same time, other elements of the *1st SS Panzer Division* plus another group consisting of the few units of the *12th SS Panzer Division* that had survived their confrontation with the Canadians at Falaise attempted an escape through Chambois. With this group was the *12th SS Panzer* commander, Kurt Meyer, his head still bandaged from the wound suffered during the defense of Falaise. Also present was the commander of the *LXXXIV Corps*, Lt. Gen. Otto

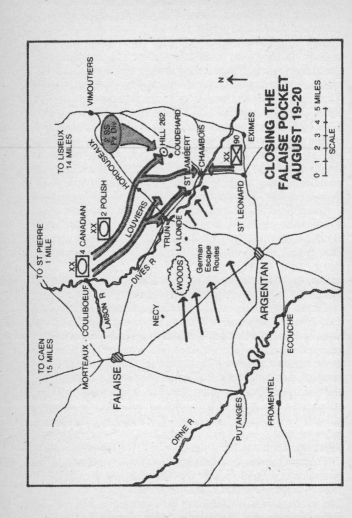

CLOSING THE
FALAISE POCKET
AUGUST 19-20

0 1 2 3 4 5 MILES
SCALE

Elfeldt. Elfeldt was a corps commander without a corps. His command had by now been reduced to the few remaining troops of the *12th SS Panzer Division*.

The group led by Meyer and Elfeldt approached Chambois only to be met with intense American fire from favorable positions south of the city. It was clear that they could make no headway as a group. Some other approach must be found. They decided to split into smaller groups and attempt to cross the river in the no-man's-land between Chambois and Saint-Lambert. Meyer was successful as were a number of the smaller groups. On the other side, Meyer gathered these small bands together and they joined in the long line of German forces working its way to the northeast past the Polish forces on Hill 262 to the safety of the lines of their own *2nd SS Panzer Division*.

General Elfeldt was not so fortunate. Separated from Meyer, he organized a small group for an attack through Saint-Lambert. They immediately ran headlong into an opposing tank battalion. Out of ammunition and facing certain death, the general and his staff surrendered. He thereby earned the distinction of being the only high-ranking German officer to be captured by the Allies in the Falaise Pocket.

As the day wore on, the two other Panzer divisions (the *2nd* and the *116th*) made their bids to escape. The *2nd Panzer* was the first to head out at dawn under its wounded commander, Lt. Gen. Freiherr von Luettwitz. With an armored force of about fifteen tanks, they were able to force their way through the town of Saint-Lambert and on past Coudehard to the northeast. One group of the *116th Panzer* followed over much the same route later on in the day. However, a second group of the *116th*, which included the division's ten remaining tanks, was less successful. It was captured as it attempted to escape near Trun.

Perhaps the most surprising aspect of the escape of the remnants of these two divisions was that their tanks and other mobile equipment were able to use the small stone bridge across the Dives at Saint-Lambert, which remained intact throughout the day. Apparently, none of the Allied forces in the Saint-Lambert area had considered destroying the bridge. The bridge crossing was an experience not soon to be forgotten by the exhausted troops struggling to get across. Luettwitz later described it as "particularly horrible, the bodies of killed men, dead horses, vehicles, and other equipment having been hurled from the bridge into the river to form there a gruesome tangled mass."[4]

By the end of the day, the feeble, scattered remnants of four once mighty Panzer divisions were across the Dives, working their way toward the safety of their own lines. There was little left in the way of equipment or manpower. One important element did remain, however. In each division, enough of the headquarters and command forces did escape to provide a framework for the later refitting and rebuilding of these divisions. The Allies had not seen the last of the *1st SS, 2nd, 12th SS*, and *116th Panzer Divisions*.

Private Don Miller was a bazooka man in Col. Warren Robinson's 314th Infantry Regiment.[5] It was a matter of little concern to him that his regiment was involved in a historic event. The U.S. 79th Infantry Division, of which his regiment was a part, had just become the first division to cross to the north side of the Seine River.

Private Miller was much more interested in the German 88s that were firing from somewhere off in the distance and in the German plane flying overhead. The regiment was located in a sugar-beet field close to the river. While this provided some cover, the exposed position of the regiment was very clear to all. Colonel Robinson had moved forward to reconnoiter, but a burst of fire sent him scurrying back. "That was a close call,"[6] he commented to the troops hunkered down among the sugar beets. The 79th Infantry had made history. They were across the Seine, but their position was far from secure.

Major General Wyche had received his orders from General Haislip about 9:30 the night before: he was to cross that night. The 79th Division along with the 5th Armored had reached the vicinity of Mantes, on the south bank about thirty-five miles downriver from Paris, two days before. The 5th Armored had been dispatched down the south bank in an effort to trap the retreating German forces, and the 79th had entered Mantes the day before, only to find that the Germans had left. As a result, General Wyche was less concerned about enemy opposition than by the fact that the width of the river ranged from 500 to 800 feet at the point where his troops were to cross.

Both good and bad fortune were the lot of the 79th Division that night. Their scouts were able to find a way across the river—a dam with a narrow footpath—but as the night progressed, heavy rainfall obscured visibility. The 313th Regiment were assigned the task of walking across the dam, and poor visibility and slippery conditions made it very hazardous. However, by moving single file with a hand on the man ahead, the regiment made it across without loss.

As dawn approached, Private Miller's 314th Regiment started paddling across in boats and rafts, some of which were provided by the Engineers, others acquired along the bank. While the men of the 314th were making their way across, the Engineers started bridging the river. By afternoon, the third regiment, the 315th, was able to cross the bridge in trucks and, by evening, tanks and artillery had also made their way to the north side.

By nightfall, the entire 79th Division was across the Seine. Had he been aware of this, Private Miller undoubtedly would have felt more secure. As it was, however, about all he had to look forward to was a long night in a sugar-beet field with all sorts of unknown dangers lurking out there in the darkness. The historic nature of what had transpired during the day was lost on Private Miller.

It was hardly a reception befitting the commander of the Free French Forces around the world—the future leader of the French nation. His party landed on a small fighter strip with a prefab metal runway in the countryside a few miles from Cherbourg. It was a gray day, with a light rain falling. One small building at the edge of the strip was the only sign of civilization. A noncommissioned officer greeted the arriving party with a demand for identification, emphasized by a submachine gun pointed in their direction.[7]

None of this mattered to Gen. Charles de Gaulle. He had been subjected to countless humiliations over the past several weeks. He was concerned with but one fact. The ground under his feet was that of France. He was home at last and he intended to stay.

This is not what he had told the American State Department

when he had requested their permission to go to France. American policy, as established by President Roosevelt, was to require that the French people decide the makeup of their government through postwar elections. To Roosevelt, allowing de Gaulle to use the power of the American army to establish himself as the leader of the French nation before such elections could take place was both distasteful and contrary to his views of proper American policy. The State Department might grant de Gaulle permission to make a short trip to France, but establishing himself there on a permanent basis was out of the question.

De Gaulle had swallowed hard and agreed that he would make a brief tour of the liberated areas of his homeland and then return to Algiers. He had no intention of abiding by this agreement. De Gaulle had no questions or doubts about his own manifest destiny to be the leader of the liberated French nation. Furthermore, he was well aware of the strength and ambitions of the Communist underground and its leaders. Without his commanding presence and authority on the scene, his forces in France were no match for Communist aggressiveness and organization. To permit his implacable enemies to assume control of the government because of the unrealistic notions of an American president was unthinkable.

He was aware also that Paris was the key to the success of his plans. To be able to assert his personal authority in the French capital as soon as it was liberated would be an absolutely essential step in his assumption of control of the government of all of France. Once on the soil of France, he had no plans to ever leave.

The double humiliation of being forced to ask for permission to return and then having to lie about his intentions was followed by further indignities as his efforts to reach his homeland continued. The Americans had offered a Flying Fortress to carry de Gaulle from Algiers to France, since it was doubtful that the general's own single-engine Lodestar had the range and fuel capacity for the trip. However, the B-17 assigned for the job had a landing accident at the Algiers airport and was unable to make the trip. The general was advised to fly his own plane to Gibraltar, where another B-17 would be waiting.[8]

On reaching Gibraltar, de Gaulle's party was informed that

the B-17 had blown a tire and there would be a twenty-four-hour delay. Convinced that this was all part of a plot by the Americans to keep him from ever reaching France, he announced that he was leaving immediately in his own plane. Against the advice of his English hosts, as well as his own pilot, the Lodestar, overloaded with fuel to provide the required range, had been just barely able to take off from the Gibraltar airport. It left shortly before midnight, taking a course for France. Precious fuel was wasted over the English Channel looking for an English fighter plane that was to escort de Gaulle to Normandy. The plane could not be located. By now, the general was absolutely convinced that the Allies intended to keep him from entering France, even if it meant he and his party would crash into the English Channel. When his Lodestar finally set down on the runway near Cherbourg, there was fuel left for only two more minutes of flying time.

The group managed to find an old automobile for transportation into Cherbourg. Here de Gaulle found the official chief of his FFI forces in France, Gen. Pierre Koenig, who brought him up to date on the uprising in Paris. De Gaulle immediately recognized this as the major effort on the part of the Communists to assume control. The pressure was mounting. It had now become imperative that the Allies move on Paris immediately. He must go at once to see General Eisenhower and convince him to change his plans.

Eisenhower, as much as any American, had experience in dealing with General de Gaulle, going back to his days in North Africa in 1943. He had, at times, become terribly frustrated and upset by the deviousness and political intrigue that were basic elements of his relationship with the Free French. On the other hand, he had developed a grudging admiration for de Gaulle's singleness of purpose and unremitting persistence in pursuit of his political goals. Ike knew full well what the general wanted to see him about this afternoon. He, as well as de Gaulle, was aware of yesterday's uprising in Paris and the complications likely to occur as a result. However, he was not about to give in. His plan to bypass Paris was sound. It would not be changed.

When de Gaulle arrived, Eisenhower took the offensive. He explained fully the Allied plan to envelop Paris rather than attack it head-on. A large supply of maps was on hand to explain exactly and in detail how this would be accomplished. De Gaulle asked that the plan be reconsidered, pointed to the Communist menace, and argued that delay could turn Paris into an unsatisfactory base for Allied operations because of an unstable and disruptive political situation. His arguments met deaf ears. De Gaulle knew Eisenhower well enough to realize he was getting nowhere. It was time to leave.[9]

He must now consider other alternatives—alternatives he had hoped to avoid. He would get in touch with Leclerc. If the Allies refused to enter Paris, he would order the 2nd Armored Division to do so under his authority as its ultimate commander. This, more than anything, illustrated his desperation to gain control of the city. He fully realized that such an action on his part would completely destroy whatever feelings of goodwill and cooperation had been developed between the Free French and the Allies over the past several years. It could not be helped. Paris must be taken.

At 6:30 in the evening, Lieutenant General Truscott was back in his command post after visits to the 3rd and 45th Divisions. It was D + 5 and things seemed to be on schedule. The French troops were on the verge of taking Toulon and were closing in on Marseilles. With his own 3rd and 45th Divisions protecting the right flank of the French forces by moving through Aix-en-Provence toward the Durance River valley, Truscott felt confident that this end of the battle was progressing satisfactorily.

He now turned his attention to the north, for it was here that, in Truscott's view, the key battle for the south of France would take place. On the east bank of the Rhone about eighty miles north of the coast lies the town of Montélimar. Just north of the town is located one of the most narrow of the numerous defiles in the Rhone valley between the coast and Lyons, another eighty miles to the north. Truscott had chosen this site to spring his trap on the Germans, who he was certain would soon be forced to attempt an escape to the north to join their comrades facing the Allied forces in northern France.

The strategy was obvious. The task was to assemble a force that was sufficient to carry it out. Key to the timely execution of his strategy was Task Force Butler, that patchwork mobile force Truscott had assembled after he concluded that CC Sudre would not be available to him for very long. (The command had indeed reverted to French control the day before.) Task Force Butler had made rapid progress north up the Route Napoleon during the past two days, having reached the vicinity of Gap, a town sixty miles east of Montélimar. From Gap there were reasonable road connections down the Drôme River, which cuts through the mountains and flows into the Rhone a few miles north of Montélimar.

There were no indications that the Germans had yet started any withdrawal to the north on the east side of the Rhone River. As a matter of fact, the *11th Panzer*, after struggling across the river, was still heading south toward the American and French forces around and above Toulon and Marseilles. Air reconnaissance indicated that all the bridges across the Rhone south of Lyons had by now been destroyed. It seemed clear that the German forces were truly surrounded by the river to the west, the mountains to the east, and the French and American forces to the south and east. All that was needed to spring the trap was to block their exit to the north.

At 8:45 in the evening, Truscott called in Colonel Conway of his staff to send him off on a 100-mile drive through the mountains in the darkness with a message for General Butler. The message read: "You will move at first light with all possible speed to Montélimar. Block enemy routes of withdrawal up the Rhone valley in that vicinity. 36th Division follows you."[10]

The last sentence was crucial. Truscott was well aware that Task Force Butler did not have sufficient strength to do more than delay a determined effort by the enemy to break through the Montélimar Gap. Further support was needed and that could come only from the 36th Division. Elements of Dahlquist's division were spread out over the 100 miles from Gap down to Draguignan near the coast. Dahlquist would be flying in by Cub first thing in the morning so the two generals could assess the problem and make their plans. Getting the entire division into an effective blocking position north of Montélimar was certainly a challenge of movement and logistics. But the potential rewards seemed incalculable.

Monday, AUGUST 21

At 03.45 hrs, we started off eastward. The pouring rain and the sound of the wind drowned any noise from the marching feet. Stumbling, stopping suddenly, close up against the man in front, there moved a mass of steaming, tired men, like a long serpent moving east-northeast. Now and then we were blinded by the glare of a burning truck, and then plunged into darkness shortly after that with the rain coming down in sheets . . . Up until 05.00 we kept the gap open, then—when the tail end had come through, it closed again. It was with a heavy heart that I found myself on the retreat at this time. The rain, still pouring down in streams, enabled us to continue our march by daytime.[1]

Thus did General Meindl describe his last hours within the Falaise Gap. By 7:00 A.M., his straggling columns had passed within the lines of the *2nd SS Panzer Division*, who had continued to apply pressure on the northern perimeter of the Polish forces on Hill 262. Other isolated groups, which had managed to cross the Dives the night before under the cover of rain and darkness, continued to head toward the north throughout the morning. Many had come from the Chambois area, and, as late as noon, a desperation attack was launched against the southern Polish perimeter without success.

By early afternoon, the movement of German soldiers had come to a halt. At about the same time, troops of the Canadian 4th Armored Division reached Hill 262 and the Poles received their first relief after three days of being surrounded on their hilltop position. The gap was now completely closed and the Allied encirclement, conceived in high hopes two weeks before, had become a part of history.

From the Allied point of view, the Battle of the Falaise Gap has been characterized as both a missed opportunity and a great victory. A strong case can be made for each characterization. Failure to approve the further advance of the XV Corps beyond Argentan on August 13 (as well as to support it to the fullest with additional troops in the area) was clearly a command error. It was a reasonable assumption that the gap could have been closed along the Argentan-Falaise road within two or three days at the most if Bradley had requested a change in army boundaries and then committed available forces to press the attack.

The strong sense of offensive strategy that had guided Bradley's decision to gamble on encirclement of the Germany army at the height of the Mortain counteroffensive had been replaced just one week later by caution and doubt. That his caution was based on faulty intelligence from his own staff on the location and intentions of the enemy can hardly serve as justification for failure to seize the opportunity.

The cost to the Allies of this missed opportunity is difficult to establish. The estimates of the number of German troops that escaped from the gap range from 20,000 to 40,000. Most of these undoubtedly escaped during the last week of the battle. In addition, most of the German army and corps commanders managed to escape along with their staffs and were to become important factors in the revitalization and reconstruction of the German forces in the months to come. The sense of lost opportunity looms so much larger in retrospect, perhaps, because the Allies came so close to the ultimate goal of all military commanders—to surround and capture or destroy the entire opposing force.

When viewed in the larger context of the campaign in western Europe, however, the Battle of the Falaise Gap was a major Allied victory. Two entire German armies—the *Seventh* and the *Fifth Panzer*—were literally destroyed as effective military units. Those German soldiers who did escape were largely individuals or small groups of stragglers, completely cut off from their units. The few organized units that escaped were merely skeletons of their original strength; as an example, seven armored divisions reported a total strength of 2,000 men, 62 tanks, and 26 artillery pieces—less than 5 percent of their normal full strength. The best estimate of the number of troops captured was approximately 50,000. The number of dead found on the field exceeded 10,000. Very little German equipment was taken out.

The devastation within the pocket during the last few days of fighting was beyond belief. A veteran of the worst battles of World War I as well as the capture of Saint-Lô described it as follows:

> None of these compared in the effect upon the imagination with what I saw yesterday southwest of Trun. . . . The grass and trees were vividly green as in all Normandy and a surprising number of houses [were] . . . untouched. That rather peaceful setting framed a picture of destruction so great that it cannot be described. It was as if an avenging angel had swept the area bent on destroying all things German. . . .
>
> I stood on a lane, surrounded by 20 or 30 dead horses, most of them still hitched to their wagons and carts. . . . As far as my eye could reach (about 200 yards) on every line of sight, there were . . . vehicles, wagons, tanks, guns, prime movers, sedans, rolling kitchens, etc., in various stages of destruction. . . .
>
> I stepped over hundreds of rifles in the mud and saw hundreds more stacked along sheds. . . . I walked through a mile or more of lanes where the vehicles had been caught closely packed. . . . I saw probably 300 field pieces and tanks, mounting large caliber guns that were apparently undamaged.
>
> I saw no foxholes or any other type of shelter or field fortifications. The Germans were trying to run and had no place to run. They were probably too exhausted to dig. . . . They were probably too tired even to surrender.
>
> I left this area regretting I'd seen it. . . . Under such

conditions there are no supermen—all men become
rabbits looking for a hole.[2]

The Battle of the Falaise Gap was the climactic event in
the effort to drive the enemy out of France. The Germans
were never again able to put up a strong defense until the
Allies approached the border of Germany itself. The spectacular advances of the next two months across France and
Belgium had their genesis between the Orne and the Dives
—between Argentan and Falaise. That the victory was not
total should in no way cloud its decisive influence on the
outcome of the European campaign.

The final wind-down of the Battle of the Falaise Gap meant
victory to some and desperate escape to others, capture to
some and relief to others. But to Maj. Gen. Philippe Leclerc,
it meant only the intensification of his feelings of frustration
and rage. For two days now, his 2nd Armored Division had
done nothing but lend support to the American 80th and 90th
Divisions in their drives on Argentan and Chambois. On top
of that, his division had been split up, with one of his combat
commands having been attached to the 90th. It was an incredible waste! Only one order would make sense for his
division—it was their historic mission, their birthright. They
should be moving now to liberate the city of Paris.

He had besieged General Patton for days with requests to
organize his march on Paris. While Patton had assured him
that no one other than the French 2nd Armored would have
the honor of liberating the city, nothing had happened to get
any such movement under way. What was worse, his new
American commanders seemed to have even less appreciation
for the special consideration his French forces deserved.

He had been to see his new corps commander, Leonard
Gerow, two days before. Gerow advised Leclerc that Paris
was not a part of his sector and that, as long as the 2nd
Armored was a part of the V Corps, it would be treated no
differently from the American divisions in the corps. Disappointed and discouraged by his talk with Gerow, Leclerc
had pressed his arguments on Gerow's boss, Courtney
Hodges, the next day. He pleaded with Hodges to send his
division immediately on the road to Paris. Hodges told him
in no uncertain terms that he was to "stay put" until he

received orders to do otherwise. Obviously, Leclerc was getting nowhere with his two immediate superiors.

What could he do? The thought had crossed his mind more than once that he could simply disregard his American superiors and start his division moving on his own authority. After all, he did have special prerogative as commander of the only French division within range of the capital. Furthermore, it had been recognized by everyone since the pre-invasion days that Leclerc's forces should have the honor of being the first to enter the city. He was also becoming increasingly concerned by the number of American divisions that were coming closer and closer to the city and who in the interest of military, rather than political, considerations might be sent in. Had not the time come to take matters into his own hands?

His division had been husbanding their fuel for several days now in anticipation of such a decision. Drawing double rations, reporting more vehicles than were actually on board, moonlight requisitioning—these and other tactics had been employed to build up a backlog of fuel and supplies. And yet, Leclerc was not so naive as to fail to recognize his absolute dependence on his American superiors for all the materials of war his division required. Even if he had enough fuel and supplies to reach Paris, what after that? While the city of Paris was extremely important, the whole of France must be liberated. Leclerc did not relish the thought of spending the rest of the war sitting idly in Paris because his division had been disowned by the Americans for being undependable and disloyal.

After a day spent wrestling with the pros and cons of all these arguments, by evening Leclerc reached a decision. He called in Maj. Jacques de Guillebon to give him his orders. He was to leave tonight in the direction of Paris with a small force of 17 light tanks, 10 armored cars, and 150 men. Officially, they were to reconnoiter the roads in preparation for a full division advance on the city. However, should other units (i.e., American) start to move on the city, de Guillebon's small force was to be with (or perhaps even ahead of) them to represent the first French military authority in the city. De Guillebon was authorized to take over as military governor of Paris.

It was the best compromise Leelerc could think of. He wished he could do more. In advising de Gaulle of his action later that evening, he cited matters of supply and the "rules of military subordination"[3] as reasons for taking only such limited action. Even so, he fully realized that de Guillebon's small task force was not so small as to escape detection. He braced himself for the expected reaction from Gerow and Hodges.

It was a hot and humid evening in Paris, and in the general's room at the Hotel Meurice the air was still. Von Choltitz was irritable and out of sorts. He was alone with his thoughts, and they brought little comfort to his troubled state of mind.

It had been two days now since he agreed with the Swedish consul and the leaders of the Paris underground to that strange cease-fire. He had to admit that the violence in the city had abated somewhat, but that was probably a result of the inability of the underground forces to sustain a significant level of activity rather than any agreement to keep their forces under control. There were still numerous instances of active resistance throughout the city, and his troops were becoming increasingly active in suppressing the violent outbreaks that did occur. The current situation represented a kind of precarious balance that could not continue. A major explosion was bound to occur at any moment. His effort to "keep the lid on" this uprising was doomed to failure.

However, the thoughts that gave von Choltitz the greatest discomfort this evening were not those of the perilous situation within the city. Rather they were thoughts of a more personal nature—thoughts that were particularly disconcerting to a general who had always prided himself on his sense of military discipline and loyalty to the service. How could he have allowed himself to drift into this state of clear and obvious insubordination? There was no doubt that he now found himself in such a position.

Four days before, his superior, von Kluge, had ordered him to start destroying the industries of Paris, and Jodl had reiterated the order since then. Yet, not one single factory had been destroyed. He had ignored orders from his new commander, Model, and done everything he could to avoid contact with him for fear of receiving some additional un-

wanted orders. He was particularly careful to make certain
that no one outside of Paris become aware of the truce he
had agreed to, knowing full well that the arrangement would
be immediately countermanded by any of his superiors who
heard about it.

Then there was that matter of the bridges. The experts sent
from Berlin to prepare the Paris bridges for demolition had
received absolutely no cooperation or support from von Choltitz. He had ignored their plans, refused to see them, and
generally made it very difficult for them to carry out their
orders. This in spite of several unequivocal orders that the
bridges be prepared for destruction, including one this very
afternoon from Jodl that "destruction of the Paris bridges be
prepared whatever the cost."[4] His actions (or inactions) on
the matter of the bridges represented a most damaging case
for insubordination or, perhaps, even treason.

How could years of strict adherence to military discipline
melt away in just two short weeks here in the City of Light?
Perhaps it could be explained in part by von Choltitz's growing conviction that his leader, the Führer, had gone mad.
Ever since his meeting with Hitler at the Wolf's Lair when
he had received his orders to come to Paris, he had been
haunted by the vision of the leader of the Third Reich raving
like a madman, his body shaking, as he railed against "his
enemies among the Generals"[5] and shouted about his conviction that he personally was destined to lead the German
people to their final victory. It had been a shocking
experience—one that seemed to blot out a lifetime of faithful
service to the fatherland. Von Choltitz's confidence in his
own sense of values had been badly shaken.

Combined with this erosion in his sense of loyalty and
discipline was the concern that his name would go down in
history as the destroyer of the city of Paris. He would certainly
earn that title if he were to carry out both the letter and the
spirit of his orders. It was hard to explain in his own mind
why the general who had been involved in so much destruction throughout the continent of Europe should now, all of a
sudden, be so concerned about the destruction of one more
city. But clearly, Paris was different. Was it the destruction
itself or merely the idea that he would be the one forever

associated with it that caused him such anguish? Whatever the reason, he did not want any part of it.

As the sleepless night wore on, there seemed no way out of his dilemma. Von Choltitz realized he could not go on much longer ignoring or disobeying orders, and yet he seemed unable to bring himself to the point of carrying them out. He could think of only one possibility that might conceivably resolve this conflict between insubordination on the one hand and inability to act on the other. If the Allies were to move quickly into the city with such overwhelming force as to make anything other than token resistance useless, then it would be impossible for him to carry out his orders, the city would be saved from destruction, and he could perhaps convince himself that he had performed his military duties to the best of his ability considering the circumstances.

But to simply open the gates of the city to the Allies was something his sense of military duty would not permit. German defense forces were in position west and south of the city, and they would have to resist any effort to enter Paris. He was well aware, however, that they were not in sufficient strength to successfully resist any such serious Allied effort. Perhaps if the major resistance took place outside the city, the destruction of Paris itself could be avoided, German forces could be saved for later defense of their homeland, and his own feeling of obligation to carry out his duties as commander of the city could be satisfied.

It was all so confusing. Being a corps commander on the Russian front or in Normandy had been much simpler. Perhaps the events of the next day or so would resolve some of his dilemmas, but there was certainly nothing to be cheerful about on this hot night in Paris.

The three Frenchmen paced up and down the airstrip outside of Omar Bradley's headquarters in Laval. They were awaiting Bradley's return this evening from a meeting with General Eisenhower.[1] They were waiting impatiently, as if their entire future depended on the answer Bradley would bring back with him. In fact, it did.

Of the three, Col. Albert Lebel was the host. He was the French liaison officer assigned to Bradley's Twelfth Army Group headquarters. His efforts through official channels to convince the Allies to abandon their established strategy to bypass Paris so far had fallen on deaf ears. His two guests were most welcome.

Leclerc had been at Bradley's CP since early morning. He had two reasons for being there. The small force he had started in the direction of Paris the day before had indeed been discovered, and, as he expected, the full wrath of General Gerow had descended upon him. Gerow, who had arrived at Bradley's headquarters during the day, threatened to take away every drop of gasoline from the 2nd Armored if Leclerc continued to refuse to obey orders.[2] Leclerc had no doubt that the threat was real. General Bradley seemed to be his best source of protection from the punishment to be meted out by the V Corps commander. The visit was also a continuation of Leclerc's campaign to receive authorization for the entire 2nd Armored to move on Paris. He had gotten nowhere with Gerow and Hodges. Perhaps Bradley could see things his way. It was worth a try, but so far he had spent the entire day in Laval and had not yet gotten the general's ear.

The third, and most unlikely, member of the trio was Maj. Roger Gallois. "A slight fellow in a grey suit with pompadour haircomb and Oxford touch to his English,"[3] Gallois was an officer in the FFI in Paris. His odyssey had been a harrowing one. He had left Paris two days before in a desperate effort to reach the Allied lines with a request for an arms and ammunition parachute drop to his FFI forces in the city. Once he reached the battle lines, he had simply walked unescorted through the German lines in full view of the troops, expecting at any moment to feel the burning sensation of a bullet between his shoulder blades. His bravado was successful, as he walked across untouched.

To the first American GI he saw, Gallois had stated his desire to see General Eisenhower with a message from Paris. The reaction was the predictable "so what?" His persistence paid off, however, and by last evening he was seated in a tent at Third Army headquarters being questioned by several staff officers.[4] By this point in time, Gallois had concluded that asking for a parachute drop was the wrong approach. He would go all the way and request an immediate Allied advance into the city. His request finally reached General Patton, only to be rebuffed with a comment about taking armies rather than cities.

Patton did agree to send Gallois on to Twelfth Army Group headquarters, and here his reception was more encouraging. After a sleepless night, he had been interviewed this morning by Brig. Gen. Edwin Sibert, Bradley's intelligence officer. Gallois's timing could not have been better. Sibert was leaving shortly with Bradley to confer with Eisenhower on the very subject of what to do about Paris.

Gallois appreciated the importance of making a convincing case. It was now or never, and he was not going to be hindered by strict adherence to the facts. He told Sibert that the FFI controlled most of the city and that the German defenses to the south and west of the city were weak. The Germans had agreed to an armistice because of the feebleness of their forces in the city and so that they could evacuate the city without having to fight their way out. The German commander, von Choltitz, was reported ready to surrender the city. On the other hand, the armistice was to expire the next day, the FFI were practically out of supplies and ammunition, and the current situation could change dramatically.[5] Gallois's message to Sibert was clear: the Allies could walk right in if they acted now. Later, who could tell?

This message went with Sibert and Bradley as they flew in their Piper Cub to SHAEF headquarters to meet with Eisenhower, who was already beginning to waver from his earlier resolve to avoid a fight for the city of Paris at all costs. Although he gave no indication at the time, his conversation several days before with de Gaulle had caused him to reconsider. A letter from de Gaulle the following day, delivered in person by the highly respected French General Juin, also had its effect. A letter from Eisenhower to Marshall written this very morning gave further indication of his change of heart: "If the enemy tries to hold Paris with any real strength, he would be a constant menace to our flank. If he largely concedes the place, it falls into our hands whether we like it or not."[6]

The Piper Cub landed at the Laval field at 7:00 P.M. Sibert yelled over the noise of the engines to Leclerc that the 2nd Armored would go to Paris. The decision had been made. The French general, who did not speak English, had to wait until Bradley approached and through an interpreter gave him his orders. The Allies would enter Paris led by Leclerc and his 2nd Armored Division. Leclerc left immediately in his own Piper Cub to put into motion the advance he had worked so diligently to bring about.[7]

Standing quietly to one side was Roger Gallois. Who could have believed two days ago, as he had set out on his highly improbable mission to obtain some supplies for his FFI forces, that he would be standing here now as one of the principal actors in a scene that was to alter the course of the Allied campaign and save his own city of Paris from the fate of so many other European cities caught in the destructive path of war? He shook his head in wonder.

For Courtney Hodges, the pace of events at First Army headquarters had picked up considerably during the past several days. With the rapid eastward movement of both the German and American forces, it had been necessary to move the army CP the previous afternoon twenty-five miles to the east from its previous location south of Mortain. The new CP was located on the grounds of the Chateau de Chantepie, about halfway on the road from Mortain to Alençon. A beautiful 200-year-old chateau, it had been used by the Germans as a hospital until their hasty exit several days before. The owners, Baron and Baroness Charles de Lauriston, welcomed Hodges with open arms. The baron had served during World War I as a French liaison officer to the Americans, and his displeasure at being required to house the Germans (even the wounded) was intense.[8]

Hodges's day in the new CP started early with a visit from his V Corps commander, Leonard Gerow. Gerow had just learned about his French subordinate Leclerc's dispatch of a task force toward Paris. He was furious and, not being able to reach Leclerc, wanted someone to whom he could vent his anger.

Hodges listened to Gerow but could spend little time with him as today's calendar was full. He had just heard that he would be visited later this morning by Under Secretary of War Robert Patterson accompanied by Lt. Gen. Brehon Somervell, chief of the United States Services of Supply. Such distinguished visitors merited careful attention, and a comprehensive review of the military situation required some advance preparation. Life was further complicated by the planned arrival of Lieutenant General Dempsey, British Second Army commander, expected shortly after noon.

The two VIPs from Washington left shortly after lunch to visit the headquarters of the 1st Infantry Division, just a few miles away, and Hodges and Dempsey were able to sit down to discuss their business. Since Bradley's meeting with Montgomery and Dempsey three days before about the so-called "second envelopment," it had been left to Hodges to work out the complications involved in sending his XIX and XV Corps across the front of the British Second Army in their effort to trap the Germans south and west of the Seine. Hodges and Dempsey had met on numerous occasions during the past month. They were, in many ways, similar personalities and had always managed to get along well together. Today was

no exception as they quickly came to an agreement on plans
and preliminary proposals for the movement of forces. Although the outcome of these movements was to produce
acrimony and recriminations between the British and Americans, the original planning was friendly and harmonious.

Dempsey had hardly left when General Bradley arrived,
unannounced. He was on his way back from Eisenhower's
headquarters to his own at Laval, and he had big news. The
decision had been made to enter Paris and to use Leclerc's
2nd Armored Division to lead the way. Hodges immediately
called V Corps headquarters for Gerow, only to discover that
he was at Twelfth Army Group headquarters looking for
Bradley. Gerow wasted no time in covering the distance to
First Army headquarters in thirty minutes, and the group
assembled in the war room, which had been established in
the ballroom of Baron de Lauriston's chateau. Maps were
spread out, orders written, routes of march decided on, and
very careful instructions developed for Leclerc's forces, who
were not known for strict adherence to orders. After Bradley
had left, the others worked well into the night putting the
finishing touches on the plans, which, until a few hours before, had been nothing but a gleam in the eye of General
Leclerc. General Hodges's day, which had started out with
recriminations about Leclerc's disobedience, ended by passing on to the French commander the very orders he had been
working so hard to obtain.

Wednesday, AUGUST 23

It was forty miles from Eisenhower's headquarters to Condé, where General Montgomery had established his forward command post. Ike had decided to drive over for his scheduled luncheon meeting with Montgomery so he would have some time to talk to Bedell Smith. He had asked his chief of staff to come over from England specifically for this meeting. He had the feeling that he was going to need support for the upcoming discussion with the peppery and often-difficult British general.

Compared to his decision the day before to order Allied forces into Paris, the issue Ike faced today was far more important, more difficult, and certainly more contentious. It had to do with the future course of the entire European campaign, including decisions on matters of command. Eisenhower had already notified both Bradley and Montgomery of his intention to assume active control of military operations (a responsibility heretofore temporarily assigned to Montgomery) as soon as he could become established in an improved headquarters location. His current situation in the apple orchard near Tournieres was not satisfactory. He had advised them that he expected this to occur at about the end of the month. He had no illusions that Montgomery would gracefully accept this diminution of his authority.

The other vital issue related to basic strategy. It had been

building up for weeks, but now that the Allies were across
the Seine, a decision had to be reached. The decision was to
be taken against a background of extreme optimism among
the Allied High Command. The SHAEF G-2 summary to be
issued later this morning would proclaim, "The August battles have done it and the enemy in the West has had it. Two
and a half months of bitter fighting have brought the end of
the war in Europe within sight, almost within reach."[1] The
mood was euphoric. It would have an important influence on
the discussions and decisions having to do with campaign
strategy.

On the one side of this discussion of strategic alternatives
was the approach generally favored by the Americans, which
foresaw the three major elements of Eisenhower's forces (the
British, the American First Army, and the American Third
Army) each driving in a three-pronged attack—the British
on the left, the First Army in the center, and the Third Army
on the right. At the other extreme was the Montgomery "single thrust" approach, which involved putting all the forces
under Montgomery and following the route through the Low
Countries into the Ruhr section of Germany and on to Berlin.

Eisenhower had heard a great deal about the "single
thrust" strategy in the past several days. Montgomery had
his persuasive chief of staff, Freddy de Guingand, camped
out at SHAEF headquarters in an effort to sell Eisenhower
and his staff on the logic and soundness of his proposal. It
was ironic that de Guingand was one of the few on Montgomery's staff who did not support the "single thrust" strategy. He was to say after the war, "This was the only major
issue over which I did not agree with my Chief. I have always
held the contrary view."[2] However, he repressed his own
views and, capitalizing on his personable nature and popularity within SHAEF, did a very respectable job of presenting
his chief's point of view. Montgomery's invitation to Eisenhower to visit his headquarters for lunch was a signal to Ike
that some accommodation of the conflicting views had to be
reached.

The meeting started off on a jarring note. Montgomery,
displaying the arrogance and irascibility for which he was
famous, demanded that Smith, whom he disliked, remain

outside. He did this in spite of the fact that Smith's opposite number, de Guingand, was to be present. Surprisingly, Ike agreed, although Smith was later brought into the meeting after the first hour of discussion. Montgomery's first point of attack was Eisenhower's decision to assume personal control of the battle. He told him that "he . . . should not descend into the land battle and become ground C.-in-C. The Supreme Commander must sit on a very lofty perch in order to be able to take a detached view of the whole intricate problem. . . ."[3] In spite of Montgomery's advice, there was little give-and-take during this part of the discussion. The answer was clear. Eisenhower would take over.

Montgomery then went on to present his own arguments for his "single thrust" theory. They were, he felt, compelling. The proposed route was the shortest way to the industrial heart of Germany. Any other proposal involved splitting the Allied forces and dispersing their strength—a cardinal sin in the art of warfare. This was also the quickest and most effective way to reach two vital objectives of the campaign—the V-2 launching sites along the coast and the port of Antwerp. Furthermore, since supply was starting to become a serious problem, it was necessary to concentrate the available supplies where they could be most effective.

Specifically, Montgomery suggested that, in addition to his Twenty-first Army Group forces, he be given the newly activated First Allied Airborne Army plus the U.S. First Army. He further advocated that all supplies for the U.S. Third Army be diverted to his forces and that Patton's army be held in place. It was to be a powerful "single thrust," utilizing the large majority of the men and supplies available, and with Montgomery clearly in command.

From his American subordinates, particularly Bradley and Patton (via Bradley) as well as senior members of his own staff, General Eisenhower had heard the counterarguments. The "single thrust" idea was a high risk strategy of putting all his eggs in one basket. The thrust would be particularly vulnerable on the flanks to counterattack from revitalized German forces. Also, to stop Patton would be foolish. His Third Army today was closer to the German border than any other force, and Montgomery's troops had not yet reached even the south bank of the Seine. It was not sound strategy to shift the bulk of the forces to the part of the attack that had to date made the least progress.

These were the arguments, pro and con. Now it was decision time. Being the great conciliator that he was, Eisenhower's answer would likely lie somewhere between the two extremes. He was impressed by the "high risk" argument; furthermore, he realized that he would open up serious political implications by putting large American forces under a British commander (this in spite of Montgomery's offer to turn the job over to Bradley if nationality was a problem—an offer of which Ike was highly skeptical). However, Eisenhower badly wanted Antwerp, in light of his growing problems of supply, and he accepted the urgent need to put a stop to the V-2 bombing attacks. He realized that the Twenty-first Army Group needed help to mount an effective drive on these objectives.

His decision was an attempt to find the most logical and effective middle ground that would be best suited to accomplish his military objectives and utilize his forces to best advantage, as well as to minimize the political fallout that was bound to occur whatever the decision. He would turn over the First Airborne Army to Montgomery's control. The British would be operating in terrain where airborne support would be the most effective, and the First Airborne Army, being recently reorganized and refitted following the Normandy landings, had not as yet been assigned to Bradley's command. Without giving Montgomery actual control of Hodges's First Army, he would assign to them the task of supporting the Twenty-first Army Group drive into the Low Countries and on to the Rhine River. This represented a northerly shift of direction for the nine divisions of Hodges's army, and a potent addition to Montgomery's forces. The bulk of the available supplies would go to this northern thrust of the armies. Patton's drive across northern France would not be shut off, but he would be required to operate on very limited rations of that precious commodity—gasoline.

As would be expected, Eisenhower's decision satisfied no one. Montgomery was to write two days later that "political and national considerations are influencing Eisenhower to take a course of action that is militarily unsound."[4] The

British chief of staff, Sir Alan Brooke, commented that "the plan is likely to add three to six months to the war."[5] But the American generals, Bradley and Patton, complained the loudest. When Patton went to visit Bradley the very day of the Eisenhower-Montgomery meeting, he found his superior in a stew. "He was quite worried, as he felt that Ike won't go against Monty and that the American Armies will have to turn north in whole or in part. . . . Bradley was madder than I have ever seen him and wondered aloud 'what the Supreme Commander amounts to. . . .' "[6] The impetuous Patton suggested that he, Bradley, and Hodges resign in protest, but Bradley quickly talked him out of that.

Bradley's anger was short lived, however. Even at the time, he had accepted the necessity to assign one of the three corps of the First Army to Montgomery to provide the support he needed. "Not long afterward . . . I was forced to concede that Eisenhower was probably right in the allotment of those two additional corps for I had underestimated the resistance that confronted Monty."[7] While still concerned about Montgomery's "extravagance in tonnage" (i.e., his demand for overwhelming superiority before initiating an advance), he could not really argue that Eisenhower should have materially altered his decision.

For Eisenhower himself, the case was clear. On the day following the meeting, he wrote to Marshall: "For a very considerable time, I was of the belief that we could carry out the operation to the northeast simultaneously with a thrust east, but later have concluded that due to the tremendous importance of the objectives in the northeast we must first concentrate on that movement."[8] The ultimate allocation of forces was his responsibility. Having heard the arguments and proposals, he had made his decision.

To war correspondent David Schoenbrun, it had sounded like a dream come true. Schoenbrun was assigned to the French forces under Gen. de Lattre de Tassigny, whose objective was the capture of the two important ports of Toulon and Marseilles. Having followed the American forces across the beaches on D + 1, de Lattre's troops had been moving steadily westward toward their objective. Then, two days ago, Schoenbrun had heard from a French officer that de Lattre's

troops had already entered Marseilles and were in the process
of mopping up the remaining enemy resistance. Having heard
nothing of this from official sources at headquarters, Schoenbrun smelled a scoop. To be the first representative of the
press on the scene at the liberation of France's second largest
city would indeed be a feather in his cap.[9]

He had quickly rounded up two fellow correspondents—
Homer Bigart of the *New York Herald Tribune* and Robert
Vermillion of the United Press—obtained a jeep with a driver,
and headed down the road from Aix-en-Provence to Marseilles, fifteen miles away. As they entered the city, the situation was not quite what they had expected. They couldn't
find any French troops, and the appearance of the local citizens clearly did not give the impression that the city was
being liberated. Then, when they spotted a German tank
coming around a corner, they became convinced that their
informant in Aix had been badly mistaken.

As the jeep carrying the three correspondents took off at
top speed to escape the German tank, they spotted a French
flag flying from the balcony of the city's prefecture. Once
within the gates, they found themselves in the midst of the
headquarters of the resistance forces, who were now attempting to take over the city. They were advised that, while a
few of de Lattre's troops were in the suburbs, none had as
yet penetrated the city itself.

Schoenbrun and his two companions had spent the next
two days as "guests" of the resistance as they fought off the
German forces still in control of the city. In fact, the Germans
would have had little difficulty taking control of the prefecture
at any time, but they were far more concerned about the
forces of de Lattre, which were forcing their way into the
city. The resistance leadership within the prefecture was confused, but their ideological leanings were not. Heavily re-
cruited from among the many dockworkers in the city, the
resistance was dominated by the Communists. During their
two-day stay in the prefecture, the correspondents heard no
mention of de Gaulle but did receive a number of briefings
about the "power of the people."

When the French troops had worked their way into the
center of Marseilles this morning, Schoenbrun and his compatriots were at last free to forego the hospitality of the re-

sistance and move about the city. The German resistance had not come to an end, however. Marseilles had been designated by Hitler as one of the fortress cities, which were to be defended to the last man. French General de Monsabert called on the German commander to surrender but to no avail. The Germans were firmly entrenched in Fort Saint-Nicholas, an old fort near the harbor, and their commander was intent on carrying out the orders of his Führer.

This loyalty to Hitler's fight-to-the-death order was to last for only four more days. French artillery was systematically destroying the walls of the fort—the only remaining protection for the German forces. On August 27, a messenger carrying a white flag would emerge from the fort, and the French general would accept the German surrender. Immediately, French and American engineers swarmed into the port and the work of reconstruction was begun. Two weeks later, the first ships entered the harbor and began unloading. The main purpose of DRAGOON was then fulfilled. The Allies had secured the use of a major port on the coast of France.

Thursday, AUGUST 24

When Patton had found it necessary to relieve Major General Cook as commander of the XII Corps because of his circulatory ailments, he replaced him with Maj. Gen. Manton C. Eddy, commander of the 9th Infantry Division. Eddy had brought the 9th to North Africa in the fall of 1942, almost two years ago, and had been its commander ever since. Active in the North African and Sicilian campaigns, the 9th had landed on Utah Beach on D + 4 and played a major part in the Cherbourg campaign, COBRA, and the fighting around Vire. Although Eddy was obviously an experienced leader and ready for corps command, Patton was concerned that he might be too conservative to suit his aggressive style of generalship. Patton wrote his wife: "He [Eddy] has been thinking a mile a day [was] good going. I told him to go fifty and he turned pale."[1]

Eddy took Patton's admonition to heart. The XII Corps occupied a position on the right flank of the Third Army movement across France, and on Eddy's first day in command, elements of his corps had moved from Orleans to Sens—a distance of more than seventy miles. The advance was so rapid that a party of German officers visiting the town of Sens's twelfth century cathedral as tourists were captured en masse. German resistance had been extremely light except at the town of Montargis, which had just been liberated earlier today by troops of the 35th Infantry Division.

In the van of Eddy's breathtaking advance was the 4th Armored Division of Maj. Gen. John Wood. Wood, who early in the month had chafed at being tied down in Brittany, was now moving in his favorite direction—to the east—at breakneck speed. By evening he was in sight of the upper reaches of the Seine at Troyes. While he knew he would find more opposition at Troyes than elsewhere along his route, he fully expected that the next day would see his 4th Armored troops across the Seine River.

Although enemy opposition had been very light, Eddy's advance was still an achievement of which he could be justly proud—from Orleans to the Seine River at Troyes—a distance of 120 miles in just three days. His armor and infantry had worked well together. The technique of sending the armor around the pockets of resistance, which would be cleared out later by the infantry, had been developed to a fine art.

To Eddy's left, equally spectacular advances were being achieved by Walton Walker's XX Corps. Leaving Chartres at the same time as the XII Corps left Orleans, and led by Major General Irwin's 5th Infantry Division, the advance covered forty miles the first day in the direction of Fontainebleau, sixty miles away. Irwin's troops had crossed the Seine the day before at Fontainebleau by small boat, canoe, and even by swimming across, and today his engineers had installed a treadway bridge. He had also dispatched other troops ten miles upstream to the town of Montereau. Word would be coming in this evening that they were about to cross the river against weak opposition.

Meanwhile, to the north, the 7th Armored was driving to Melun, also on the Seine, about ten miles downstream from Fontainebleau. Melun was to prove a tougher nut to crack because the river is wider there and its banks considerably steeper. The Germans had concentrated what little strength they had available in Melun in recognition of its defensive possibilities. They had managed to destroy the bridge yesterday before Major General Silvester could get any of his 7th Armored troops in position to attack.

Dissatisfied with the progress of the 7th, Walker had come

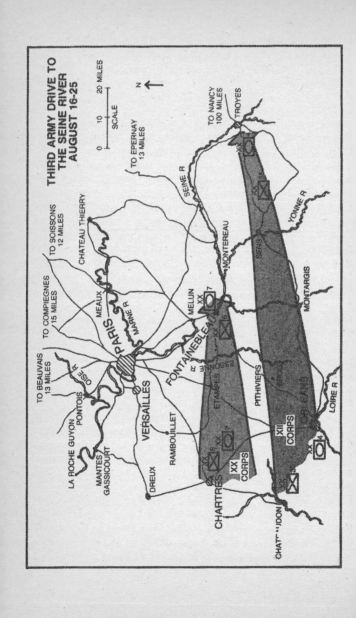

THIRD ARMY DRIVE TO
THE SEINE RIVER
AUGUST 16-25

SCALE

0   10   20 MILES

N

TO EPERNAY
13 MILES

TO NANCY
100 MILES

TROYES

SEINE R

YONNE R

TO SOISSONS
12 MILES

CHATEAU THIERRY

MONTEREAU

SEINE

MONTARGIS

TO COMPIEGNES
15 MILES

MEAUX

MARNE R

PARIS

OISE R

MELUN

FONTAINEBLEAU

ESSONNE R

PITHIVIERS

ORLEANS

LOIRE R

TO BEAUVAIS
13 MILES

PONTOIS R

VERSAILLES

ETAMPES

XII
CORPS

LA ROCHE GUYON

MANTES
GASSICOURT

RAMBOUILLET

XX
CORPS

DREUX

CHARTRES

CHAT"'JDON

to Melun yesterday and virtually taken over. He ordered an attack today over the wreckage of the bridge, which was not successful and which produced the only significant casualties since the advance began. However, while the attention of the enemy was focused on this attack at Melun, engineers quietly completed a treadway bridge a few miles further downstream, and 7th Armored troops began crossing at once. Walker was now in a position to outflank the Melun defenders and continue the advance.

By this evening, Patton's Third Army forces had managed to make three separate crossings of the upper Seine River over an arc of twenty miles. In addition, Wood's 4th Armored Division approaching Troyes was well to the east of any other Allied force—at a point almost a third of the distance from Paris to the German border. If they could sustain their present pace, they could be looking at the Rhine rather than the Seine in a matter of a week or two. It was an intoxicating thought but overlooked one very ominous fact: they were using gasoline at a rate faster than it could be supplied. Major General Eddy's XII Corps had calculated that they had used 200,000 to 300,000 gallons of gasoline to move fifty miles. A check of their supplies today indicated 31,000 gallons on hand.[2] And, the farther east they went, the more difficult the supply problem would become. If their supplies of fuel were further limited by decisions of the higher command, their days of whirlwind dashes across the French countryside would be at an end.

The prize had been so tempting. It had prompted Bradley five days before to obtain permission from Montgomery and Dempsey to cut across their front with two of his corps. The movement was called the "second envelopment." The intent was to trap the German forces that had escaped from the Falaise Gap before they could find some degree of safety across the Seine River. The XV Corps from Patton's army followed by the XIX Corps from the First Army were to drive down the south side of the Seine, closing off escape routes across the river or, at the very least, forcing the Germans to cross the river between Rouen and the sea, where the width of 1,000 feet or more and the tides would make the crossing much more difficult.

After the 79th Infantry had crossed the Seine four days before at Mantes, the 5th Armored Division (which constituted the remainder of the XV Corps) was to head for Louviers, twenty to twenty-four miles down the river. Speed was, of course, essential if the retreating enemy was to be trapped. A day, or two at the most, was thought to be sufficient for an armored division of the Third Army to cover that distance.

Major General Oliver, the division commander, was soon to find out otherwise. The country to be crossed was far different from the open terrain over which the XII and XX Corps sped on their eastward advance. It was heavily wooded, and a succession of ravines leading down to the winding river made rapid movement difficult. Steady fog and rain added to Oliver's problems.

However, the chief difference that General Oliver faced compared to his compatriots Eddy and Walker was a skillful and tenacious defense on the part of the enemy. In spite of the generally chaotic condition of the German retreat from the Falaise Pocket, several officers acting on their own initiative were able to assemble a polyglot force from three or four of the Panzer divisions in the area. Taking advantage of the terrain and the weather, they gave ground to the 5th Armored Division very grudgingly. It was only by today that Oliver had been able to reach his objective at Louviers: four days of tough fighting to cover twenty miles, during which time the escaping troops of the enemy were streaming across the river in anything that would float.

Pete Corlett's XIX Corps met fewer obstacles, but they had a greater distance to cover. A stronger force consisting of the 2nd Armored and the 28th and 30th Infantry Divisions, their objective was the town of Elbeuf, on the Seine just a few miles upstream from Rouen. Their advance had met little resistance until this morning, when they reached the southern outskirts of Elbeuf. Once more, the Germans, recognizing the danger of being denied the last few decent river crossings, had gathered remnants of the decimated Panzer divisions and organized a last-ditch defense of the town. The XIX Corps was too strong to be denied for long, but here again precious hours were gained for the escaping enemy troops and equipment.

According to arrangements previously made, the Ameri-

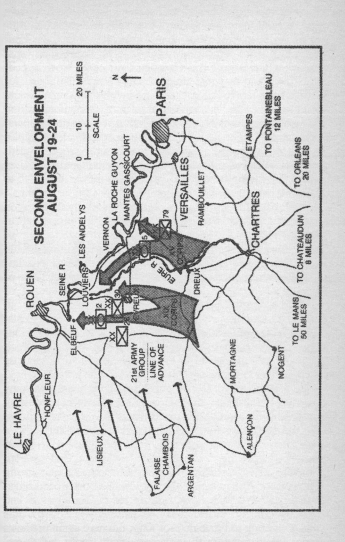

SECOND ENVELOPMENT
AUGUST 19-24

cans were now to reverse direction and withdraw back up the
river, turning over the territory that they had gained to the
advancing British and Canadian forces. Recriminations between the Allies were soon to follow. The Americans were
critical of the British and Canadians for being slow in occupying ground they had already taken. The British, in turn,
complained that the Americans were in their way and slowed
their progress. The beneficiaries of these recriminations were,
of course, the Germans. In spite of chaotic conditions (often
approaching panic) at all the crossing locations, a large number of German troops did manage to make it across the river.
In the period between August 20 and 24, the Germans were
also able to transport 25,000 vehicles to the far bank. The
"second encirclement" had to be considered of dubious
value, at best. In a maneuver where speed and aggressiveness
were essential, neither seemed to be present in sufficient
degree.

One final and potentially embarrassing question was raised
later by students of the battle—both German and American.
Why had the American command not exploited the early
crossing of the Seine by the 79th Division on August 20?
According to Lt. Gen. Hans Speidel, chief of staff to von
Kluge and Model, "A thrust westward along the north bank
of the Seine would have certainly enabled General Hodges
to cut off a great mass of *Army Group B* and destroy it. This
omission was the salvation of German forces."[3] If several
divisions (particularly the 5th Armored, which was nearby)
had followed the 79th Division across the river and then swept
down the north bank, there is certainly reason to speculate
that the results would have been much more fruitful. However, no one seems to have considered that possibility at the
time.

In the six days since Field Marshal Model had assumed
command of *Army Group B*, very little had gone according
to plan. He had been chased out of his headquarters at La
Roche Guyon on the first day he arrived. He had moved
almost 100 miles to the rear to Margival, near Soissons. Here
there was a specially constructed but hardly used command
post that Hitler had ordered built in 1940 to serve as his
headquarters from which to direct the invasion of the British

Isles.[4] It was to be the scene of a far different mode of battle during the days that it would be occupied by Model.

The field marshal had originally planned to establish a defensive line along the Seine with his *Seventh Army* on the right stretching to the Atlantic coast, the *Fifth Panzer Army* in the center with its left reaching Paris, and the *First Army* from southwestern France to the upper Seine. When he discovered that Hausser, commander of the *Seventh Army*, was wounded, he assigned the entire responsibility of defending the Seine from Paris to the sea to Sepp Dietrich, commander of the *Fifth Panzer Army*. It was apparent almost immediately that Dietrich's job would not be to defend the Seine, but rather to protect as many crossings as possible, enabling the maximum number of troops and vehicles to reach the north bank. All thought of establishing any defensive line along the northern bank would be dispelled within a couple of days when the full extent of the German losses became known.

Effective organization of the remnants of numerous Panzer divisions had succeeded in keeping the crossings open near Rouen. Troops and equipment were still crossing. Model realized, however, that the complete collapse of any effective defenses along the lower Seine was only hours or, at best, a day or two away. He had attempted to send as many as possible of his shattered divisions to the rear so that rehabilitation and reorganization could begin, but the pressures along the Seine had severely limited the number of divisions he could spare regardless of their weakened condition.

The question of where to establish the next line of defense had been under consideration at German army headquarters for some time, in spite of the Führer's admonitions to his generals against any consideration of retreat. A line along the Somme and Marne rivers had been selected for the building of field fortifications. This line of defense became known for the man in charge of its construction—the military governor of France, Gen. Karl Kitzinger.[5] However, Kitzinger was having very little success in finding the materials or the labor to erect even the beginnings of an effective system of defense. Model was hardly pleased when Jodl had called the day before to advise that construction of the Kitzinger

Line was being added to his list of responsibilities. By now, Model was thinking more about the Rhine than the Somme or the Marne as the proper location for defensive fortifications.

The question of the defense of Paris had been another thorn in Model's side. With all his other problems, he had little time to devote to the defense of the French capital. Model favored defensive lines to the north and east of the city, but as recently as two days ago, Hitler had made it abundantly clear that Paris was to be defended. "The defense of the Paris bridgehead is of decisive military and political importance. . . . Paris must not fall into the hands of the enemy except as a field of ruins."[6] That this order was not carried out by von Choltitz can be explained in part by the actions of Model's chief of staff, Speidel, who later admitted suggesting to von Choltitz that the order be ignored. Refusal to carry out a direct order from his Führer seems very much out of character for the loyal Model. Yet it is difficult to believe that he could have been completely unaware of the activities of his own chief of staff.

If Model was, in fact, unaware of Speidel's machinations, it was probably because his attention was drawn to his most difficult problem of all—the defense of the upper Seine. Here all his defensive plans had crumpled like a deck of cards. The *First Army*, which had been assigned to provide defense along the upper Seine, was completely unable to cope with the rapidly advancing American Third Army. They had provided token resistance at a few places like Chartres and Melun. However, the American tactics of rapid movement and bypassing pockets of resistance kept the defenders completely off balance and unable to deploy in time to counter the next threat. If the Americans could maintain their pace of the last several days, Model wondered how they could be stopped.

The only thing to do was to ask for help. He had been working feverishly all day to outline his needs, and it was almost midnight when the message to Jodl was put on the wire. It requested fifteen divisions to be placed in the path of the Third Army in the vicinity of Troyes and Dijon. If the Kitzinger Line was to be of any use at all, he needed thirty to thirty-five divisions to man the line. He also asked for twelve Panzer divisions to serve as a mobile reserve, as well as the various army and corps headquarters staff to provide the necessary command organization.[7]

Model undoubtedly knew that this request, just like the one he had made the week before, went completely beyond the resources that could be made available. He was aware, however, that OKW had been working since July to organize reserve and replacement troops in rear areas for effective use at the front. He certainly intended to get his share.

Major General Jacques Philippe Leclerc chose the Prefecture of Police as the site for the formal capitulation of the German forces in Paris. Just six days before, the Gaullist forces had sought to assert authority over the uprising in the city by establishing control over the building. This symbol of authority in the capital was a fitting place to officially recognize the liberation of Paris.

It was a moment of supreme satisfaction for Leclerc—the climax of a four-year struggle to return to the capital of his beloved France. As he prepared to receive the German general for this most historic occasion, one annoying complication did arise. Demanding not only entrance to the building but official participation in the ceremony as well was Colonel Rol, the powerful leader of the Communist underground forces. Leclerc was well aware that Rol was the person General de Gaulle feared most as a roadblock in his program to assume authority as the undisputed leader of France. Any official recognition of Rol's position or authority would not be looked upon favorably by de Gaulle. However, Rol was also commander of the Paris FFI, which by now had developed considerable strength and authority throughout the city. To exclude him would invite trouble at a critical time. Leclerc relented. Rol would not only be present at the ceremony but would be a cosignor of the document of capitulation along with Leclerc.[1]

Leclerc's desire for a peaceful, rapid, and trouble-free conclusion of hostilities was partly the result of the difficulties and frustrations he had faced in getting his 2nd Armored Division into the city. When Leclerc had dashed to his plane at Bradley's Laval airstrip the previous Tuesday with orders to enter the city, he, and everyone else, had expected an easy time of it. After all, the representative from the Paris underground, Roger Gallois, had told them that the routes to the city were only lightly defended and that the German commander was ready to surrender as soon as the Allies arrived. They had only twenty miles or so to cover. There should have been nothing to prevent a rapid conclusion of the operation.

At noon the following day, when he arrived in Rambouillet, fifteen miles from Paris, Leclerc found that the situation was quite different. Reports from his own reconnaissance units and from French civilians indicated that a solid line of defense was in place south and southwest of the city. In addition, his division was having problems getting under way and would not reach Rambouillet until that evening. Regrettably, any attack would have to be postponed until the following day.

Leclerc had received orders from his superior, General Gerow, to send his division through Versailles into the southwestern section of the city. As Leclerc studied the situation Wednesday evening, however, he decided to depart from Gerow's instructions. He would split his force, sending the smaller group along the designated route but swinging his major force around to enter the city directly from the south. He undoubtedly made this change on the basis of information he had received about the strength of the defending forces. In fact, as he was to find out the following day, the strongest defensive position that the Germans had established was on the very road Leclerc had selected—the one that entered the city from the south.

German defenders were not the general's only problem, however. As his forces headed toward the city, they were inundated by the joyful French citizens who rushed into the streets to greet them on their way. Climbing onto the tanks, showering flowers, kisses, and wine on the troops, they caused monumental traffic jams as well as a severe strain on the discipline of Leclerc's troops, many of whom were coming home to Paris after an absence of as much as four years.

When by yesterday evening his troops had still not entered the city itself, Leclerc realized something must be done. He decided to send a small force into the city through side roads and back streets in the hope that they might be able to move in fast and establish some French army presence in the heart of Paris before the day was over. At least part of his reason for this decision was that the Americans, frustrated by Leclerc's lack of progress, had decided to take action on their own. Earlier in the day, Bradley had authorized the 4th Infantry Division to move into the city. ''To hell with prestige,'' he told his chief of staff, ''tell the 4th to slam on in and take the liberation.''[2] The 4th was nearby, and Leclerc had little doubt that they would move rapidly. For the Americans to be the first soldiers to reach the Champs-Elysées was absolutely unthinkable.

Leclerc's small force under Captain Dronne did indeed make rapid progress. Crossing the Seine at Pont d'Austerlitz, they drove down the right bank and pulled up in front of the Hotel de Ville at midnight.

By morning, the logjam had seemed to melt away. Except for a few small pockets of heavy fighting within the city, the German resistance faded away. Leclerc's tanks raced for the center of the city and had the German headquarters at the Hotel Meurice surrounded by noon. The general headed for the Montparnasse railway station, where he planned to establish his headquarters, but then left immediately for the Prefecture of Police and his appointment with history.

Major General Leonard Gerow, commander of the V Corps, was not one of those generals who had never been exposed to the vagaries of political considerations or conflicting national interests. During 1941, he had served as chief of the War Plans Division of the War Department and was heavily involved in the prelude to the attack on Pearl Harbor as well as the subsequent misunderstandings, conflicts, and accusations that grew out of the effort to assess blame for this unprecedented national defeat. In fact, in less than a month, Gerow was to return to the United States to testify before the Army Pearl Harbor Board, one of the many investigative bodies that were established in the years following the attack. He was to have a rough time of it before the board.[3]

However, to him, at this point, even testimony before the board might have seemed preferable to dealing with the French. The past several days had been a nightmare of disobedience, deceit, and just plain incompetence. It had all started on the previous Tuesday, August 22, when Bradley and Eisenhower had decided to send the 2nd French Armored Division into Paris. Gerow had called Leclerc immediately with orders to get his division on the road that night. He told Leclerc that orders would be forthcoming the following morning and that he was to use the road through Versailles for his main force. The primary purpose of the call, however, was to get the French troops under way that night.

When Gerow heard the following evening that the 2nd Armored had covered only a few miles to Rambouillet in the twenty-four hours since he had talked to Leclerc, he was deeply concerned. He really hit the roof the next morning when he received a copy of Leclerc's orders to his troops. He had completely ignored Gerow's orders and selected an entirely different route of march. For an American division commander, this would be considered gross insubordination, worthy of dismissal, perhaps even court-martial.

The change of routes created difficulties beyond the mere question of obedience to orders. The U.S. 4th Infantry Division, which later that day would be given orders to "slam on in"[4] to Paris, had already been alerted to start a cautious move toward the city to protect the right flank of the French division. Leclerc's change of orders had sent his division on the roads previously assigned to the 4th. General Haislip could have reminded Gerow that this same thing had happened a little more than ten days before near Argentan. The French seemed to have a special knack for cutting across their neighboring division's lines of advance.

After warning the 4th Division commander, Ray Barton, Gerow climbed into his jeep and headed for Rambouillet to straighten out matters with Leclerc. By the time he arrived, Leclerc was gone. Gerow followed toward the front in an effort to find him, but the traffic was so heavy he had to give up the chase. By this time, his level of frustration with his French subordinate was at an all-time high.

After the 4th Division had been given its "slam on in" orders (the result of Gerow's request to Bradley because of the 2nd Armored's slow progress), Barton made adjustments to the east in his division's line of advance and put his 12th Infantry Regiment in the lead. They succeeded in reaching the Cathedral of Notre Dame at about the same time that Leclerc's forces were surrounding the Hotel Meurice. The 12th then pushed on into the northeastern section of the city.

Gerow, coming into the city with the American forces, established his headquarters at the Gare Montparnasse and proceeded to assume his authority as commander of all the regular troops in the city. He had been there but a short while when Barton arrived, irritation showing all over his face. Barton had heard that Leclerc was at the Prefecture of Police and had gone there to coordinate the activities of the two divisions. He found Leclerc at lunch. Leclerc came outside to meet Barton, acting quite disturbed at having his lunch interrupted, and suggested that Barton go to the Gare Montparnasse. Chagrined by Leclerc's superior attitude, Barton uttered a few unfriendly comments and left.[5]

Gerow was not so naive or narrow-minded to fail to recognize that this was the Frenchman's day of triumph. He also realized that allowances must be made for national pride and the long period of separation from his homeland. He understood the importance of the Americans adopting a low profile on this historic day for the French soldiers and the citizens of Paris. He knew all that, but the French general was certainly making it difficult to be forbearing and sympathetic.

Gerow did not allow himself to dwell on such thoughts. Paris may be liberated, but it remained a potentially dangerous place. Isolated pockets of German resistance still existed within the city, although French and American troops assisted by the FFI were busy clearing them out. Counterattack from German forces to the north and east of the city was not out of the realm of possibility. There was also the problem of control of the now wildly celebrating civilian population as well as the military personnel, many of whom had joined the festivities. Yes, Gerow had much serious work to attend to amidst the joy and holiday atmosphere that surrounded him. He had better get on with it.

The route down the Rue de Rivoli from the Hotel Meurice to the Prefecture of Police on the Ile de la Cité was a distance of only slightly more than a mile. The trip should normally take ten minutes or less. To von Choltitz, it seemed like an eternity. Spat upon, cursed, reviled in every imaginable way, the German general felt at times that he might very well be lynched or trampled to death on the spot. However, his captors, now turned protectors, had no thought of missing the chance of a lifetime—to deliver the former commander of occupied Paris to its liberator, General Leclerc.

As he walked through the door of the prefecture, von Choltitz was only slightly disheveled from his harrowing ride down the Rue de Rivoli. As a matter of fact, he felt that he looked much more presentable for the occasion in his dress uniform than did Leclerc in his khaki shirt open at the neck and his unpolished GI boots. Von Choltitz did not question the propriety of capitulating to the French general. He had no choice. He was also unaware that Leclerc's superior officer was installed in headquarters at the Gare Montparnasse, just a short distance away.

The surrender ceremony was brief. Leclerc's terms were much as expected—an order from von Choltitz to all German forces for an immediate cease-fire plus the availability of German officers to accompany the French and Americans to the various strong points to ensure enforcement of the order. After these matters were attended to, von Choltitz was taken, along with Leclerc in his command car, to the Gare Montparnasse.

As they drove through the city he had commanded for the past several weeks, von Choltitz had a few moments to reflect. In spite of the humiliation of surrender and the indignities in the streets that he had experienced during the past hour or two, he had reason to be pleased with the way things had worked out. He was now a prisoner of the Allies—the only condition that gave him any reasonable hope of remaining alive. His actions of the past few weeks would surely mean court-martial and death at the hands of the Nazis. On the other hand, he wanted to be absolutely certain that the Allies were aware he could have carried out Hitler's orders to destroy the bridges and public buildings of Paris if he had been of a mind to do so. He wanted his captors to understand that it was he who had saved the city from destruction and that he had even done so without the cooperation of the various French factions within the city, who frequently seemed more intent on destroying each other than on opposing their German captors. All in all, he felt that he had a good case to make, which would enhance his position with his captors.

Von Choltitz was still troubled by a gnawing sense of guilt—that he had been disloyal to his country or, perhaps more important, to his profession as a military officer. Yet, even here there were compensations. He was satisfied that his troops defending the southern and western outskirts of the city had acquitted themselves well. Given the fact that they were facing two Allied divisions, they had made entrance to the city both difficult and costly. In fact, Leclerc's division lost 71 killed, 225 wounded, and 21 missing as well as 35 tanks, 6 self-propelled guns, and 111 vehicles destroyed— heavy casualties for one day's fighting. Only the night before, when it was clear his troops were about to be overwhelmed, did von Choltitz order them to withdraw to the north and west. Militarily, he had done what he could with the means at hand to defend the city.

When the young French lieutenant had burst into his quarters at the Meurice this morning demanding surrender, he was ready. His period as commander of the city of Paris was over. It had been a difficult time for him, but it had ended about as well as could be expected.

The citizens of Paris were not the only ones to be liberated on this glorious Friday in late August. Lieutenants Alan Willis and Hank Gladys of the U.S. Army Air Corps had equal cause for celebration. It was their liberation day as well.[6]

Their B-17 bomber had been shot down over Germany in the first major raid on Berlin on March 6. Willis, the pilot, and Gladys, the bombardier, had been fortunate to escape the burning plane and parachute safely to the ground. Six of their crew members had not been so fortunate—one killed in the plane and five killed by fighter plane machine-gun fire on the way down.

After numerous harrowing experiences and narrow es-

capes, the two airmen made connections with an underground
escape organization, which had successfully led many airmen
to safety over the Pyrenees through Spain to Portugal. Willis
and Gladys were moved successfully through Belgium and
Holland into northern France during the spring and early
summer. Conditions within the French underground were far
from secure. The Normandy invasion had encouraged an increase in activity as well as a relaxation of security among
the various resistance units. The German counterintelligence
forces were ready and waiting. Resistance units were being
exposed and captured at an alarming rate, and hundreds of
underground leaders who had successfully avoided capture
throughout the war were being run to ground. The more
leaders captured, the more exposed all the rest became. This
was the most difficult period of the entire war for the French
resistance.

While the pilot escape plan normally avoided all large cities
and plotted its routes through the countryside, the situation
in the underground had become so dangerous by early August
that it was decided to send Willis and Gladys into Paris. Their
odds of meeting up with the advancing American troops were
as good there as anywhere else, and it was felt that the greater
risk of capture in a large city was worth taking to increase
their opportunity of finding their fellow countrymen.

A farm truck loaded with vegetables for the citizens of
Paris (or more likely for their German occupiers) left a farm
near Sedan in the middle of the August night. Underneath
the mounds of potatoes and onions were the two American
fliers on their way to a new safe house in the French capital.
They were dropped off at a row house in the middle of the
city and led quietly to a room on the third floor. This was to
be their home for the next ten days.

They were not ever let out of their room, but the Americans
could tell immediately that the floors beneath them were the
scene of considerable activity. It did not take them long to
find out why. Their room was on the third floor of a
brothel—a house patronized mainly by German officers. The
underground had always felt that places frequented by the
enemy usually made excellent hiding places. A brothel
seemed to offer an unusual degree of security.

Willis and Gladys spent most of their time as residents of

the house looking down into the streets from the one window
of their room. The ladies provided them with two meals a
day. They were also kept up-to-date on the progress of the
Allied forces—information that the ladies received from the
underground radio and from the more talkative of their regular
customers. The two men knew that their liberators were not
far away.

Then this afternoon, Al Willis saw it. A tan-colored jeep
with U.S. military insignia came rolling down the street.
Behind a mounted 30-caliber machine gun sat a captain and
a sergeant—both obviously Americans. Willis and Gladys
took the stairs three at a time, dashed into the street, and
leaped into the jeep. Willis tugged madly at the lining of his
shoe where he had hidden his dog tag all these months. He
wanted no doubt about his identity at this stage. They found
out that their rescuers were members of the 101st Cavalry,
part of a small group sent in with the 2nd French Armored
Division to show the American flag in Paris. Once identified,
Willis and Gladys were put in the back seat while the captain
and sergeant continued their task of rounding up (or shooting)
German stragglers. As the day ended, they were taken to the
Hotel Meurice, now emptied of its German occupants to make
room for, among others, two American fliers.

In the secrecy of their arrival and the haste of their departure, Willis and Gladys never found out in what section
of the city they had been housed for the past ten days. In the
joy of their liberation, they probably did not care. Their house
was on a block-long street called the Rue du Chat Qui Pesche.
The street dead-ended into the Quay Saint-Michel, which in
turn ran along the left bank of the Seine. Directly across the
river on the Île de la Cité was the Prefecture of Police. The
two airmen had been living less than two city blocks from
the historic building that had played such a vital part in the
final days of the German occupation of Paris.

Saturday, AUGUST 26

General Charles de Gaulle was a politician with few equals. His finely developed sense of power and politics told him emphatically that if he were to finally assume his rightful place as leader of France, he must act quickly and dramatically to establish himself as the clear, logical, and only choice for that position in the eyes of the French people.

He had carefully planned his return to Paris as he waited patiently in the Chateau de Rambouillet—that vast country estate frequented by the kings of France, Napoleon, and even the hated masters of the Vichy government. Then the previous afternoon, with word of the German capitulation, he had entered the capital and headed directly for the Gare Montparnasse to greet Leclerc. When he was shown a copy of the surrender agreement, he was furious. Not only did it include the name of the dangerous Colonel Rol as a signatory, but nowhere in the entire document was there any mention of the name of de Gaulle or the government he proposed to establish. However, Leclerc's contributions to the liberation of Paris were too great and the emotions of the moment too strong to permit animosity to develop with his general, whose status as a hero of France had by now been clearly established. After carefully explaining to Leclerc the importance of his mistake, de Gaulle warmly embraced his general and congratulated him for his achievements.

De Gaulle made several other visits that afternoon—to the War Ministry, the Prefecture of Police, and the Hotel de Ville. At each place, he met with various resistance leaders. As the afternoon drew to a close, he made a public appearance before the teeming crowds in the streets from the second-floor balcony of the Hotel de Ville.[1]

His activities of yesterday, however, were merely a prelude to the major event of today. The parade was to start at the Arc de Triomphe at 3:00 P.M. and proceed all the way to the Cathedral of Notre Dame. Preparations for the parade produced complications. Ordered by de Gaulle to provide security along the parade route, Leclerc had to advise General Gerow that he would be unable to pursue the German forces north of the city, as he had been ordered to do. Gerow was furious. A parade would not only interrupt ongoing military operations but would also dangerously expose the city to possible German counteractions. He sent a sharp note to Leclerc: "I understand you have been directed by General de Gaulle to parade your troops this afternoon. . . . You will disregard those orders and continue on the previous mission assigned you."[2]

Being caught in the middle was certainly not a new experience for Leclerc, but his primary loyalty at this point was clearly to de Gaulle. When apprised of the situation by Leclerc, de Gaulle was reported to have said to an American present, "I have given you Leclerc; surely I can have him back for a moment, can't I?"[3] The 2nd Armored Division troops would join the parade. Gerow could do little but acquiesce. He did tell General Barton to take his American troops off the streets and hold them in readiness for whatever trouble may occur.

De Gaulle arrived at the Arc de Triomphe promptly at 3:00 P.M. He was joined by Leclerc as well as the military leader of the Free French forces, General Koenig, other military figures, and most of the leaders of the French resistance. De Gaulle majestically led the march down the broad Champs-Elysées, his tall figure clearly standing out above all the rest to the hundreds of thousands who had gathered along the curb and in all the buildings bordering the route. Walking all the way to the Place de la Concorde, he boarded a car at the Rue de Rivoli for the last portion of his trip, following the same route down which the deposed commander of Paris, General von Choltitz, had been led the day before.

At the square in front of the cathedral, de Gaulle stepped out of his car, and immediately there came the sound of gunfire. The huge crowd panicked—people screamed, fell to the ground, ran for safety in all directions. Unperturbed, the general walked slowly toward the cathedral as if nothing had happened. Once he was inside the building, more sounds of gunfire were heard. Once again, de Gaulle seemed completely oblivious to the danger and confusion. He took his place in the front row of the cathedral as a Magnificat was sung (without benefit of the organ, since there was no electricity). Sporadic firing continued throughout the short service. At its conclusion, the general arose and slowly left the cathedral.

No one was ever able to determine the source of the gunfire. It may have been nothing more than the combination of the aura of celebration and nervous tension among the members of the resistance, many of whom had guns. The few remaining German troops in the vicinity were considered a possible source. Another suggestion was that the firing was planned by the Communists, who hoped to create a condition of hysteria and a state of emergency from which they could somehow or other benefit.

Whatever the cause, the events of the afternoon made Gerow's concern about the security of the city seem very real. Another potential danger was averted when, late in the afternoon, 2,600 German soldiers came out of their hiding places in the Bois de Boulogne with their hands up. They certainly had the means at their disposal to have shelled the parade, rather than choosing that time to surrender. Then, that night, the Germans launched a last-ditch air attack on the city, which destroyed 500 homes and caused 1,000 casualties.

To General de Gaulle, there was never any question of giving way to concerns about safety within the city. It is true that, in the interest of improving relations, he later apologized to the Americans for having insisted on the parade.[4] But the parade was at the very heart of his plan to establish his leadership. It fulfilled both of his conditions: it was immediate and dramatic. He recognized that he faced a difficult period of negotiations with many factions within the city, both friendly and otherwise, before he could assume the mantle of authority. In those negotiations, he would now be dealing from a position of strength. The overwhelming display of enthusiasm and support along the parade route from the Arc de Triomphe to the Cathedral of Notre Dame had guaranteed that.

When Omar Bradley moved his forward command post eastward to Chartres two days ago, it was done in order to keep him in closer touch with his rapidly moving forces, particularly Patton's Third Army, whose most advanced units had reached positions still 120 miles farther to the east. The move, however, had the effect of increasing Bradley's separation from another element of his forces—Troy Middleton's VIII Corps, still engaged in the effort to capture the port of Brest at the tip of the Brittany peninsula. Middleton's headquarters at Lesneven, 15 miles north of Brest, was now separated from Bradley's new CP by approximately 300 miles. This "forgotten battle" of the war was even more isolated from the military mainstream.

Travel to visit Middleton would have been very difficult for General Bradley had it not been for the delivery the day before of a new plane for the general's use. It was a C-47, the military equivalent of the famous DC-3. A gift from American Air Force General Tooey Spaatz, the offer grew out of a trip Bradley had made to London back in July while planning the COBRA operation. Unable to borrow a larger plane from the air force, the general had to make the trip in a small two-engine trainer called a C-78, known to airmen as a "double-breasted cub with a built-in headwind." He and his aide, Chester Hansen, could just barely squeeze in along with the maps and plans for COBRA. When he was met at the airfield near London by Air Force Lieutenant General Brereton and Air Marshal Coningham of the RAF, the point was made. The commander of the Twelfth Army Group needed something a little more substantial than a C-78. Bradley would be assigned a new C-47 as soon as one could be made available. Named the *Mary Q* for his wife, the plane and crew would remain with Bradley for the rest of the war. One of its most useful features was a self-contained system for unloading a jeep so that the general would not be dependent on someone else for ground transportation once the plane had landed.[5]

For the plane's maiden flight, Bradley headed for Brest and a visit to Middleton, whose VIII Corps troops were engaged in a major effort to breach the Brest defenses. Almost three weeks had gone by since Grow's 6th Armored Division had attempted unsuccessfully to enter the city after their whirlwind march across the Brittany peninsula. Since then, the 6th Armored had been sent elsewhere, and the job of capturing the port city had been taken over by three infantry divisions—the 8th, 2nd, and 29th. The 8th had been in Brittany since the breakthrough early in August. The 2nd and 29th had been pinched out of the line south of Vire with the reduction of the Falaise Pocket and had been sent to Brittany to augment Middleton's forces. The two divisions had arrived within the past week. They were badly needed.

When Major General Grow had confronted Brest three weeks before, he estimated that as many as 6,000 German troops could be in the city. Middleton later increased that estimate to 16,000. In fact, both missed the mark by a wide margin: the correct number was 30,000. To make matters worse, these were not just the expected ineffective garrison troops. The *2nd Parachute Division* represented the heart of the city's defenses—a field-quality division with young, well-trained troops. Their commander, Lt. Gen. Herman Ramcke, was in overall charge of the city defenses. Contrary to the reaction of many German generals, Ramcke was in full accord with the orders he had received from the Führer to defend the city to the last man. He fully intended to do so.

For Middleton, the battle for Brest had taken on all the aspects of siege warfare. This meant heavy use of artillery and an ample supply of artillery ammunition. For his major attack on the city, he had requested 20,000 tons of ammunition from Third Army headquarters, who in reply authorized only 5,000 tons, one quarter of his request. An inadequate supply of ammunition was one of the most serious problems faced by all the American forces in France. Failure to properly estimate usage rates during the original pre-invasion planning, as well as failure to acquire the expected port facilities (Brest being one of the most important), had left the entire Twelfth Army Group short of ammunition ever since the D-day landings. Ammunition rationing had become a way of life.

The VIII Corps faced additional problems in acquiring their share of the rationed supplies. The higher command had thought that Brest would fall easily. A major battle was not expected. The rapid advances of the other American forces during the month of August had tended to siphon off larger supplies of ammunition than expected, cutting into the VIII Corps' share. Transportation of supplies was another problem for the entire army, but most particularly for the VIII Corps. It was a long way from Brest to Omaha Beach, where most Allied supplies were still being landed. Efforts to relieve this problem by establishing landing ports along the north shore of the Brittany peninsula were only marginally effective.

Middleton's request was simply beyond the capacity of the army to deliver. However, several days before, he had been successful in convincing Bradley and Patton to increase his allotment from 5,000 to 8,000 tons. With this promise, he planned a major attack with all his forces to commence on August 25. He arranged for heavy air support, as well as support from the HMS *Warspite*, a British battleship equipped with 15-inch guns.

The attack the day before had made little progress. Part of the air attack had to be cancelled because of bad weather, but the bombardment was still extremely heavy. The coordination between the three attacking infantry divisions was all the general could ask for. Still, the German defenders held their ground.

Middleton had repeated the heavy air attacks last night and again this morning. However, when Bradley arrived at his CP late in the morning, he had little progress to report. Discouragement mounted when he learned that there were delays in delivering even his reduced allotment of ammunition, and that artillery support had to be cut back. The answer was clear. The German defenses were too strong for a successful frontal attack by three divisions with limited artillery support. The major attack was called off. Some other strategy would have to be devised if this strongly defended city was to be taken.

The trip back to Chartres was not a pleasant one for Bradley in spite of the relative luxury of travel in his new C-47. The failure of Middleton's attack raised some very difficult questions. Was any likely outcome of this battle going to be worth the substantial effort it was obviously going to require? If the major goal of the campaign was use of the port, was it not obvious that the port facilities would be so destroyed as to be useless for months after it was captured? Could not three divisions and all the supplies they required be put to better use with the rest of Patton's Third Army forces? Was he following a plan of action simply because it had been a major part of the original OVERLORD plan, which he was too inflexible to change?

Tough questions—all of them. But then Bradley thought about the character of the German defense—the *2nd Parachute Division* commanded by the able and fanatical Ramcke. Would Ramcke be content to sit still within his garrison defenses if Bradley removed all but a light screening force from the area? Not likely. The thought of the *2nd Parachute Division* loose in Brittany and raiding against his lines of supply was not a pleasant one. As he was later to write, "I went ahead with the costly siege at Brest . . . not because we wanted the port, but because Ramcke left us no other solution. If unable to contain Brest, we had no choice but to take it."[6]

This argument would be greeted with much skepticism by many of General Bradley's later critics. They more readily accepted another explanation recorded by Patton in his diary: "He said to me, with reference to the Brest operation, 'I would not say this to anyone but you, and have given different excuses to my staff and higher echelons, but we must take Brest in order to maintain the illusion of the fact that the U.S. Army cannot be beaten.' More emotion than I thought he had. I fully concur in this view. Anytime we put our hand to a job we must finish it."[7]

Whatever the reason, Brest was a painful thorn in the general's side. The battle to take the city was to continue for almost another month and cost him 10,000 casualties. The euphoria of victory on all other fronts was considerably dampened by this troublesome, expensive, and frustrating campaign.

* * *

Lucian Truscott was in a very bad mood when he walked into Dahlquist's CP near the Montélimar Gap. He left no room for doubt about how he felt. "John, I have come here with the full intention of relieving you from your command. You have reported to me that you held the high ground north of Montélimar, and you had blocked Highway 7 [the key road running along the east bank of the Rhone River]. You have not done so. You have failed to carry out my orders. You have just five minutes in which to convince me that you are not at fault."[8]

Actually, Truscott had been unhappy with the performance of the 36th Division commander ever since their meeting five days before to plan the division's crucial role in Truscott's plan of entrapment. It all started with Dahlquist's failure to concentrate on getting as much strength as possible to the Montélimar area as quickly as possible. He had been distracted by unfounded rumors of enemy advances. He had sent elements of the division as far as fifty miles north to Grenoble in response to reports of enemy movements in that area. Truscott had written Dahlquist a letter on August 22 reminding him of his primary responsibility—to get the maximum number of troops into the gap right away. He pointed out the vital importance of the ridge north of Montélimar and indicated that it would undoubtedly take his entire division to effectively block the gap.

By now the Germans were clearly moving north to escape the trap. They were moving in strength, with the *11th Panzer* in the vanguard. The early dissipation of the 36th Division's strength had been costly. The valuable ground north of Montélimar, which could have been readily taken several days before, was now fiercely contested by the Germans as they sought to protect their retreat up the Rhone valley.

In Dahlquist's reply to his superior's pointed questions, he indicated that he had received a report two days before that his troops had occupied the key ridge overlooking Highway 7. Unfortunately, he did not discover until a day later that they were on the wrong ridge. Subsequent efforts to take the correct one had met with strong resistance. Nevertheless, he did now have a toehold on the northern edge of the ridge and also had four battalions of artillery in position to cover the highway. While there had been problems, Dahlquist felt that he had done as well as could be expected. Truscott did not agree but decided under the circumstances to leave him in command. Better to make the best of the current situation than to lose crucial time in the confusion and delay of a change of command. But from now on, he would keep a close watch on Dahlquist and the activities of Montélimar. Perhaps some of the blame was his for giving too much leeway to a division commander in his first battle. If so, he did not intend to make that mistake again.

Sunday, AUGUST 27

For Chester Hansen, it had all the earmarks of a very exciting day. The group left Chartres at 7:45 A.M.—destination Paris. It was quite a convoy. In the van driving a jeep was Edwin Sibert. As Bradley's intelligence officer, he had already visited the city and was best able to lead the way. General Eisenhower's Cadillac followed with its British, French, and American flags flying in the breeze. Two armored cars were placed on either side of the general's car. Eisenhower, Bradley, Hansen, and Eisenhower's British aide, Jim Gault, were all in the Cadillac, along with Ike's driver, Kay Summersby.

The whole idea of the Paris trip had come up late the previous afternoon. Eisenhower had arrived at the Chartres headquarters before Bradley had returned from Brest. While waiting for Bradley to return, Ike learned that General de Gaulle had established headquarters in Paris, and this together with his natural curiosity to see the French capital prompted the idea of the trip.[1] He commented to a member of Bradley's staff, "I'll ask Brad. He thinks straight on things like that and he'll know what to do."[2]

When the idea of a trip was suggested to Bradley on his return, he was something less than enthusiastic. However, when Ike pointed out that it would be Sunday and they could probably sneak into the city "without any fuss,"[3] Bradley had agreed. Protocol demanded that Montgomery also be included, and an invitation was sent off by wire. His negative reply came in at 3:30 in the morning in a secret code that only Hansen could decipher. Still, lack of sleep did little to dampen the enthusiasm of Bradley's aide as the group set off for their day in Paris.

As the entourage approached the city, Hansen's eye was naturally attracted to women along the way. ''The men looked thin and dowdy by comparison. A freshness in the women that seemed to shout Paris. Certainly they were chic with beautiful complexions and many of them with blonde hair, well turned legs, gracefully fashioned bodies, wide warm and disarming smiles as they waved prettily.''[4] Bicycles were everywhere—many of them heading for the countryside in an effort to find food. A truck passed loaded with armed FFI men, carrying food labeled for Paris. Roadblocks were still in evidence at the intersections, along with many German 88s not yet removed from their positions pointing down the roads.

Just inside the city near the Porte d'Orleans, Generals Gerow and Leclerc joined the group. The first stop on their itinerary was de Gaulle's headquarters at the Prefecture of Police. As they ascended the stairway leading from the courtyard to de Gaulle's office, they passed between lines of the men of the Garde Republicaine, standing stiffly at attention in their Napoleonic tunics and black patent leather hats with large red plumes. At the top of the stairs, they were met by an aide and ushered into the general's office. As Eisenhower and Bradley entered, they detected the faint glimmer of a smile of welcome on the usually dour face of the general. The welcome was brief, and de Gaulle quickly got down to business.[5] He pressed the two American generals for food and supplies for the citizens of Paris, as well as uniforms and equipment for his Free French forces. He pointed out that it was extremely important to quickly establish order in the city, and that his Gaullist forces be recognized officially as the accepted source of power and authority. He also requested the temporary loan of two American divisions as a show of force to demonstrate to the people of Paris that their city was now secure from any German retaliation. The Americans had no such divisions to spare, but Eisenhower and Bradley did agree to parade one division through Paris on its way to the front lines. Bradley indicated that he could arrange to do this within a day or two.

After leaving de Gaulle, the two generals were joined by General Koenig, who had just been appointed military governor of Paris. After a brief visit to the tomb of Napoleon, the group crossed the Seine to the Place de la Concorde and then down the Champs-Elysées to the Arc de Triomphe. Here the two American generals stepped out of their cars for a picture-taking session. Hansen described the scene: "Someone asked who they were. The report spread through the crowd and soon the crowd was upon them. Ike was blocked from the door of his car by a cheering clawing mob, Brad was completely cut off from the front. Brad climbed into his jeep, stretching his long frame quickly into it for a getaway. As he attempted to, a woman leaned across the back of the jeep, put her arms around the general and kissed him. Brad reached for his hat, his face came away from her embrace, reddened and smarting with embarrassment as he laughed loudly. Ike was similar[ly] snatched by a man who kissed him on the cheek. As they finally fought free from the throng and left the crowded Place de l'Etoile, Chester Hansen kidded Bradley about his experience. With a laugh, the General responded, 'Well, I did better than Ike; he had a man kiss him.' "[6]

It was by now early afternoon, and word had spread about the presence of American dignitaries within the city. Large crowds lined the streets as the cavalcade headed out of Paris. Dropping off Gerow and Koenig at the edge of the city, the group returned to Chartres and the more somber business of running a war. For Chester Hansen, it had been a wonderful interlude—an exciting experience—and indeed everyone seemed to feel a certain sense of exuberance as a result of the trip. Hansen commented that "he [Bradley] was likewise in good spirits and Paris seems to have the faculty of making people feel that way most of the time."[7]

As Courtney Hodges flew back to his CP from a visit to the VII Corps near Melun, he was feeling better about his situation. The past few days had been full of confusion and uncertainty, but now things were beginning to straighten out. His First Army mission had been clearly established following the discussions several days before on overall strategy between Eisenhower and Montgomery. The First was to support the right wing of Montgomery's forces in a move to the northeast into Belgium and toward the Ruhr valley. Their starting point for this movement was the Seine River both above and below Paris. He would have three corps to carry out the advance—VII under Joe Collins on the right, V under Gerow in the center, and XIX under Pete Corlett on the left. The XV Corps, which had been temporarily under his command, would be returned to the Third Army.

Understanding his mission was one thing. Getting his forces properly aligned to carry it out was another, and this had presented some problems for Hodges over the past few days. The least of his problems was that represented by the VII Corps. Involved in the cleanup at the Falaise Pocket, the VII Corps had been the last to head for the Seine. Their movement was slowed somewhat by their route, which took them eastward to the south of Paris, across the roads used by the 2nd French Armored on their way into the city. Naturally, Leclerc's forces had priority.[8]

Nevertheless, Collins's forward elements had reached the Seine at Melun two days before, replacing the XX Corps's 7th Armored Division, which had just taken the city. In spite of Collins's complaints about the poor quality of the Third Army bridges, his troops began crossing the river yesterday. By today, his 3rd Armored Division was approaching the town of Meaux, twenty miles to the northeast. His two infantry divisions, the 1st and the 9th, were across the river and following closely behind. With Collins's proven penchant for aggressiveness, Hodges felt no qualms about the condition on his right flank.

The center corps was another matter. Here Hodges was suffering from political rather than military complications. At the moment, the V Corps consisted of Leclerc's armored division and the 4th Infantry Division of Ray Barton. Both had been diverted from previous assignments by the decision of the higher command to enter Paris. Hodges had no hope of getting the French division freed for active military operations for some time. However, he did expect the 4th Infantry to begin clearing the city in the next day or two.

He was equally concerned that his V Corps commander

was being swallowed up by the political complexities within
the French capital. He was well aware that the past few days
had been extremely frustrating for Gerow. Not knowing who
was boss, having his orders ignored or countermanded, being
treated as the forgotten man in the city where, by all rights,
he was the military commander—these were trying experiences to say the least. Hodges had done his best to support
Gerow, but the situation had passed well beyond his control.
Then, to top it off, Hodges knew that he was soon to lose
his V Corps commander, at least temporarily, to the Pearl
Harbor investigation in Washington, D.C. It was difficult for
Hodges to feel confident about his situation in the center.

On the left, Hodges's complications had been predomi-
nantly military in nature. His first task had been to successfully withdraw the three divisions of Corlett's XIX Corps
across the front of the advancing British Second Army as
agreed upon some time ago. He had held daily meetings for
the last several days with Lieutenant General Dempsey, and
he was expecting Dempsey at his CP for a final meeting later
this afternoon. In spite of all the concerns Bradley had expressed about the difficulty of this sort of movement (and in
spite of later recriminations on both sides about interference,
tardiness, et cetera), Hodges was pleased about what he and
Dempsey had accomplished. They had developed a system
of alternate use of important crossroads, giving each side a
two-hour interval of use. It had worked well. True, Corlett
had issued a few complaints about British interference, but,
in Hodges's view, Corlett tended to be a chronic complainer.
The fact was that, at this moment, only a few support troops
remained to be withdrawn from the British front. They should
be cleared today, and Dempsey would be free to cross the
Seine and launch his advance to the north and northeast.

With the impending departure of the XV Corps to the Third
Army, Hodges still had to sort out the corps command responsibilities, but things were beginning to fall into place.
There were no plans to shift any divisions to the Third Army
along with the XV Corps headquarters. One of Hodges's first
actions as the XIX Corps withdrawal progressed was to order
the 30th Infantry Division across the Seine at Mantes to join
the 79th Division. This had been accomplished today, thus
ending the 79th's lonely one-week vigil on the north bank of

the river. Hodges had already ordered the 2nd Armored Division to cross the following day. As soon as the XV Corps had cleared the area, the XIX Corps could assume command of these three divisions and commence their drive to the northeast on the right flank of Dempsey's Second Army.

This left Hodges with two divisions (the 28th Infantry and the 5th Armored), who were obvious candidates to join the 4th Infantry to make up a newly constituted V Corps. It was beginning to look as if the problem of complicated withdrawals, political entanglements, and jumbled-up corps organizations was coming to an end. Hodges could now turn his full attention to the advance to the German border. The terrain north of Paris was favorable to rapid advances, and significant resistance from the enemy did not seem likely. Perhaps, Hodges thought, it was the First Army's turn to grab a few headlines. It certainly was about time.

Monday, AUGUST 28

If there was a likely candidate to grab some headlines for Hodges's First Army, it was the 3rd Armored Division (better known as the Spearhead Division) and its new commander, Maj. Gen. Maurice Rose. His superior, VII Corps commander Joe Collins, thought that Rose had built the 3rd Armored "into a marvelous thing . . . built up morale, taught the division how to . . . fight."[1]

Son of a rabbi, Rose had joined the army as a private in 1916, received a field commission the following year, and gone to France with the 89th Division. Wounded at Saint-Mihiel, he had returned to active duty in time to serve during the entire Meuse-Argonne offensive. Between the wars, his service in the cavalry led him into the tank corps during its years of development in the 1930s. He had served in North Africa and Italy with the 1st Armored Division. He was transferred to the 2nd Armored in November 1943 as commander of its Combat Command A and came ashore in Normandy on D + 1 with the division. He sealed his reputation as an outstanding commander in the three days following the breakout at Saint-Lô. His Combat Command A, operating independently, broke out on the left flank of the American forces and drove all the way to the town of Percy, fifteen miles south of Saint-Lô, wreaking havoc in the enemy's rear and contributing significantly to the collapse of the German defenses.

At about this same time, Collins was becoming disenchanted with his 3rd Armored Division commander, Maj. Gen. Leroy Watson.[2] He was critical of Watson for remaining in his headquarters when his presence was needed to make crucial decisions at the front. He asked Bradley for a replacement—a difficult request for Bradley as Watson was a West Point classmate in whom he had a great deal of confidence. Bradley stated, ''This was one decision I did not believe was correct, but because Watson was under Joe's command, I had to back him up. We gave the division to Maurice Rose.''[3]

Collins no longer had to worry about his 3rd Armored commander being at the front line. Rose's normal procedure was to direct the division from a jeep at or near the head of his forward column. This was his style of leadership and, while effective, it was also to prove very costly. The following spring, Rose would be killed by German gunfire when his jeep wandered beyond the forward position of his 3rd Armored forces during the encirclement of the German army in the Ruhr valley.

The 3rd Armored Division under its new commander participated in the closing battles at the Falaise Pocket. They then moved east to the Seine to join the drive for the German border, crossing the river on the night of August 25. The division was held up for several hours during the following morning by enemy resistance, but, by noon, they broke out. They managed to cover the thirty miles to the Marne River during the next day, crossing the river on bridges that were still intact at the small crossroad village of La Fiere sous Jouarre, and moving on to capture the town of Meaux.

While not on the division's direct line of advance, Château-Thierry, of World War I fame, was just a few miles to the east, and General Collins asked Rose to send a small detachment to liberate the town. Apparently, the same idea had occurred to Walton Walker's XX Corps of Patton's army, and a detachment from the 7th Armored Division showed up at about the same time—a situation that would naturally lead to an interminable and unsolvable argument as to who liberated Château-Thierry. On noticing the presence of 7th Armored troops in the town, Capt. Theodore Black of the 3rd Armored detachment dashed to the public square and located the mayor, who was more than happy to give Black a signed statement that read ''2nd taking of Château-Thierry by the Americans: all our gratitude.'' After a trading session with the local resistance leader in which Black acquired a German Luger pistol, he ''smiled benignly on the furious staff officer of Gen. Patton's out-maneuvered XX Corps and returned to the 'Spearhead' Division very well pleased.''[4]

Having crossed the Marne yesterday, the division spent today covering the forty to fifty miles to the next river barrier, the Aisne, and the cathedral city of Soissons. German resistance, at least for the moment, had vanished. ''The countryside was littered with all types of equipment, cosmetics, clothing, and wine bottles abandoned by the loot-laden German soldiers in their panic.''[5] By afternoon, the Aisne River was reached at Soissons and Pont D'Arcy. While the main highway bridge at Soissons had been destroyed, other bridges were not. Several were thought to have been damaged, and Maurice Rose was the first to cross one of them to demonstrate that it was in usable condition. By evening, most of the division was across the river. The 3rd Armored had covered seventy to eighty miles and crossed two major rivers in just a little more than two days.

The rapidity of their advance caught the Germans completely by surprise. Sergeant Hollis Butler of the 486th Armored Antiaircraft Battalion was entering the small town of Braine, a few miles east of Soissons, when he spotted a German troop train headed into the town.[6] Opening fire on the train with their AA guns, Butler's group succeeded in blowing up the boiler in the engine. With that, SS Panzer troops poured out of the coaches and headed for a tank on one of the flatcars. Butler's guns were ineffective against the tank, but, in spite of that, the Germans soon surrendered. The train consisted of twenty-one flatcars, nine passenger coaches, the baggage and equipment of a German Panzer company, and a staff car and tank. Seventy SS Panzer troopers were taken prisoner.

The Germans had no idea that American troops were in the vicinity, nor were they able to sound the alarm. A few hours later, the 32nd Armored Regiment captured another train pulling into Braine. This time, the booty consisted of, among other things, four Mark VI Tiger tanks—the Germans' latest and best armored vehicle. That night in Soissons, still another freight train was captured by other elements of the 3rd Armored.

Catching the enemy by surprise was a key part of Rose's strategy, and this could be accomplished only by rapid movement and constant pressure. These past two or three days had demonstrated how successful that strategy could be, and also showed what an incredible strain it placed on the men of the Spearhead Division. As chronicled by the division's historian: "The nightmare drive through France and Belgium seemed like the beginning of the end. Their days merged into one long stream of fatigue and weariness in the endless pursuit. They followed the white road all day long with their eyes streaming from sun and wind and dust. At night they drove in total blackout, often with no better guide than ordinary road maps of the give-away type—into territory where the only certainty was the dubious knowledge that the enemy might, or might not, be at any given point. The strange realization of this was only overcome by accumulated, gnawing fatigue, and the sureness that Jerry was on the run."[7]

Few, if any, of the Spearhead Division's soldiers would question that it was all worthwhile if Jerry was truly "on the run." They had seen plenty of evidence during the past several days that such was the case. The troops had to admit that, in spite of the constant pressure their new commanding general put them under, he had an air about him that inspired confidence. They would not have argued with Collins's assessment. The Spearhead Division was being rapidly developed into a "marvelous thing."

For Omar Bradley, the previous day's excursion to Paris had been a pleasant diversion from his normal round of problems to be solved and decisions to be made. Today promised to be much less enjoyable. The job ahead of him was going to be difficult and unpleasant. It was something that he strongly regretted having to do. He was going to put the shackles on George Patton.

The drive took about an hour, and it was 10:30 A.M. when

he arrived at Patton's CP, deep in the woods near the small town of Brou, just south of Pithiviers. He had brought his chief of staff, Lev Allen, with him. He had the feeling he would need his support during the discussions with his Third Army commander.

Bradley started out by explaining to Patton the strategic decisions that had been reached by Eisenhower following his discussion with Montgomery several days before.[8] Primary Allied support would be given to Montgomery's forces in their drive toward the Low Countries and the Ruhr Valley. Hodges's First Army was to support Montgomery's right flank and was to receive sufficient support to carry out that mission. While Eisenhower had not agreed with Montgomery's proposal to cut off all support to the eastward thrust of the Third Army, his decision had clearly left Patton's forces at the bottom of the priority list.

The problem had been intensified with the liberation of Paris. Bradley had been ordered to provide the city with 3,000 tons of supplies a day. These supplies would obviously come from the allotment that would otherwise have gone to the Third Army. Patton's allocation of supplies was going to be extremely tight—certainly too tight to permit the continued use of fuel at the rate of the past several days. Bradley emphasized his point by requiring that the Third Army infantry move by marching rather than by riding on trucks—a change that would surely slow down the rate of advance.

Patton listened with anger and growing impatience. He pointed out that, at this moment, his 7th Armored Division was crossing the Marne River on its way to Rheims, and the 4th Armored was approaching the Marne near Châlons. Once on the Marne, they had only fifty miles to go to the Meuse River, the last significant natural barrier before the Siegfried Line, the German border, and the Rhine Valley. The Siegfried Line was a particularly important target. Patton felt certain that it was only lightly manned at the present time, a condition that could not be expected to last very long. At the rate his forces had been moving during the past week, these targets were only days away.

In spite of Patton's strong penchant to exaggerate, Bradley knew full well that most of what he said could not be questioned. The Third Army had covered almost 200 miles in the past week from their starting points near Chartres and Orleans. Their movements had been so rapid that it had been literally impossible for the enemy to organize any effective resistance. This situation had not changed. Light, scattered resistance was all that Patton's troops were encountering as they sped across the French countryside. Only one thing could stop Patton's forces now —lack of fuel. Unfortunately, that was exactly the situation they faced.

Bradley did authorize Patton to continue his advance toward the Meuse. He was unable, however, to promise anything other than a shrinking supply of fuel. Patton would have to do the best he could with what he had.

After Bradley's departure, Patton could do little but lick his wounds. "The British have put it over again," he wrote in his diary. "We get no gas because, to suit Monty, the 1st Army must get most of it, and we are also feeding the Parisians."[9] He felt that his achievements should have earned him more generous support. "I had to beg like a beggar for permission to keep on to the line of the Meuse. What a life."[10]

His wounded ego did receive some therapy later on that evening. "Today was the first day that I have received letters and clippings from home which appeared subsequent to the announcement of my commanding the 3rd Army, and I spent a very pleasant evening reading them."[11] The future might appear bleak at the moment, but this public recognition of past accomplishments helped to ease the pain.

Tuesday, AUGUST 29

The name on the masthead of the paper was *The Invader*. Directly underneath were printed the words "Special Paris Edition." It was the newspaper of the 28th Infantry Division—the National Guard Division of the Keystone State of Pennsylvania—and the lead article had a special significance for the troops of the Keystone Division.

> The trample of soldier feet echoed in Paris yesterday for the first time since the victory parade of 1918—and it was the trample of the feet of the sturdy fighting men of our own Division.
>
> History was made in Paris this bleak rainy Tuesday—the 29th of August 1944—for with the entry of our Division the French capital, symbol of French liberty and center of European civilization, really became free once more.
>
> For us—the fortunate American troops selected to take this initial pilgrimage into Paris—it was a day that will live forever in our memories.
>
> In the reviewing stand rigidly at attention in tribute to our boys were General de Gaulle, leader of the French government, Lieutenant General Omar Bradley, commander of American ground forces, Lieutenant General George S. Patton, 3rd Army Commander, and Brigadier

General Norman D. Cota, our Divisional Commander.

Tall, thin General de Gaulle, wearing the light tan uniform of the French Army, acknowledged the salute of every passing unit, occasionally waved at the hysterically happy Parisians.

With all the festive spirit however, the war was not entirely forgotten. While bands played lively martial tunes while the crowds cheered and men marched, tanks parked by grim-looking gun crews occupied strategic roadways and ack-ack crews were at their stations.

And standing solemnly, yet majestically over the scene like a sentinel was the Eiffel Tower seeming, as it were, high in the rainy sky to symbolize the reinstated freedom of France.

Overhead as this procession marched droned Piper Cub observation planes guarding against a possible air attack by the Luftwaffe.

It was truly a great day—

Just four years two months and 15 days previous the Germans blitzing through the Low Countries and bursting through the Maginot Line marched in triumph down the same route our boys marched yesterday.

That route was past the 107-year old Arc de Triomphe down broad tree-lined Champs Elysees branching off at the towering memorial to Louis XIV at the Place de la Concorde.

It was virtually impossible to estimate the number of Parisians who went wild with joy and enthusiasm at the entry of our troops but at a rough guess the crowd numbered at least half a million people.

Marching battalions abreast, with bayonets fixed and slung arms, the procession of infantry made an impressive sight as it swung down the thronged thoroughfare.

For the French it was a holiday and they made the most of it. For us it was a tremendous honor and privilege and we made the most of it also.

The Division band once more playing the Division marching song, saluted the marching men, paid tribute in song to the armed might of the American soldiers on parade.[1]

The 28th Division reporter should perhaps be credited more for his enthusiasm than for his accuracy. The 2nd French Armored Division as well as the 4th U.S. Infantry would undoubtedly take umbrage at his statement about soldiers' feet echoing for the first time since 1918. A more serious mistake was his identification of the people on the reviewing stand. Patton was not there, and indeed had no reason to be, as the 28th Infantry was part of the First rather than the Third Army, and the Third Army was in no way involved in the liberation of Paris. However, Hodges and Gerow were on hand along with de Gaulle, Bradley, Leclerc, and the Division's own Norman Cota.

For the 28th, it was indeed a proud day, although it is doubtful that the degree of enthusiasm displayed by the reporter was equally shared by the soldiers in the ranks. The division was in a period of transition from the XIX Corps and the campaign along the lower Seine to the V Corps in their drive north from Paris. By midafternoon of the day before, they had moved thirty miles to Versailles. Expecting to stop there for the night, they were notified at 3:00 P.M. that they were to parade through Paris the following day. The 28th Division had been selected by Bradley to provide the show of force de Gaulle had requested two days before when Eisenhower and he had visited Paris. The division was to proceed to the Bois de Boulogne that night, where it was to assemble for the parade—hardly a pleasant prospect on a dark and rainy night.

Orders for the parade were issued to the troops early this morning. Among the instructions were the following:

a. Vehicular mounted weapons will be manned.
b. There will be no riding by miscellaneous personnel on the loads in the vehicles.
c. All vehicles uncovered—windshields down.
j. Dismounted elements will double time for 300 yards immediately after passing reviewing stands.
k. All personnel will be impressed with the honor conferred on the division and with the importance of putting on the parade in the exceptional 28th Division manner.[2]

After following the parade route, the division kept right on marching until they reached the Paris suburb of Saint-Denis. Here they stopped for reassembly, preparatory to moving out the following morning to join the 4th Division, already moving northward toward Senlis and Compiègne. To remind them that life was more than a parade, the Germans north of the city greeted their arrival in Saint-Denis with a short artillery barrage.

While the parade was no picnic, it was still an enjoyable and memorable experience for the troops of the Keystone Division. For soldiers who had fought at Vire, the southern flank of the Falaise Pocket, the lower Seine crossings, and who would within a few months experience more than 6,000 casualties at a grim place called the Heurtgen forest, a day spent swinging down the Champs-Elysées to the martial airs of the division band and the cheers of thousands of enthusiastic onlookers was not all that hard to take, after all.

The battle was winding down. General Truscott had spent much of the past two days flying by Cub between his corps and division CPs. This gave him a good view of the battle area, and his acute disappointment of several days before was somewhat lessened. The past few days had seen considerable improvement in the position of the 36th Division at Monté-limar, and the 3rd Division was now putting heavy pressure on the Germans from the south as well.

The enemy forces now attempting to make their way north through the gap were receiving terrible punishment. Highway 7 was a mass of tanks, guns, trucks, and other vehicles. The railroad that paralleled the highway was equally jammed with equipment of all kinds. Traffic had literally come to a halt, and there was a constant rain of tank and artillery shells on the beleaguered columns.

While it had become virtually impossible for any more Germans to break out, the disappointment remained that most of the *11th Panzer* and much of the *198th Reserve Division* had escaped. Being in the vanguard of the German retreat, they had reached the gap before the 36th Division had established strong blocking positions. Quick and aggressive action, particularly by the *11th Panzer*, had enabled most of these troops to escape.

In spite of this, the action at Montélimar was still an impressive victory for the American forces. In excess of 5,000 prisoners were taken. More than 4,000 vehicles were destroyed, and two German divisions—the *338th* and the *189th*—were literally eliminated.[3]

In addition, the action of Montélimar was the key to victory in the overall campaign in southern France. In just fourteen days, the French and American forces had captured the major ports of Toulon and Marseilles, where, within less than a month, Liberty ships would be docking to unload their cargo. In addition, they had captured 23,000 prisoners and almost destroyed the German *Nineteenth Army* east of the Rhone. Those troops west of the Rhone were now outflanked and hastily retreating toward the German border.

Truscott's VI Corps was now more than 100 miles north of the beaches, with some elements still another 100 miles farther ahead. The Americans would continue their rapid drive to the north until they had reached a junction with Patton's Third Army in the middle of September. The book would then be closed on Operation DRAGOON.

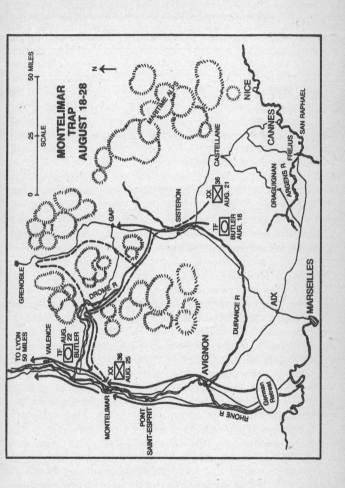

Wednesday, AUGUST 30

When Patton returned to his CP in the afternoon, he was told by his chief of staff, Hugh Gaffey, that the XII Corps was questioning the wisdom of continuing its advance toward the Meuse River and the town of Commercy. Its commander, Maj. Gen. Manton Eddy, had pointed out to Gaffey that even if he had enough gas to reach Commercy, his tanks would certainly be empty by the time he got there. Patton would have none of it. Gaffey was to tell Eddy to "run till his engines stop and then go on, on foot. We must and will get a crossing on the Meuse. In the last war I drained ¾ of my tanks to keep the other ¼ going. Eddy can do the same."[1]

For Eddy, the past several days had been a series of ups and downs as far as his fuel supplies had been concerned. He was aware that the Third Army had been placed at the bottom of the priority list for available supplies of gasoline as a result of Eisenhower's decision to put the major support behind Montgomery's advance to the north. Then yesterday, he discovered that he had not received even his reduced share of the gasoline allotment. Deliveries to the XII Corps were 140,000 gallons short. He felt certain this had been an administrative error that could be straightened out, but in the meantime his 4th Armored Division was operating with little, if any, reserve.

John Wood's 4th Armored tanks had indeed been consuming fuel at a rapid rate during the past several days. Since leaving Troyes the day before yesterday, they had sped fifty miles to the vicinity of Vitry and Châlons on the Marne. Leading the advance was the division's Combat Command A under Col. Bruce Clarke. A coldly reserved individual and strict disciplinarian, Clarke had his own ideas about how to fight Germans. The war correspondent, Wes Gallagher, had spent some time with him during the drive through France and in an article in *Liberty Magazine* quoted him as follows: "Warfare is mental, not physical. When you upset the enemy you have him licked, particularly the German. He is big and slow to react, and if you cut his communications and lines of contact, he will just take to the woods. But if you give him time to sit down and get out the rule book, he is tough as hell."[2]

Clarke was self-confident to the point of cockiness and gave no thought to protecting the rear or defending the flanks. He went on to tell Gallagher: "We received the other day a battle experience note in which some joker wrote that the American Sherman [tank] with its 75 [mm gun] is no match for the German 45-ton Panther with its heavy armor. That would have scared hell out of us if we hadn't just knocked out more than a hundred Panthers with our Shermans and tank destroyers in a three-day battle."[3]

A measure of Clarke's aggressiveness had been demonstrated several days before when CCA approached the town of Troyes on the Seine. To his surprise, he found the town strongly defended. At first glance, a frontal assault looked suicidal. However, recalling his training in desert-style warfare, Clarke spread his tanks across a wide front facing the German defenses and made a mad dash for the town. Hurdling the tank ditches and brushing aside other antitank defenses, Clarke's tanks overwhelmed the German defenders by the speed of their attack and took the city in a matter of hours.

In his advance toward the Marne, Clarke had divided CCA into two groups—Task Force Jacques under Lt. Col. George Jacques and Task Force ABE under Lt. Col. Creighton Abrams. The day before, TF Jacques had captured Vitry and TF ABE had secured Châlons. It was while patrolling in the vicinity of Châlons that a most fortunate discovery was made. The troops came upon a first-class airport that had been recently used by the Germans. The runways had been wired for demolition and three German aircraft were still on the ground. In addition, there was a large ammunition dump and—the most prized treasure of all—a cache of 115,000 gallons of gasoline.[4]

This was less than a day's supply for the 4th Armored at current rates of usage, and the gasoline was of poor quality by American standards. However, to Clarke's tank commanders, whose eyes were constantly on their fuel gauges, this was a real bonanza. Without this addition to the division's fuel supplies, further advance would have been severely restricted. The Meuse River and Commercy would have been out of reach regardless of Patton's exhortations.

Clarke's TF Jacques reached the town of Saint-Dizier by noon today. After clearing some German tanks from the woods northwest of the town, they were ready to resume the advance toward Commercy, just thirty miles away.

Eddy now had his orders to proceed to the Meuse, no matter what. Wood's 4th Armored was well on its way toward reaching that important river with help from the "liberated" gasoline supplies. But to Patton, this was still well short of the mark. "It is terrible to halt, even on the Meuse. We should cross the Rhine in the vicinity of Worms, and the faster we do it, the less lives and munitions it will take. No one realizes the terrible value of the 'unforgiving minute' except me. Some way I will get on yet."[5]

The man who strode into Omar Bradley's mobile office was short, somewhat stout, and walked with a swagger. While most general officers wore one set of stars—on the front of their combat helmets—he wore a set both front and rear. He was all spit and polish, radiating arrogance and strutting like a martinet. He was Lt. Gen. John C. H. Lee (West Point '09), deputy commander of the European Theater of Operations—U.S.A. (ETOUSA) and Eisenhower's chief of supply.

Lee had come to London on orders from General Marshall in May 1942 to assume the role of supply chief and had been in the job ever since. He was a stickler for military regulations (earning the nickname "Court House")[6] and a very hard taskmaster. He was a strongly religious man, one who wore his religion on his sleeve. Eisenhower referred to him as a "modern Cromwell."[7] His troops were less respectful, using his initials to frame the nickname "Jesus Christ Himself."[8] After the war, he was to become a lay brother in a monastic order.[9]

Lee was a prodigious worker, keeping busy as many as eight secretaries. He also was a pretentious person. In the pre-invasion days, he had used a private train of twelve cars to carry him and his staff on tours of inspection around the British Isles. His popularity at SHAEF and with Eisenhower had not been enhanced when in March he received a promotion to lieutenant general directly from the War Department and without Eisenhower's advance approval. This put him, at that time, second behind Eisenhower in the ranks of the officers serving in Europe. Yet, in spite of Lee's many annoying personal characteristics, Eisenhower resisted the temptation to relieve or reassign him and kept him in his position throughout the war. "He was determined, correct, and devoted to duty; he had long been known as an effective administrator," Eisenhower wrote.[10]

Bradley's relationship with Lee went back to last winter when he came to England to prepare for the invasion. He referred to Lee as "brilliant," as an "energetic and imaginative commander with bold executive talents,"[11] but his personality was particularly offensive to the unpretentious Bradley. The two generals had been involved in numerous disagreements before the invasion, largely over the division of responsibility between their two commands. To this day, the division of responsibility remained unclear and a continuing source of friction between Bradley and all his field generals and Com Z (communications zone), the title given to Lee's supply organization. And now, the recent increase in supply problems all across the fighting front further aggravated the relationships.

As if this were not enough, Lee added one more source of friction, which was to cause lasting damage to the relations between Com Z and Bradley's forces. Lee had been quick to move his large staff organization to France after D day. Established in a Quonset hut city near Cherbourg, his organization could be more effective being that much closer to the zone of active military operations. This move had been generally applauded by the forces in the field. Then, just the day before, he had made another move which was to bring him universal disapproval and condemnation. Without even asking for Eisenhower's approval, he moved his forward headquarters to Paris. At a time when transport of supplies for the troops was painfully short, Lee had used 200 of his trucks to make the move. He advised General Koenig in Paris that he would need accommodations for 8,000 officers and 21,000 enlisted men. He requested use of all the city's hotels.[12]

To Bradley, Patton, Hodges, and others, the thought of all that transport and fuel being put to such a use was painful in the extreme. To the troops, the thought of some supply sergeant living in luxury in a Paris hotel was more than painful: it was infuriating. Eisenhower was livid. He wanted the Paris hotels used for rest and recuperation centers for front-line troops. He considered requiring Lee to pull his people out, but soon realized that this would just compound the problems already created by the move. He merely put strict controls on moving additional people and instructed Lee to make a careful investigation and remove all individuals whose presence in Paris was not absolutely required.

Against such a background, the meeting between Lee and Bradley could not be expected to be pleasant. The first subject was gasoline supply. Both men knew that the problem was not one of available supplies on the Continent. As of the week before, there were 27,000,000 gallons in Normandy—an eleven- to twelve-day supply and an increase of more than 1,000,000 gallons from the figure of two weeks before.[13] The problem was one of transportation to the front-line forces, whose distance from the coast was increasing at a rapid rate with every passing day. There simply were not enough fuel-supply trucks available (trucks which, of course, used increasing amounts of fuel themselves to make their runs), and the French railroads were still far too damaged to provide any significant help.

To the ever-confident Lee, the answer was clear—build a pipeline. He proudly announced to Bradley that his pipeline from the Normandy beaches now ran all the way to Alençon and was being extended as rapidly as possible. Lee would have been badly embarrassed had he known that, just the day before, as a result of shoddy workmanship brought about by the pressure for rapid construction, the line had sprung a major leak and was now usable only as far as Saint-Lô, almost 100 miles to the west. Bradley would know soon enough that the pipeline would be of little help in solving his short-term fuel problems.

The other problem was ammunition for the VIII Corps at Brest. Yesterday, following his trip to Brest, Bradley had sent Lee a memo complaining about the failure to deliver the promised amounts. Another memo from Middleton had just reached Bradley's desk, pleading for some action to relieve his shortage. Bradley and Middleton were suspicious (and rightly so) that the people at Com Z were no longer interested in the port facilities at Brest, now that both Le Havre and Antwerp appeared to be within immediate reach. They questioned the degree of commitment on the part of Com Z to support the Brest operation.

However, Lee was all cooperation. After contacting his chief of operations, Brigadier General Stratton, he proposed the following: 2,500 tons per day for seven days delivered by LST to be landed on the north shore of Brittany, to be followed by 1,500 tons per day thereafter. In addition, he offered 1,500 tons per day for four days via the railroad that runs across the north shore to Brest.[14] It was a bold offer, and one that would go a long way to fulfill Middleton's needs. It had one problem. The stocks on hand even in the rear areas were not sufficient to fill this order for many of the types of ammunition required. The shortage of ammunition for the VIII Corps attack on Brest would be eased somewhat but would continue to be a problem.

After Lee had left, Bradley tried to be generous in his thoughts about Eisenhower's supply chief. After all, he had an extremely difficult job, and the problems they all faced were not of his making. He was intelligent, dedicated, hard-working, and apparently had Ike's full support. If only he could demonstrate empathy, humility, or understanding, perhaps some of these supply difficulties would be easier to resolve.

Thursday, AUGUST 31

General Eisenhower had flown to London from the Continent on Tuesday. Yesterday, he had worked on his report for the Combined Chiefs of Staff and met with Prime Minister Churchill, who had just returned from an extended tour of the Mediterranean front. His meeting with Churchill had been brief, for the prime minister was suffering from his third attack of pneumonia since the beginning of the war and was also scheduled to leave for Quebec and a conference with Roosevelt within a few days.[1]

The main purpose for the general's trip had to do with the announcement of command changes to be made effective the following day. This was the day on which Eisenhower planned to assume direct control of the land battle in accordance with the plan established some time ago and outlined to his subordinates about a week ago. General Montgomery would be relieved of that responsibility and would now exercise command over only the Twenty-first Army Group on equal terms with Bradley and his Twelfth Army Group.

In many respects, the change was more symbolic than real as, for all practical purposes, Bradley had been receiving most of his direction straight from Eisenhower for some time. In the eyes of the general public, however, the change was real and was of major significance. This was particularly true in Great Britain, where people viewed the change as a de-

motion for the hero of El Alamein. Eisenhower was well
aware of the British sensitivity on this matter and realized
the importance of setting the record straight.

In order to achieve the maximum publicity for this announcement, he had arranged a press conference to take place
in the building of the Ministry of Information in London. As
he and his British Deputy Commander, Arthur Tedder, entered the auditorium, they were greeted by a group of 200 or
more correspondents. Pleased by the size of his audience, Ike
opened the conference with a straightforward explanation of
the change in command structure. In anticipation of questions
about Montgomery's status, he continued his statement by
praising Montgomery as "one of the great soldiers of this or
any other war" and as a "great and personal friend."[2] He
ridiculed the idea that this command change was to be considered in any way a demotion for Montgomery. It was simply
the natural result of the great expansion of the area of Allied
control in France and the need to adapt the command structure
for the coming drive toward Germany.

Eisenhower touched on another subject that had received
much attention in the British press—the apparent lack of
progress by the British forces in the Caen area during July
and August. He pointed out that it was basically Montgomery's plan to draw the majority of the German forces to the
defense of the Caen area, thus opening the way for the American breakout at the western end of the line. The Germans
had responded to the Montgomery strategy. "Every piece of
dust on the Caen front was more than a diamond to them,"[3]
he declared. Montgomery should be praised for the success
of his strategy rather than condemned for the failure of the
British forces to make large territorial advances.

A question from the floor touched on another sensitive
subject—the "American parade" through Paris on Tuesday.
Why were no British units involved? To answer this question
Ike reviewed the whole train of events leading up to and
following the liberation of Paris: the decision to use the 2nd
French Armored Division as the liberating force, the need to
add the U.S. 4th Infantry Division to assure the rapid surrender of the German defenders, the invitation to Montgomery
to attend the parade as well as to join Bradley and himself
on their earlier trip to Paris (both of which he had been unable

to accept), the request from de Gaulle for a show of strength in the city. He emphasized the fact that the decision to use the U.S. 28th Division for the Paris parade was made without regard to nationality. This division happened to be so situated that the march through the city was as quick a way as any for it to join up with the V Corps attack north and east of Paris. There were no British units in a similar situation. He concluded by pointing out to the press that nothing was done at SHAEF headquarters on the basis of British versus American. It was a truly Allied command, and he fully intended to keep it that way.

At the conclusion of the press conference, Ike spotted his naval aide, Harry Butcher, in the audience. Butcher had not seen his boss for about ten days, having been in London on a special assignment. Ike suggested they ride out to Telegraph Cottage for lunch before he left for France later in the afternoon.

During the ride, they discussed, among other subjects, the risk of overoptimism as a result of the succession of victories throughout the month of August. Butcher asked Eisenhower if he felt that the Allied armies could now move right on into Germany. Ike was doubtful. He cited inadequate port capacity, clogged roads, damaged bridges, and poor signal communications as several factors that would make it difficult to maintain the present rate of advance. However, he pointed out to Butcher, as he had to the gentlemen of the press earlier, that today—D + 85—his forces were well beyond the line scheduled in the original invasion plan to be reached by D + 90.[4] Whatever problems he may face in the coming months, Ike had ample reason to be pleased with the present state of affairs as he prepared to officially assume his duties the following day as overall ground forces commander.

While Eisenhower was in London explaining why the British had gained so little ground around Caen, across the channel Lt. Gen. Brian Horrocks was making it clear that, given another set of circumstances, the story would be entirely different. His XXX Corps of the Second British Army had just taken the French city of Amiens, seventy miles northeast of the Seine River and almost halfway to the Belgian border. When the American XIX Corps had cleared the path of the

British forces approaching the Seine, XXX Corps was in the lead. The tone for the upcoming operation had been set by General Montgomery, who wrote in his orders: "The proper tactics now are for strong armoured and mobile columns to bypass enemy centers of resistance and push boldly ahead, creating alarm and despondence in enemy rear areas. Enemy bypassed will be dealt with by infantry columns coming on later. I rely on commanders of every rank and grade to 'drive' ahead with the utmost energy; any tendency to be 'sticky' or cautious must be stamped on ruthlessly."[5]

Crossing the river would be the XXX Corps' first task, and not an easy one. Horrocks's troops reached the Seine in the vicinity of Vernon and Louviers, where the river is wide and the banks steep. No bridges were left standing. By utilizing their own equipment and some borrowed from another corps, they were able to force the crossing and were ready to resume their advance by August 29—two days ago.

At first, the XXX Corps found it very difficult to "push boldly ahead." Enemy mines had been scattered strategically across their lines of advance. There were numerous pockets of German resistance and the weather was poor. By evening of the 29th, Horrocks's leading armored columns were only twenty miles beyond the river.

Then, late the next morning, the weather began to clear, and at the same time the German resistance seemed to melt away. Horrocks had fifty miles to go to Amiens, and one thought dominated his mind—the bridges across the Somme River. The Somme was the last major natural barrier before the Belgian border. If, by chance, he could surprise the Germans and reach the city before they had an opportunity to blow the bridges, it would be a major victory.

With the exhortation from Montgomery ringing in his ears and the lure of the bridges across the Somme in front of him, Horrocks sent his 11th Armoured Division on a nonstop race for Amiens.[6] As day wore into night, the weather worsened and the rain started to come down again. However, the long columns kept moving and, except for a few lone tanks and scattered truck convoys, enemy resistance was nonexistent. By dawn, they were in the city; the citizens of Amiens had the unusual experience of going to bed in an occupied city and waking up in one that had been liberated.

There were four bridges crossing the Somme. The 11th Armoured raced for the center of the city to see if any of them were still intact. They found three of the four undamaged. The French resistance had done its job well. Aided by the rapid approach of the British forces, they had managed to protect all but one of the bridges. The troops immediately secured the three bridges and kept right on moving. Destination—Lille and the Belgian border.

When Horrocks arrived in Amiens, he learned that the Somme River bridges were not the only prizes that had been captured this day. As his troops poured into the city, a meeting between two German generals was in progress in a building just a few blocks away. It was the headquarters of the German *Seventh Army*, and its commander, General Eberbach, had just taken over command of the Somme River defenses from Gen. Sepp Dietrich. He was busily writing an order for the defense of the Somme when word reached his headquarters that the British were entering the city. Both generals fled. Dietrich managed to escape, but Eberbach, heading out of town in a Volkswagen, was captured. The British also captured maps and documents not only outlining the plans for the defense of the Somme but also indicating the generally confused and chaotic state of all the German defenses in northern France.[7]

A seventy-mile advance in two days, the Somme Line breached, a leading German general captured. This was the kind of war that the fiery and colorful Horrocks reveled in. And now, it was on to Belgium.

For the second time in two weeks, Field Marshal Model had been unceremoniously chased out of his headquarters by advancing Allied forces. When Maurice Rose's 3rd Armored Division crashed into Soissons two days before, the *Army Group B* headquarters at Margival had to be abandoned. This time, Model moved sixty miles to the north and established his headquarters in the Chateau de Havrincourt, just west of Cambrai and within twenty-five miles of the Belgian border.[8] He would spend even less time here.

Shortly after his arrival at the chateau, he received new orders from the High Command outlining the future strategy he was to follow. With relief, Model read that the former rategy of fighting to the last ditch for every foot of ground as finally being abandoned. The directive spoke about such ings as avoiding encirclement, harboring strength, and ghting their way to the rear. It did, however, establish a ew line of defense that was to be held "at all costs." It ran ughly from Antwerp across southern Holland via the Albert anal, down the western edge of the Argonne Forest, through Metz and Nancy to the Swiss border.[9] For the first time, the igh Command seemed to recognize the extent of the Allied dvances and were offering Model some breathing room in hich to establish a defense.

The field marshal needed more than breathing room, however. Although it came as no surprise, he had received none f the reinforcements he had requested a week ago. This did ot mean that nothing was being done to replace the huge sses experienced during the last month. Actually, herculean fforts were being exerted to rebuild the military strength of e Reich, and many of these efforts were close to fruition. tretching of the recruiting age limits to include both older en and younger boys, as well as use of naval forces and ar-echelon troops, had increased the supply of manpower or the front-line forces, and tank production (as a result of e use of impressed foreign labor) had reached a high of ore than 1,500 tanks in the combined months of July and ugust. However, Hitler and the High Command took the pproach of building entirely new divisions, both infantry nd armored, rather than reinforcing the depleted divisions urrently in the field.[10] Time expended in recruitment and aining meant that these forces were not immediately available to Model. With few exceptions, he had to face the Allied nslaught with the shattered remains of the divisions and rmies already in the field.

It was a patchwork collection, and the situation was changg so rapidly that Model was really unable to exert much ontrol over events. The least battered of his forces, the *ifteenth Army*, had been assigned to the Pas-de-Calais area nd had seen limited action until the Allies began to cross e Seine. With a command to deny the coastal ports of Le lavre, Boulogne, Calais, and Dunkirk to the Allies, as well s to protect the V-2 launching sites, the *Fifteenth Army* forces ere restricted to the coastal areas and were in increasing

jeopardy of being cut off and isolated as the British advance
into Belgium. The remnants of the *Seventh Army* and th
Fifth Panzer Army had made an effort to establish a Somme
Marne River defense line. This effort had collapsed over th
past several days as the American Third Army storme
through Châlons, the First Army took Soissons, and, ju:
today, the British captured Amiens. With its leadership i
disarray with the capture of Eberbach and with Sepp Dietric
on the run, the troops saw just one feasible course to follow
That was to retreat to the German border. This meant headin
to the east and northeast across northern France and Belgiur
The movement was badly disorganized. Crowded roads, cor
gested intersections (which on occasion produced nasty dis
putes over rights-of-way), a shortage of bridges and ferries
and, most of all, bone-numbing fatigue made the retreat
nightmare for the German troops. Only one factor was i
their favor—the weather. Rain, clouds, and generally poo
flying conditions severely limited Allied air reconnaissanc
and attack. The pilots of the few planes that managed to ge
into the air reported large numbers of German troops movin
eastward and northeastward across the front of the advancin
American First Army.

Meanwhile, in front of Patton's Third Army advance, th
situation was somewhat different. Although Patton's force
had made spectacular gains during the past week, the Germa
First Army forces in his front showed no sign of disorgani
zation or collapse. They were, in fact, very successfully trad
ing territory for time as they looked to establishing a
effective defense in the Metz-Nancy area. The few new di
visions that had become available as a result of Hitler'
buildup were assigned to the German *First Army* because th
High Command recognized the threat provided not only by
Patton's forces but also by the forces of Lieutenant Genera
Patch's Seventh Army, now heading up the Rhone valley t
join the right flank of the Third Army. The *First Army* also
had a new commander, Lt. Gen. Otto von Knobelsdorff, a
Panzer specialist with a fine reputation acquired on the Rus
sian front. With its stable command situation and priority i
receiving reinforcements, the *First Army* at the end of Augus
was the strongest German force on the western front. Patto

would soon discover that more than a shortage of fuel stood between him and the Rhine.

General Bradley had always been a strong advocate and a staunch defender of airborne operations. His support may have been the deciding factor in the decision to schedule the drop of the 82nd and 101st Airborne Divisions into the Cotentin Peninsula as the prelude to the invasion of Utah Beach on D day. The senior air advisor on Eisenhower's staff, British Air Marshal Leigh-Mallory, was violently opposed to this airborne operation, feeling that it could not succeed and would be a disaster of major proportions. He pressured Eisenhower constantly to give up the idea. Bradley dug in his heels and declared that he "would not land on Utah Beach without the support of the U.S. 82nd Airborne Division."[11] It was an agonizing decision for Eisenhower, warned as he was by his chief advisor of the likely destruction of two first-class American fighting divisions. Without Bradley's strong and unequivocal support, the decision might have gone the other way.

Bradley's enthusiasm for airborne operations had cooled considerably during the past several months. Part of his change of heart could be attributed to the recent establishment of the First Allied Airborne Army under the command of Lt. Gen. Lewis Brereton, former commander of the U.S. Ninth Air Force. Brereton was no favorite of Bradley's, at least in part as a result of the dispute over the short-bombing experience during COBRA that had killed and wounded so many of Bradley's troops. It was Brereton's Ninth Air Force that had delivered the attack.

Bradley also felt that removal of control over airborne operations from ground force commanders was a mistake. He considered that the primary purpose of the paratroops was to provide support for his ground forces, and he was concerned that a separate airborne command would look at its mission in an entirely different light. "Almost from the day of its creation," he said, "this Allied Airborne Army showed an astonishing faculty for devising missions that were never needed."[12]

However, Bradley's main reason for growing cool toward the use of airborne operations had to do with questions of

supply. In the constant battle to keep his forces adequately
supplied, Bradley had come to rely more and more on the
use of airlift for the delivery of all types of supplies but most
particularly of gasoline. The same planes that delivered his
gasoline were required for use in airborne operations, not
only for the day (or days) of the drop itself, but usually for
a number of days of planning and preparation beforehand.

This was the reason he was furious when he heard about
LINNET—an airborne operation scheduled for a September
3 drop in the vicinity of Tournai, Belgium, just a few miles
north of the French border. Already, the planes had been
withdrawn from his airlift to prepare for this operation. It did
not take Bradley long to calculate that he was losing 823 tons
of gasoline a day—the equivalent of 250,000 gallons, which
represented almost a full day's supply for Patton's Third
Army.[13]

Bradley was particularly disturbed because he felt the air-
drop was unnecessary. He was confident that Hodges's First
Army troops could reach Tournai by September 3. He pleaded
with Eisenhower to call off the operation. "When the paratroopers come down," he predicted, "they'll find us waiting
on the ground."[14] But Eisenhower held firm. The operation
was part of his commitment to support Montgomery's forces
in their drive toward Belgium, and he would not give it up.

Bradley saw only one way to get LINNET cancelled, and
that was to carry through on his threat to take Tournai before
September 3. In fact, such an effort to reach Tournai fitted
in well with two other strategic considerations that had been
running through the general's mind. He felt certain that the
left flank of Hodges's First Army would become exposed
over the next several days as the Americans outdistanced the
British forces in their movement to the north and northeast.
In spite of the fact that Tournai was a few miles inside the
British zone of advance, Bradley felt it must be taken by his
troops to avoid a threat to the First Army flank.

A drive on Tournai would necessitate an important change
for the First Army—a swing from a northeasterly to a more
northerly direction. This fitted in nicely with Bradley's third
consideration—which would turn out to be the most important
of all. Intelligence on the location of enemy forces had been
sketchy and difficult to obtain during the past several days.

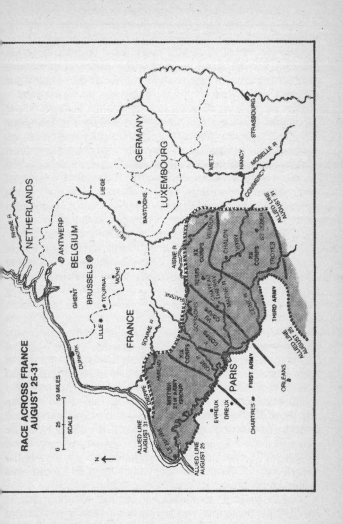

RACE ACROSS FRANCE
AUGUST 25-31

SCALE
0   25   50 MILES

N

NETHERLANDS

RHINE R.

ANTWERP

BELGIUM

BRUSSELS

GHENT

GERMANY

LIÈGE

BASTOGNE

LUXEMBOURG

MEUSE R.

STRASBOURG

MOSELLE R.

METZ

NANCY

COMMERCY

ALLIED LINE
AUGUST 31

TROYES

XII
CORPS

XX
CORPS

THIRD ARMY

CHÁLON

VITRY

AISNE R.

MARNE R.

ALLIED LINE
AUGUST 31

TOURNAI

LILLE

MONS

SOMME R.

ARRAS

XIX
CORPS

WESTERN
BR. FIRST ARMY GROUP

DUNKIRK

DIEPPE

ALLIED LINE
AUGUST 31

CHARTRES

DREUX

ÉVREUX

PARIS

FIRST ARMY

ORLEANS

ALLIED LINE
AUGUST 25

FRANCE

The poor weather had been one factor; it had given the German troops cover from the ever-present Allied air force. The rapid movement of his own troops had also made collection and assessment of worthwhile intelligence difficult. However, Bradley was intrigued by the bits and pieces of information he had received, which seemed to indicate that a significant number of German troops were moving across the front of Hodges's army in an effort to retreat to the German border. A change in direction to the north would put the First Army in a much better position to interdict this movement and perhaps accomplish still another encirclement of the German forces retreating out of Normandy.

Word went out from the Twelfth Army Group to Hodges, and almost immediately Stubby Thorson, Hodges's operations officer, was off to Pete Corlett's XIX Corps headquarters with a new plan. Instead of continuing to the northeast, the XIX Corps was to change direction to the north and head for Tournai, 100 miles away. Corlett was given forty-eight hours to cover the distance and take the city. Midnight, September 2, was his deadline. When Corlett called in his 2nd Armored Division commander, Maj. Gen. Edward Brooks, to give him the assignment of leading the 100-mile dash, he got the kind of answer he liked to hear. "Get a good night's sleep and don't worry," said Brooks. "It's in the bag."[15]

Meanwhile, Courtney Hodges was on the phone to Joe Collins, whose VII Corps was on Corlett's right. "Joe, you've got to change directions at once toward Mons to help cut off the German 7th Army," Hodges said. Collins, whose front extended from the XIX Corps on his left to the Third Army on his right (the V Corps had not yet reached the front lines), was concerned. "But who will fill the gap that will develop between my right and the 3rd Army?" he asked. "Joe, that's your problem," replied Hodges as he hung up the phone.[16] Collins headed his three divisions toward Mons and then set about devising a way to plug the gap.

For Bradley, a month that had begun with great victories and high expectations was ending in the same way. The XIX Corps was on its way to prove the futility of an airborne drop in Tournai, and the VII Corps was headed for the Belgian town of Mons and an opportunity to deal the retreating German army still another crushing blow. His change in army direction had been implemented in a matter of hours, and he had no doubt whatsoever that the objectives he had laid out would be achieved. What a marvelous fighting machine this Twelfth Army Group had become since he took over as its commander thirty-one days ago! His troops had accomplished things he would not have believed possible on that day when he had stepped out of his jeep near Coutances to assume command. August 1944 had indeed witnessed the coming of age of the greatest military organization in American history, and the general was mighty proud to have had a part in it.

EPILOGUE

The spectacular advances that marked the final days of August continued into September, and the contagious optimism that pervaded the Allied armies at all levels was unabated. The 2nd Armored Division did reach the city of Tournai in time to bring about the cancellation of the planned airborne operation, LINNET. Joe Collins's VII Corps succeeded in establishing blocking positions in the vicinity of Mons and, before the first week of September was over, had captured 25,000 German soldiers—coming close to rivaling the number of prisoners trapped in the Falaise Pocket. Brian Horrocks's XXX Corps sped through Brussels on their way to Antwerp, which fell into their hands on September 4. Patton's Third Army managed to acquire sufficient gasoline not only to cross the Meuse River but also to reach the Moselle in the vicinity of Metz and Nancy by September 5. Six days later, the XV Corps, now on the Third Army right flank, made its first contact with the Seventh Army of General Patch coming up from the Rhone valley.

On September 2, the day after assuming direct control of the ground forces, Eisenhower flew to Bradley's headquarters near Chartres, where he met with both Bradley and Patton. The result of this meeting was a slight "bend" in Allied strategy in favor of Patton. Eisenhower gave authority for the Third Army to cross the Moselle, pierce the Siegfried Line, and advance toward Frankfurt. To back up this authorization, he increased the Third Army fuel allowance. As a result, more than 1,500,000 gallons were delivered to Patton's forces during the first week of September.

The high-water mark of the Allied sweep to the east came around the middle of September. On September 15, Eisenhower wrote, ''Clearly Berlin is the main prize, and the prize in defense of which the enemy is likely to concentrate the bulk of his forces. There is no doubt whatever, in my mind, that we should concentrate all our energies on a rapid thrust to Berlin.''[1] By then, Patton's Third Army was across the Moselle in the vicinity of Nancy. To the north, both the V and VII Corps of the First Army had penetrated the West Wall (Siegfried Line) into German territory at several points in the area from the Ardennes forest north to Aachen. The British, meanwhile, had driven through Belgium and were poised on the southern border of the Netherlands, ready for a new leap forward. Last, but certainly not least, on September 19, after weeks of bitter fighting, the Germans surrendered the port city of Brest to Troy Middleton's VII Corps.

It was at this time, in an atmosphere of optimism approaching euphoria, that Operation MARKET GARDEN was launched. The largest airborne operation of the war (more than 35,000 airborne troops were landed during the week-long battle), MARKET GARDEN involved three separate landings in the Netherlands—the British 1st Airborne Division near Arnhem, the American 82nd near Nijmegen, and the American 101st near Eindhoven. The purpose of these landings was to secure the important bridges along the sixty-mile stretch of highway from the Belgian border to Arnhem and the Rhine River. Down this highway, Horrocks's XXX Corps was to rapidly advance, reaching Arnhem and crossing the Rhine before the end of D + 3.

The operation was a disaster. Failure to secure the crucial bridge over the Rhine at Arnhem, the slowness of the advance of the XXX Corps, the presence of greater German strength in the area than had been anticipated, miserable flying weather during most of the period of the battle—these were just some of the many problems that plagued MARKET GARDEN from the start. When the attack was called off after one week, there was very little to show for the 15,000 casualties among the airborne forces. Of these, 7,500 occurred in the British 1st Airborne, out of a total of 10,000 men committed to the operation.

MARKET GARDEN was not Montgomery's only problem. In taking the port of Antwerp early in September, his forces had failed to capture the estuary of the Schelde River, which lies between Antwerp and the sea. Although the harbor was seized with minimal damage, the port was unusable as long as the Germans held the ground along the estuary. Considered a minor problem by Montgomery, he sent his Canadian First Army to clear out the opposition. The Germans put up a strong defense, aided by reinforcements by sea from the French channel ports. The Canadians made little headway. In fact, it would not be until early December, and until Montgomery had committed most of his forces (including the British Second Army) to the task, that the port of Antwerp would at last be opened for use by the Allies.

While Montgomery was having his problems in the Netherlands, the Americans were faring no better along the German border. Their progress came to a virtual halt during the latter part of September and October. They found surprisingly strong German resistance all along the front from the Belfort Gap near the Swiss border to the city of Aachen. Pitched battles reminiscent of World War I became the norm as bad weather and increasing supply difficulties hampered efforts to force a break in the German defenses.

Bradley and Eisenhower agreed that the most promising place for a breakthrough in this stiff line of German defenses was the valley to the south of Aachen. Not only was the terrain suitable for an attack, but a breakthrough in this area would lead into the southern flank of the Ruhr valley. There was, however, one problem that had to be dealt with. Just to the south of the Aachen valley was the Huertgen forest, a dark, densely wooded area full of ridges and ravines. The forest presented two problems to an advance through the Aachen plain. First, it offered an ideal place for concealment of German forces in a position to swoop down on the flank of any American attack. Second, the forest was the site of several dams near the source of the Roer River, which flows directly across the Aachen plain. Bradley, Hodges, and their staffs were concerned that the enemy might open the dam gates and flood the plain, complicating any advance through the area. It was decided that the Huertgen forest must be cleared.

In October, a series of attacks began that were to last more than a month. It was the most costly and unproductive offensive of the entire European campaign. As a result of their dazzling successes of the summer and early fall, the American High Command seemed to feel that there was nothing their troops could not accomplish. The lure of ''Berlin by Christmas'' had fastened its grip on the decision makers. They decided that a break through the Huertgen forest would be achieved—and achieved without delay. Division after division was sent into the forest, only to be chewed up by the Germans who very effectively used all the defensive advantages the Huertgen forest had to offer. American casualties amounted to 33,000 men—24,000 were battle casualties and 9,000 succumbed to trench foot and respiratory diseases resulting from the miserable weather conditions.[2] The 28th Infantry Division was literally destroyed. The 4th, 8th, and 9th Divisions were badly shattered.[3] After almost two months of fighting, there was little to show for this tremendous sacrifice of fighting men. The American military leadership was faced with its most stunning reverse and most serious blunder since Normandy had been invaded six months before.

MARKET GARDEN, the Battle of the Huertgen Forest, and the Battle of the Bulge, which followed immediately, marked the end of the period of unlimited optimism and supreme confidence that had become so clearly evident during the month of August. The war of movement—of sweeping envelopment and lightning advances—gave way to a grisly war of attrition, during which the enemy demonstrated remarkable recovery of his fighting capabilities and a grim determination to defend his homeland with all his strength. However, after initial successes, Hitler's all-or-nothing gamble in the Battle of the Bulge failed in the face of heroic resistance on the part of the American forces. By early spring, momentum was regained and the race for Berlin was on.

As the Allies sped across Germany to destroy the shattered

remnants of the German army and end the war, they once again could put to use those uniquely American strategies of speed and mobility, which had been developed and so successfully employed during the campaign across France in August 1944.

NOTES

PROLOGUE
1. Alfred D. Chandler, Ed., *The Papers of Dwight David Eisenhower* (Baltimore, Md.: Johns Hopkins Press, 1970), 206.
2. Leonard Mosely, *Marshall* (New York: Hearst Books, 1982), 203.

THURSDAY, AUGUST 1
1. Mosely, *Marshall*, 96.
2. Ibid.
3. Dwight Eisenhower, *Crusade in Europe* (Garden City, N.Y.: Doubleday & Co., 1948), 262.
4. Omar Bradley, *A Soldier's Story* (New York: Henry Holt & Co., 1951), 296.
5. Ibid., 302.
6. Quesada debriefing, Lt. Col. Steve Long and Lt. Col. Ralph Stevenson, May 1975, U.S. Army Military History Institute, Carlisle Barracks, Pa.
7. Bradley, *A Soldier's Story*, 338.
8. Omar Bradley and Clay Blair, *A General's Life* (New York: Simon & Schuster, 1983), 279.
9. Louis L. Snyder, *Historical Guide to World War II* (Westport, Conn.: Greenwood Press, 1982), 372, for von Kluge biographic details.

10. Martin Blumenson, *Breakout and Pursuit*, United States Army in World War II, The European Theater of Operations Office of Chief of Military History, United States Army, Washington, D.C., 1961, 326.
11. Ibid., 280.
12. Ibid., 323.
13. Martin Blumenson, *The Patton Papers*, Vol. II (Boston: Houghton Mifflin Co., 1974), 337.
14. Ibid., 326.
15. Ibid., 332.
16. Ibid., 337.
17. Ibid., 397.
18. Ibid., 402.
19. Ibid., 496.
20. Ibid.
21. Bernard Montgomery, *Memoirs* (Cleveland, Ohio: World Publishing Co., 1958), 232.
22. Ibid., 235.
23. Ibid., 234.

WEDNESDAY, AUGUST 2

1. Blumenson, *The Patton Papers*, 231.
2. Russel Weigley, *Eisenhower's Lieutenants* (Bloomington, Ind.: Indiana University Press, 1981), 122.
3. Bradley, *A Soldier's Story*, 226.
4. Blumenson, *The Patton Papers*, 498.
5. Major William C. Sylvan Diary, U.S. Army Military History Institute, Carlisle Barracks, Pa., 45.
6. Bradley, *A Soldier's Story*, 226.
7. Blumenson, *Breakout and Pursuit*, 444.
8. Walter Warlimont, *Inside Hitler's Headquarters 1939–45* (New York: Frederick A. Praeger, 1964), 46.
9. Eddy Florentin, *Battle of the Falaise Gap* (London: London Elke Books, 1965).
10. Harry Butcher, *My Three Years with Eisenhower* (New York: Simon & Schuster, 1946), 630.
11. SHAEF Msg. Form Ref. #S-56667, 8/2/44, Dwight D. Eisenhower Library, Abilene, Kan.

THURSDAY, AUGUST 3

1. Chester Hansen Diary, U.S. Army Military History Institute, Carlisle Barracks, Pa.
2. Blumenson, *Breakout and Pursuit*, 431.
3. After action interview of General Eberbach by Major H. P. Hudson, 10/44, U.S. Army Military History Institute, Carlisle Barracks, Pa.
4. Florentin, *The Battle of the Falaise Gap*.
5. Blumenson, *Breakout and Pursuit*, 370.
6. Ibid.
7. Anthony Cave Brown, *Bodyguard of Lies* (New York: Harper & Row, 1975), 578.
8. Ibid., 779, 780.

FRIDAY, AUGUST 4

1. Blumenson, *Breakout and Pursuit*, 362.
2. Weigley, *Eisenhower's Lieutenants*, 180.
3. Hobart Gay Diary, U.S. Army Military History Institute, Carlisle Barracks, Pa., 439.

SATURDAY, AUGUST 5

1. Butcher, *My Three Years with Eisenhower*, 634.
2. Ibid., 634, 635.
3. Winston Churchill, *Triumph and Tragedy* (Boston: Houghton Mifflin, 1953), 66–71.

SUNDAY, AUGUST 6

1. Chester Wilmot, *The Struggle for Europe* (London: Collins, St. James Pl., 1952), 470.
2. Ibid., 409.
3. Blumenson, *Breakout and Pursuit*, 458, 459.
4. Personal interview with Colonel Melvin Helfers, 11/23/84, Charleston, S.C.
5. Blumenson, *The Patton Papers*, 502.

MONDAY, AUGUST 7

1. Blumenson, *Breakout and Pursuit*, 464.

TUESDAY, AUGUST 8

1. Chester Hansen Diary.
2. Hobart Gay Diary, 446.

3. Ibid., 447.
4. Chester Hansen Diary.

WEDNESDAY, AUGUST 9
1. Chester Hansen Diary.
2. Bradley, *A Soldier's Story*, 375, 376.
3. Chester Hansen Diary.
4. Sylvan Diary, 52.
5. John Blum, *Years of War 1941–1945* From the Morganthau Diaries (Boston: Houghton Mifflin Co., 1967), 336.
6. Eberbach After Action Interview.

THURSDAY, AUGUST 10
1. Ralph Bennett, *ULTRA In The West* (New York: Charles Scribner's Sons, 1979), 118.
2. Hobart Gay Diary, 448.
3. Louis L. Snyder, *Historical Guide to World War II*, 385, for Leclerc biographical information.

FRIDAY, AUGUST 11
1. Blumenson, *Breakout and Pursuit*, 484.
2. Ibid., 495.
3. Butcher, *My Three Years with Eisenhower*, 637.
4. Bradley, *A Soldier's Story*, 374.
5. Ibid., 377.
6. Chester Hansen Diary.

SUNDAY, AUGUST 13
1. Eberbach After Action Interview.
2. Blumenson, *Breakout and Pursuit*, 515.
3. Ladislas Farago, *Patton, Ordeal and Triumph* (New York: Paperback-Dell, 1970), 521.
4. Bradley, *A Soldier's Story*, 376.
5. Hobart Gay Diary, 457.
6. Bradley and Blair, *A General's Life*, 299.
7. Blumenson, *The Patton Papers*, 508, 509.
8. Bradley, *A Soldier's Story*, 303.
9. Snyder, *Historical Guide to World War II*, 710.
10. Lucian K. Truscott, Jr., *Command Missions* (New York: E. P. Dutton, 1954), 383.

11. Jacques Robichon, *The Second D Day* (London: Arthur Baker Ltd., 1962).
12. Ibid.
13. Ibid.

MONDAY, AUGUST 14
 1. Max Hastings, *Overlord* (New York: Simon & Schuster, 1984), 302.
 2. Wilmot, *The Struggle for Europe*, 418.
 3. Bradley, *A Soldier's Story*, 378.
 4. Blumenson, *The Patton Papers*, 510.
 5. Ibid., 509, 510.

TUESDAY, AUGUST 15
 1. Truscott, *Command Missions*, 414.
 2. Robichon, *The Second D Day*.
 3. Hans Speidel, *We Defended Normandy* (London: Herbert Jenkins, 1951), 143.
 4. Eberbach After Action Interview.
 5. Blumenson, *Breakout and Pursuit*, 521.

WEDNESDAY, AUGUST 16
 1. Blumenson, *Breakout and Pursuit*, 523.

THURSDAY, AUGUST 17
 1. Hobart Gay Diary, 464.
 2. Hobart Gay Diary (subsection, Diary 3rd Provisional Corps), 1–3.
 3. Sylvan Diary, 57.

FRIDAY, AUGUST 18
 1. Blumenson, *The Patton Papers*, 519.
 2. Ibid., 517.
 3. Ibid.
 4. C. P. Stacey, *The Victory Campaign*, Vol. III, *The Operations in Northwest Europe 1944–1945* (Ottawa, Canada: The Queen's Printer, 1960), 252.
 5. Weigley, *Eisenhower's Lieutenants*, 212.
 6. Speidel, *We Defended Normandy*, 144.
 7. After Action Interview, Gen. Rudolph Von Gersdorff by

Major Kenneth Hechler, 10/45, U.S. Army Military History Institute, Carlisle Barracks, Pa.
8. Eberbach After Action Interview.
9. Blumenson, *Breakout and Pursuit*, 533.
10. Eberbach After Action Interview.
11. Von Gersdorff After Action Interview.
12. Speidel, *We Defended Normandy*, 144.
13. Milton Schulman, *Defeat in the West* (London: Secker & Warburg, 1947), 152–154.

SATURDAY, AUGUST 19
1. After Action Interview, Gen. Eugene Meindl by Maj. Kenneth Hechler, 1/46, U.S. Military History Institute, Carlisle Barracks, Pa., 26.
2. Ibid., 30.
3. Ibid., 33.
4. John Keegan, *Six Armies in Normandy* (New York: Viking Press, 1982), 275.
5. Meindl After Action Interview.
6. Bradley, *A Soldier's Story*, 380, 381.
7. Chester Hansen Diary.
8. Bradley and Blair, *A General's Life*, 313, 314.
9. Bradley, *A Soldier's Story*, 387.
10. Larry Collins and Dominique La Pierre, *Is Paris Burning?* (New York: Simon & Schuster, 1965), 38, 39.
11. Ibid., 148.
12. David Schoenbrun, *Soldiers of the Night* (New York: E. P. Dutton, 1980), 427.
13. Collins and La Pierre, *Is Paris Burning?* 23.
14. Ibid., 129, 130.

SUNDAY, AUGUST 20
1. Meindl After Action Interview, 36.
2. Ibid., 41.
3. Ibid.
4. Blumenson, *Breakout and Pursuit*, 549.
5. Personal Interview, Don Miller, Spartanburg, S.C., 6/4/85.
6. Ibid.
7. Collins and La Pierre, *Is Paris Burning?* 138, 139.
8. Ibid., 131, 132.

9. Ibid., 144, 145.
10. Truscott, *Command Missions*, 426.

MONDAY, AUGUST 21
1. Meindl After Action Interview.
2. Blumenson, *Breakout and Pursuit*, 558.
3. Ibid., 601.
4. Collins and La Pierre, *Is Paris Burning?* 181.
5. Ibid., 27.

TUESDAY, AUGUST 22
1. Collins and La Pierre, *Is Paris Burning?* 203, 204.
2. Chester Hansen Diary.
3. Ibid.
4. Collins and La Pierre, *Is Paris Burning?* 168, 169.
5. Blumenson, *Breakout and Pursuit*, 604.
6. Ibid., 603.
7. Chester Hansen Diary.
8. Sylvan Diary, 60, 61.

WEDNESDAY, AUGUST 23
1. Stephen Ambrose, *Eisenhower* (New York: Simon & Schuster, 1983), 336.
2. Francis de Guingand, *Operation Victory* (London: Hodder & Stoughton, 1947), 411.
3. Montgomery, *Memoirs*, 341.
4. David Irving, *The War between the Generals* (New York: Congden & Lattes, 1981), 252.
5. Ibid.
6. Blumenson, *The Patton Papers*, 526.
7. Bradley, *A Soldier's Story*, 401.
8. Blumenson, *Breakout and Pursuit*, 659.
9. David Schoenbrun, *Soldiers of the Night* (New York: E. P. Dutton, 1980), 414–417.

THURSDAY, AUGUST 24
1. Blumenson, *The Patton Papers*, 522.
2. Blumenson, *Breakout and Pursuit*, 666.
3. Speidel, *We Defended Normandy*, 148.
4. Wilmot, *The Struggle for Europe*, 333; Speidel, *We Defended Normandy*, 147.

5. Blumenson, *Breakout and Pursuit*, 661.
6. Ibid., 598.
7. Ibid., 662.

FRIDAY, AUGUST 25
1. Collins and La Pierre, *Is Paris Burning?* 321.
2. Bradley, *A Soldier's Story*, 392.
3. Gordon Prange, *At Dawn We Slept* (New York: McGraw Hill, 1981), 652, 823.
4. Bradley, *A Soldier's Story*, 392.
5. Blumenson, *Breakout and Pursuit*, 617.
6. Personal Interview, Alan Willis, Spartanburg, S.C. 10/2/85.

SATURDAY, AUGUST 26
1. Brian Crozier, *De Gaulle* (New York: Charles Scribner's Sons, 1973), 310.
2. Blumenson, *Breakout and Pursuit*, 620.
3. Ibid.
4. Ibid., 621.
5. Bradley, *A Soldier's Story*, 340; Chester Hansen Diary.
6. Bradley, *A Soldier's Story*, 367.
7. Blumenson, *The Patton Papers*, 532.
8. Truscott, *Command Missions*, 430.

SUNDAY, AUGUST 27
1. Eisenhower, *Crusade in Europe*, 297.
2. Chester Hansen Diary.
3. Bradley, *A Soldier's Story*, 394.
4. Chester Hansen Diary.
5. Eisenhower, *Crusade in Europe*, 297, 298.
6. Chester Hansen Diary.
7. Ibid.
8. J. Lawton Collins, *Lightning Joe* (Baton Rouge, La.: Louisiana State Press, 1979), 258.

MONDAY, AUGUST 28
1. Blumenson, *Breakout and Pursuit*, 672.
2. Collins, *Lightning Joe*, 246.
3. Bradley and Blair, *A General's Life*, 281.

4. *Spearhead in the West, 1941–1945, The Third Armoured Division* (Frankfurt am Main, Germany: Kunst & Werverdruck, 1945), 184.
5. Ibid., 204.
6. Ibid.
7. Ibid.
8. Hobart Gay Diary, 479, 480.
9. Blumenson, *The Patton Papers*, 531.
10. Ibid., 530.
11. Ibid.

TUESDAY, AUGUST 29
1. *Historical and Pictorial Review of the 28th Infantry Division in World War II* (Nashville, Tenn.: Battery Press Inc., 1980).
2. Ibid.
3. Truscott, *Command Missions*, 433.

WEDNESDAY, AUGUST 30
1. Blumenson, *The Patton Papers*, 531.
2. *What They Said about the Fourth Armored Division*, Public Relations Section, 4th Armored Division (Landshut, 1945).
3. Ibid.
4. HQ, Combat Command A, 4th Armored Division, After Action Report for July and August 1944, U.S. Army Military History Institute, Carlisle Barracks, Pa.
5. Blumenson, *The Patton Papers*, 531.
6. Weigley, *Eisenhower's Lieutenants*, 84.
7. Eisenhower, *Crusade in Europe*, 236.
8. Weigley, *Eisenhower's Lieutenants*, 84.
9. Irving, *The War between the Generals*, 88.
10. Eisenhower, *Crusade in Europe*, 236.
11. Bradley, *A Soldier's Story*, 405.
12. Forrest C. Pogue, *Supreme Command*, United States Army in World War II, The European Theater of Operations (Office of the Chief of Military History, U.S. Army, Washington, D.C., 1954), 322.
13. Roland G. Ruppenthal, *Logistical Support of the Armies*, United States Army in World War II, The European

Theater of Operations (Office of the Chief of Military
   History, U.S. Army, Washington, D.C., 1953), 509,
   510.
14. Ibid., 532–534.

THURSDAY, AUGUST 31
 1. Warren F. Kimball, *Churchill and Roosevelt, The Com-
    plete Correspondence*, Vol. III (Princeton, N.J.: Prince-
    ton University Press, 1984), 302.
 2. Butcher, *My Three Years with Eisenhower*, 652.
 3. Ibid., 653.
 4. Ibid., 655.
 5. Blumenson, *Breakout and Pursuit*, 370.
 6. Brian Horrocks, *A Full Life* (London: Leo Cooper,
    1974), 197.
 7. Wilmot, *The Struggle for Europe*, 471.
 8. Speidel, *We Defended Normandy*, 151.
 9. Ibid.
10. Weigley, *Eisenhower's Lieutenants*, 256.
11. Clay Blair, *Ridgeway's Paratroops* (Garden City, N.Y.:
    Dial Press, Doubleday & Co., 1985), 208.
12. Bradley, *A Soldier's Story*, 402.
13. Ibid., 403.
14. Ibid., 402.
15. Blumenson, *Breakout and Pursuit*, 680.
16. Collins, *Lightning Joe*, 261.

EPILOGUE
 1. Weigley, *Eisenhower's Lieutenants*, 347.
 2. James Gavin, "Bloody Huertgen," *American Heritage
    Magazine*, December 1979, 44.
 3. Weigley, *Eisenhower's Lieutenants*, 368, 420.

BIBLIOGRAPHIC ESSAY

In addition to the source material listed in the Notes, I should mention several sources in particular that provided background material for this book. The most important was Martin Blumenson, *Breakout and Pursuit* (Office of the Chief of Military History, United States Army, Washington, D.C., 1961). This volume from the series *United States Army in World War II, The European Theater of Operations*, is the definitive history of the campaign in northern Europe during the summer of 1944 and was used extensively to better understand the military events that occurred during the month of August.

Larry Collins and Dominique La Pierre, *Is Paris Burning*? (Simon and Schuster, New York, 1965) was the major source used for the events leading up to and including the liberation of Paris. For the campaign in southern France, Lucian K. Truscott, Jr., *Command Missions* (E. P. Dutton, New York, 1954) provided most of the background material.

Much assistance was provided by the U.S. Army Military History Institute, Carlisle Barracks, Pa. Their extensive collection of unpublished manuscripts, unit histories, and published works was made freely available. Richard J. Somers, Archivist-Historian, David Keough, and Louise Arnold were particularly helpful.

Finally, I would like to thank Col. Melvin Helfers, Don Miller, and Alan Willis. Each freely shared his experiences with me and was helpful in answering my questions about his activities during the month of August 1944.

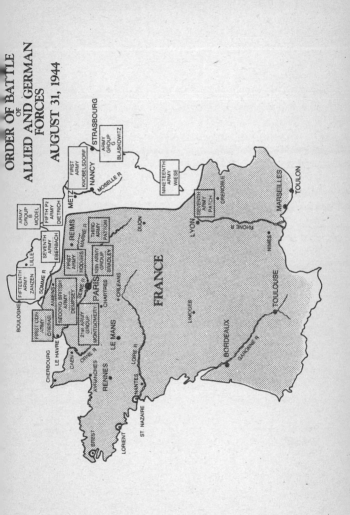

ORDER OF BATTLE
OF
ALLIED AND GERMAN
FORCES
AUGUST 31, 1944